Approaches in Public Policy

Edited by
STEVE LEACH and JOHN STEWART
Institute of Local Government Studies, University of Birmingham

For the
Institute of Local Government Studies
University of Birmingham

GEORGE ALLEN & UNWIN
London Boston Sydney

**George Allen & Unwin (Publishers) Ltd,
40 Museum Street, London WC1A 1LU, UK**

George Allen & Unwin (Publishers) Ltd,
Park Lane, Hemel Hempstead, Herts HP2 4TE, UK

Allen & Unwin, Inc.,
9 Winchester Terrace, Winchester, Mass. 01890, USA

George Allen & Unwin Australia Pty Ltd,
8 Napier Street, North Sydney, NSW 2060, Australia

First published in 1982

British Library Cataloguing in Publication Data

Approaches in public policy.
1. Local government — England
I. Leach, Steve II. Stewart, John
III. University of Birmingham. *Institute* of *Local Government Studies*
306'.2 (expanded) JS3095
ISBN 0-04-658236-3
ISBN 0-04-658237-1 Pbk

Library of Congress Cataloging in Publication Data

Main entry under title:
Approaches in public policy.
Bibliography: p.
Includes index.
1. Local government — Addresses, essays, lectures.
2. Regional planning — Addresses, essays, lectures.
3. Policy sciences — Addresses, essays, lectures.
I. Leach, Steve. II. Stewart, John David, 1929–
III. University of Birmingham. Institute of Local Government Studies.
JS91.A65 352'.00047'2 82-3980
ISBN 0-04-658236-3 AACR2
ISBN 0-04-628237-1 (pbk.)

Set in 10 on 11 point Times by Alan Sutton Publishing Ltd, Gloucester
and printed in Great Britain
by Mackays of Chatham

Contents

Contents

Acknowledgements

We owe a very considerable debt to those who have assisted us by their criticism, comment and help. We are especially indebted to Professor George Jones, whose criticisms helped us at a formative stage in the work. Rod Rhodes helped us particularly in forcing us to think carefully about the nature of the work. We would also like to thank Professor Peter Self and William Plowden for their helpful comments.

Our colleagues at the Institute have contributed in the process of debate and discussion – as have that wide range of local government officers and councillors with whom the Institute has continuing contact.

We also have to thank the Department of the Environment whose research awards made possible the work on which Chapters 5, 6, 7, 9 and 11 are based.

We are grateful to the editors of *Policy and Politics, Public Administration* and *Local Government Studies* for permission to publish material that originally appeared in those journals.

We are very appreciative of the help we have received from the Institute Secretarial Staff and the University Central Typing Services.

In the end, with all the help and assistance, criticism and comment, the responsibility remains that of the editors and the authors. Nevertheless, the acknowledgements are warmly given.

ACKNOWLEDGEMENTS

Introduction

I

This book is as a contribution to the study of policy-making. It focuses on the processes by which policy is derived, maintained, analysed and justified.

There is, of course, a range of different perspectives from which processes of policy-making can be studied. They can be studied in terms of the actors involved and the interests they represent. Such a perspective could be described as a study of the politics of policy-making. This book is not such a study, although it recognises that the processes of policy-making with which it is concerned take place in a political setting and that improvements in such processes must take cognisance of that setting.

The processes of policy-making can be studied in terms of the detailed tools of analysis that can be used to assist the processes of policy-making. This book is not such a study. It is, however, concerned with the way such tools of analysis have been used and misused in processes of policy-making, and with the role they could and should play.

Neither is the book a study of the policy content of specific policies although, particularly in the later chapters, a range of substantive policy areas are discussed as examples of approaches to policy-making. What the book is about is rather the range of processes which organisations have developed or can develop to make policies. It is concerned with the design of such processes. It stresses the processes by which policy problems are identified, alternatives are arrayed, evaluations are carried out and monitoring is undertaken. The field is one which has been conceptualised as 'metapolicy-making' – the determination of the processes by which policy is made.

Although primarily concerned with understanding and interpreting processes of policy-making, the authors share a common concern with how these processes can be improved. (They may, however, differ in the meaning they would attach to the concept of improvements.) The book is both descriptive and prescriptive in nature.

II

The book consists of a series of papers written by members of the staff of the Institute of Local Government Studies. Some have already been published elsewhere: others have been developed from as yet unpublished reports of particular research projects; still others have been written specifically for the book. They all focus on the processes of policy-making in the agencies of community government, that is to say, those governmental institutions set below the national level.

Although they focus primarily on local authorities they do not do so exclusively. For example, Chapter 7 focuses on regional planning while Chapter 11 is concerned with the health service. The particular institutional focus of the various chapters is, however, of less importance than the themes they explore. Local authorities, health authorities and regional planning teams provide different institutional arenas within which common themes concerned with policy processes can be analysed.

The chapters are arranged in a sequence which moves from a general perspective on metapolicy-making to a more specific discussion of the subject in terms of particular problems and particular settings. The first chapter, by Steve Leach, argues that the 'rational model', and in particular the conceptual framework and language associated with it, provide an essential basis for attempts to counteract the tendencies within public organisations to perpetuate existing policies and resist innovation and change. This is followed by a chapter by John Stewart which takes up some of the same themes in a rather different way. Stewart argues that while it will be unusual to find policies which have been derived or bargained for in terms of the rational model, it is common for policies to be justified by reference to that model. In the domain of justification the rational model has a key role. Different guidelines are required in the domain of policy derivation (and by implication the domain of policy adoption). The discussion is given a more empirical grounding in the next chapter, by Chris Skelcher, which explores the changes in the types of rationality-based methods which have been used in local authorities in recent years. Using the annual policy planning and budgetary cycle as the main focus, Skelcher shows that there has been a move to greater selectivity in policy analysis and an increasing tendency to link policy issues with resource considerations.

While Skelcher notes that the monitoring of policy outcomes has been slow to develop both conceptually and in practical experiments, Barbara Webster's chapter is a detailed conceptual examination of the distributional effects of local government services. It provides a framework for the analysis of such effects and argues strongly for their systematic study. It is suggested that such studies would have an important practical role in reviewing the performance of local authority policies and services. Steve Rogers's chapter looks at similar issues from the perspective of how information needs may most appropriately be identified in policy and management systems. He concludes that the most appropriate strategy involves a combination of a 'hard' and, where possible, quantitative analysis with a 'soft' process of evaluation and negotiation.

Felix Wedgwood-Oppenheim focuses on the 'monitoring function within public organisations', and explores ways in which the capacity of such organisations to receive and use information can be improved. Distinctions are made between implementation monitoring, impact monitoring and strategic monitoring. The argument is developed in the context of regional planning. Regional planning is also the substantive area of concern of the next chapter, by Chris Skelcher, which explores the linkage between the form of planning or policy-making processes and their context. He argues that the dominant methodology that has been used in regional planning involves certain concepts which are inappropriate in that context and proposes a context-appropriate type of methodology.

The next four contributions all look at arenas of policy-making and focus on the problem of policy derivation and implementation in particular intra- and inter-organisational settings. The problems of land use policy formulation and its implementation, in a two-tier system of local government, are discussed by Steve Leach, who argues that the districts possess most of the key resources in disputes between the two levels. The limited impact of area management approaches on policy-making is pointed out by Barbara Webster, who demonstrates that while such approaches have often led to the increased recognition of specific local issues and needs, and have resulted in limited changes in policies and service provision, a more systematic response to area needs and priorities has not generally been achieved. Ken Spencer examines the comprehensive community programmes (CCPs) which were developed jointly by central and local government in Gateshead and Bradford. The need for adequate political understanding of and commitment to the aims of CCP activity is highlighted. The chapter illustrates that effective inter-agency co-ordination is difficult to achieve at central and regional levels of government as well as at local authority level. Bryan Stoten looks at the experience of planning health care services and argues that the conditions of uncertainty facing the national health service, and the variety of policy-making cultures, mean that the task of maintaining existing patterns of health service is likely to take precedence over analysis aimed at adapting the service to the needs of those who receive it.

Finally, John Stewart provides a postscript which links together the themes emerging from the preceding chapters.

III

The various authors share an interest in the study of the processes of policy-making; they share in different ways a concern to improve such processes; they share a focus on local authorities as the main agencies of community government.

It is not claimed, however, that the work of the various authors constitutes a common viewpoint. They differ in their approaches to the processes of policy-making. Because they work in the same Institute it does mean, however, that they share the same arena of debate and discussion. It is therefore possible to identify certain themes which recur in a number of the chapters. Although the views of those themes differ among the chapters they are generally recognised as important themes in the study of the processes of policy-making. They may be summarised as follows: the restrictiveness of the rationality/incrementalism paradigm; the significance of the differing contexts of policy processes; the interrelationship of political and management processes; the distinction between hard and soft data; and the multidimensional nature of the processes of evaluation and assessment.

Much analysis of the process of policy-making has been posed in terms of a choice between a disjointed incremental model and a rational comprehensive model. These models are outlined in Chapter 1. Most of the subsequent chapters are marked by attempts to escape from such a simple choice. It can be argued that the use of these two models has been restrictive in the development of thinking about policy. The variety found in different policy-making situations precludes such a simple and restrictive dichotomy. Both 'rationality' and 'incrementalism' have their uses in appropriate circumstances, but there are other important dimensions to the study of policy processes which do not easily fit within these models.

Processes of policy-making have to be discussed in the context in which they are set. Suggestions for improvements in these processes must take into account the constraints and opportunities involved in these contexts. This awareness and basis for prescription is implicit in most of the contributions to this book and is a perspective developed explicitly by Skelcher (in relation to corporate planning and regional planning processes) and by Rogers (in relation to information systems). The design of policy systems and supporting management structures might usefully be seen as a creative process which exploits the space between what exists and what might be desirable. The recognition of the differing patterns of constraints and opportunities, which can be exploited in different ways in different circumstances, is an essential feature of this process.

Political and management processes are often discussed as separate processes. Many of the chapters which follow explore the interplay between such processes. Policy processes are analysed in political as well as managerial terms in, for example, the contributions by Webster (on area management) Leach (on county–district relations in planning), Spencer (on comprehensive community programmes) and Stoten (on health care planning). The inherently political nature of management processes is recognised.

Policy processes involve not merely the hard data of quantitative analysis but also the softer data of opinion, complaint and even hunch. This position is taken in the two contributions by John Stewart. The theme of how these different types of information can be used in policy processes is explored in the contribution by Rogers (on information systems), Wedgwood-Oppenheim (on the monitoring of regional strategies) and Webster (on the distributional effects of local government services).

Finally, it is important to recognise the multidimensional nature of evaluation and assessment activities within policy-making. The effect of policies can – and will – be judged differently by different interests. Processes of evaluation can be informed by the recognition of such differences and of the differences in values underlying them. This theme is one which recurs in a number of ways throughout the book.

IV

The search for improvement in policy-making has to be sensitive to the complex of forces involved in any policy-making situation. That involves consideration of political, organisational, resource and environmental context. It involves an appreciation of the way in which different models of policy-making can provide guidance in different situations.

This book is an attempt to contribute to that search for improvement through the exploration of differing approaches to policy-making in different situations. It reflects an awareness that the different dimensions of policy processes can only sensibly be understood in the context of a changing environment. The chapters in this book have been strongly influenced both by 'academic' writers on public policy and by practitioners of it. We hope it will prove of interest and use to both groups.

1

In Defence of the Rational Model

STEVE LEACH

INTRODUCTION

This chapter takes as its starting point the familiar dichotomy between the 'rational' and 'incremental' models of policy-making. It is important to summarise at the outset what is meant by this distinction.

The rational model, whose roots can be traced back through classical economic choice theory to Aristotle,[1] can most usefully be seen as a cyclical process involving a series of logically related stages which prescribe how policy-making should ideally be undertaken. The stages identified usually comprise, in one form or another, the following: identification of needs/problems; setting of objectives; identification of alternative choices; evaluation of alternatives; choice of preferred alternatives; implementation; and monitoring feedback and review. There exists a wide range of recent statements of the model, ranging from the very rigorous and demanding interpretation outlined by Dror (1968) to the more limited and flexible interpretations set out by Stewart (1971, ch. 4), Eddison (1973, p. 18) and Hambleton (1978, p. 48). Many of the prescriptive statements about planning and policy-making utilising the concept of rationality have been developed in land use planning (see Meyerson and Banfield, 1955; Davidoff and Reiner, 1973; McLoughlin, 1969; Chadwick, 1971; Faludi, 1973b), and more recently in the context of local authority corporate planning procedures. Frequently, though not inevitably, the rational model is presented with connotations of 'comprehensiveness', 'technicality' and 'quantification'.

In the 1950s there began to develop a critique of this model which stressed the political, organisational and financial realities which constrain the process of decision- and policy-making in public authorities. This critique, which came to be known variously as 'incrementalism', 'disjointed incrementalism', or 'muddling through', has been widely used both descriptively and normatively – that is, as a statement of how policy is customarily made and as a prescription of how it should be made (Faludi, 1973a, p. 120). The rational model is criticised from a variety of standpoints but particularly the following: unreasonable demands on the intellectual capacities of policy-makers; impossibility of setting objectives prior to and distinct from a consideration of alternative policies; financial and time costs; and its unrealistic view of the realities of inter- and intra-organisational behaviour. The incremental model as put forward by its most celebrated adherents (Lindblom, 1959, 1979; Wildavsky, 1964; Wildavsky and Dempster, 1979) eschews any real attempt at long-range planning, comprehensiveness, means/ends analysis, or a wide-ranging identification and evaluation of alternatives. It takes as its basis for decision-making the nature of existing policies and considers only incremental sideways shifts from such policies. The formulation of this approach is not dissimilar to Popper's (1957) concept of 'piecemeal social engineering'.

The argument of this chapter may be summarised as follows. There is a range of different conceptual frameworks (or heuristics) which are useful as aids to discussing and developing ideas about policy-making. One central and indeed essential conceptual framework is that provided by the linked set of ideas which comprise the rational model. This set of ideas is valuable not as an accurate description of how policy is made in practice, but rather as a mode of thought which can be used to 'open up' critical discussion about processes of policy-making. In particular, it is most usefully seen as a countervailing force to the well-documented tendencies within organisations and departments to perpetuate existing policies and resist innovation and change. The language and basic tenets of the rational model are widely accepted within public organisations as an appropriate way to talk about policy-making and policy justification. Although policy may be made and justified in practice in ways which owe very little to the rational model, battles can be fought using the generally accepted terminology of rationality. As with any presciptive model or technique of policy-making, the various stages of the rational model are open to a wide range of potential misuses and distortions. This potential, however, does not invalidate the benefits of the model. Indeed, the case for its advocacy rests on the perception that there is very little else available which is appropriate to cope with the complex and turbulent environment within which most public sector organisations operate.

The rational model has been criticised from a variety of perspectives, but usually on the basis either of the impossibility of the realisation of some perfect or ideal version of the model, or of shortcomings which have been observed in particular attempts to apply it. The appropriate response to these criticisms is not to reject the model *per se*, but to accept the *boundedness* of rationality and to be prepared to use the rational model flexibly. Units within public organisations striving to introduce a perspective on policy-making informed by the rational model will inevitably find themselves operating within a series of constraints. It is useful to develop an awareness of the nature of these constraints and the way they operate, as a means of developing appropriate strategies for the introduction of more context-appropriate approaches to policy-making and justification. The strength of these constraints, and the possibilities of changing them, will vary from organisation to organisation. One of the most important skills of the advocate of the rational model is an ability to comprehend and exploit the area of uncertainty which exists in all organisations, and to make the most of the opportunities which present themselves.

The rational model rests, of course, on the more fundamental concept of 'rationality' itself. This term has been used in a large number of different ways. In the policy-making literature it is often prefixed by a qualifying epithet, sometimes, one suspects, to convey a flavour to the concept which the author subsequently wishes to use as a basis for criticism; for example, Lindblom's (1959) use of 'comprehensive rationality', Marcuse's use of 'technical rationality' (1964, ch. 6). In this chapter the term 'purposive rationality' is preferred to indicate a concern that the heuristics of the rational model should embrace discussion about the ends being pursued by a policy (see Habermas, 1971, p. 91; Offe, 1975, p. 136). Self argues that the word rationality has three different, though related, meanings.

> First, it stands for the notion of *reflection as a prelude to action*. Instead of acting upon hunches, the decision-maker should analyse the situation carefully, consider alternative options, list their pros and cons, and so on . . . secondly, rationality is an *instrumental value* concerned with the maximisation of some goal or the application of some value judgement . . . thirdly, rationality stands sometimes for a principle of *harmony between conflicting aims* or values . . . or at a more mundane level, the popular idea of 'reasonableness'. (Self, 1975, p. 196)

The concept of rationality used in this chapter embraces a combination of Self's first two meanings. Rationality in policy-making is seen as a reflective activity which tries to relate policy means to particular ends, but which keeps the ends themselves under critical review. It does not incorporate any built-in assumptions about a unified public interest, or any spurious attempts to generate harmony between conflicting interests. Where the term 'the rational model' is used in this chapter it is intended to cover the cyclical process, encompassing a series of stages, referred to earlier.

THE CENTRALITY OF THE RATIONAL MODEL

One of the most significant aspects of the rational model of policy-making is the difficulty writers about policy have in ignoring it, even when critical of it. The model has already been mentioned in the Introduction, where it was argued that the use of the rationality/incrementalism dichotomy has become something of a straitjacket, restricting the development of a constructive discussion about policy processes. It is considered in Chapter 2, where the argument is put forward that the rational model has a special role to play in justifying a policy, while being much less appropriate to a discussion of policy derivation. It is subsequently used, in a variety of ways, in the remainder of the chapters in this book. The rational model seems to survive, here and elsewhere, as a starting point for discussion, even when it is then subjected to a good deal of criticism.

The recent spate of criticism is to be welcomed. Ten years ago, in the field of British local government at any rate,[2] it would hardly have seemed necessary to advocate the centrality of the rational model in the development and evaluation of policy. It was firmly installed as *the* basis for discussion. Indeed, in retrospect, it was often too uncritically accepted, as an unqualified piece of conventional wisdom. In recent years the model and its range of associated techniques have come in for increasing criticism (see Benington, 1976, pp. 16ff.; Cockburn, 1977, ch. 1; Dearlove, 1979, p. 179). However, concepts may often develop a renewed vitality from being subjected to criticism. Certainly the utility of the rational model has now to be reargued and re-emphasised from more fundamental premises.

One of the effects of the channelling of academic debate about policy-making into a rationality/incrementalism dichotomy has been to give the impression that the rational model operates as an all-embracing philosophy of policy-making which *in itself* can provide the basis for the derivation and justification of policy (see Lindblom, 1959; Hart *et al.*, 1978, pp. 36ff.) No such claim is made for it here. It is a necessary condition for the development of an environmentally sensitive policy process, but in no sense a sufficient one. There are a number of stages in the policy process where the heuristics of the rational model are of limited use. The rational model cannot tell us what values or objectives *should* be inserted into a particular substantive policy although, as we argue later, the model provides a useful mechanism for highlighting the implications of choosing particular values. There is little the rational model can do to help develop alternative policies to cope with a particular problem, although its use may demonstrate the need to search for alternatives. As John Stewart points out later in this book, the rational model may be a lot more useful in policy justification than in policy derivation. The rational model will not help us do everything. Many of the skills involved in the policy process are 'extra-rational'.[3] But to reject a model on the grounds of an inability to achieve a comprehensiveness of scope rarely claimed for it is to throw out the baby with the bathwater.

A number of writers have commented on the fact that the way in which policy processes operate in practice bears little resemblance to the sequential logic of the rational model (Lindblom, 1959, p. 153; Banfield, 1973, pp. 145–6; Wildavsky, 1964, p. 128, fn.). As description, the rational model is found wanting. This view is not disputed. Political opportunism, departmental inertia and muddling through clearly exist and will go on. Models which stress such organisational and political factors are much more convincing guides to reality than the rational model (see Allison, 1971, ch. 5). Paradoxically this conclusion strengthens the case for the use of the rational model, in a normative or prescriptive rather than a descriptive role. If public policy-making is to move in the direction of the organisational learning paradigm advocated by Schon (1973, ch. 5) and Hambleton (1978, ch. 10), it will not do so by means of political opportunism, departmental interest protection or muddling through, although all these processes will have to be recognised and coped with; indeed, they all may have their uses. The utility of the rational model lies in the questions it raises about these more familiar processes and in the alternative direction it provides to the constraint-bound emphasis of the incrementalists. It may be seen as a countervailing force to the tendencies within organisations to perpetuate existing policies and to resist innovation and change (or if change does take place for it to be change on the basis of political ideology).

The importance of retaining some conception of the rational model in any discussion which considers policy-making from a prescriptive standpoint is highlighted when one considers the alternatives. One feature of Lindblom's advocacy of incrementalism on which those who have commented on his work, favourably or otherwise, seem to be agreed, is its tendency to perpetuate the status quo. In Lindblom's own words, 'simplification is achieved through limitation of policy comparisons to those policies that differ in relatively small degree from policies presently in effect' (Lindblom, 1959, p. 161). This approach surely cannot respond adequately to the turbulent, unstable and fast-changing environment in which most public agencies operate, although it may ensure organisational survival. Consider the implications of an incremental approach for the development of an energy policy for Britain . . . or a local authority response to the closure of a major local employment source, or a spiralling set of outbreaks of race riots. Something more innovative, far-seeing and sensitive to change is required in such circumstances than can be provided by an incrementalist perspective.

A review of other available prescriptive models is not encouraging. Simon's 'satisficing' model is convincing as an explanation of much observable policy-oriented behaviour in organisations. It is, however, more useful as an exposition of the organisational forces constraining the development of a more innovative and sensitive approach to policy than as a guide to how such an approach might be developed (Simon, 1957). 'Satisficing' has many of the 'limited search', 'status quo' connotations of Lindblom's incrementalism. Indeed, the same might be said of Vickers's use of the concepts 'regulation' and 'balance' (Vickers, 1965, pp. 25ff.). They accept the limits set by the operation of organisational and departmental self-interest. To improve the quality of policy analysis and to open up debate about policy choice, something much less inward-looking is required.

It is significant that two of the writers most aware of the organisational forces which operate against the development of more rational methods of policy analysis are also the most convinced about the need to improve the quality of policy analysis. Wildavsky is often linked with Lindblom as a proponent of incrementalism. This categorisation does him less than justice. In an influential and perceptive paper, Wildavsky argues as follows.

> Everyone knows that the nation needs better policy analysis. Each area one investigates shows how little is known compared to what is necessary to devise adequate policies . . . however, a belief in the

> desirability of policy analysis – the sustained application of intelligence and knowledge to social problems – is not enough to ensure its success . . . if we are serious about improving public policy, we will go beyond the fashionable pretence of PPBS to show others what the best policy analysis can achieve. (Wildavsky, 1969, p. 190)

These are hardly the words of a man committed to the desirability of 'muddling through' or convinced of the impossibility of moving towards a more radical and innovative approach to policy-making. Banfield has a similar perspective. After demonstrating forcibly that in the Chicago Housing Authority he and Meyerson studied 'there is very little planning, and even less rationality' (Banfield, 1973, pp. 143–4), he concludes:

> The reader may by now have come to the conclusion that since organisations are so little given to the rational adaptations of means to ends, nothing is to be gained from constructing a model [of rationality] . . . But if the interest is normative – if it is in describing how organisations would have to act in order to be in some sense more effective or efficient – it is hard to see how reference to such a model can be avoided, or indeed, why its lack of realism should be considered a defect. (ibid., p. 149)

The stance of these two writers is very similar to that adopted in this chapter. Banfield explicitly defends the use of the rational model. Wildavsky's concept of policy analysis is based on and compatible with the set of sequential stages which we have characterised as the rational model (Wildavsky, 1969, p. 200). The problem for them, as for us, is to develop more realistic ways of applying the ideas inherent in the rational model to improve the quality of public policy-making.

The language of rationality is invariably used by those who criticise its use. As John Stewart points out: 'Those who attack rationality in decision-making or in public policy-making do not argue irrationally. They argue by rational argument that rationality is impossible or undesirable in policy-making' (see Chapter 2). It is noticeable that when the rational model is presented as a guide to policy-making in our courses for local government managers, the dismissive responses are often outweighed by the reactions that claim 'this is the way we go about things anyway'. The suspicion that such a claim is often far from warranted does not detract from the fact that the language of rationality has been incorporated, superficially at least, by those who make the claim. The acceptance of the language of rationality carries with it, of course, the susceptibility to attack in those terms. If rationality is one of the languages of discourse in public organisations, then any policy analysis unit trying to open up a debate about an entrenched area of departmental policy maintenance[4] has a legitimate weapon with which to operate.

Much that is undesirable has been done in the name of the rational model. Benington (1976, pp. 16–21) in a perceptive paper shows how each of the conventional stages of the rational model (identification of need; setting of objectives; considering alternatives; monitoring outcomes) is susceptible to manipulation in the interests of certain groups within and outside a local authority. Similar comments have been made about the techniques associated with rational policy-making such as cost-benefit analysis and the planning programme budgeting system (PPBS). Hart, Skelcher and Wedgwood-Oppenheim have illustrated the tendency of objectives to become 'unmoving movers' (Hart *et al.*, 1978, p. 38). Links between centralisation processes and corporate planning (and hence, by implication, between centralisation and the rational model) have also been portrayed by a number of writers (see especially Dearlove, 1979, ch. 8; Cockburn, 1977, pp. 37ff.).

An awareness of the potential and actual distortions of the constituent concepts of the rational model has led some to reject it completely as a basis for analysis or prescription. However, it is surely an unwarranted leap of argument to claim that because a model – or any particular part of it – demonstrates a potential for misuse it should therefore be rejected. Any prescriptive model will inevitably possess such a potential. Neither the rational model nor any alternative can sensibly be seen as 'neutral' or 'objective'. Just as there is nothing intrinsically centralist, elitist, consensual, or technical-expertise-biased about corporate planning, so it can be argued that the rational model does not intrinsically possess any of these features. It equally has the potential to be interpreted in these ways; but then it also has the potential to be interpreted in a number of other very different ways, for example, decentralist,[5] councillor-oriented,[6] and so on.

THE RATIONAL MODEL: LINES OF CRITICISM

The rational model has come under attack from three main directions. There is now a relatively long history of criticism of the model on account of its *complexity*. The argument here is that the rational model, which is usually in such arguments linked with the idea of comprehensiveness, is so complex and demanding in its 'pure' form as to be beyond the capabilities of any public agency. Simpler, more manageable alternatives must, it is claimed, be sought. This kind of criticism is familiar from the works of Simon (1957, ch. V) and Lindblom (1959, pp. 152–3) and reappears in various forms in the writings of Schon (1973, ch. 5), Jenkins (1978, pp. 138ff.) and Allison (1971, p. 254). More recently the model has come under attack from different standpoints. It has begun to be argued that the rational model cannot in effect handle values satisfactorily. Sometimes it is claimed that the model assumes a consensus, that is, an agreed set of public values (see Hart *et al.*, 1978, p. 37); sometimes it is claimed that the sequence of the stages of the model requires a definition and weighting of values prior to a consideration of policies, which is thought by the writers concerned to be extremely difficult (Lindblom, 1959, pp. 157–8; Gutch, 1972, p. 25).

In the recent renewal of interest in the relationship between policy and implementation a further type of criticism has begun to emerge. A problem of implementation has begun, somewhat diffusely, to be identified which stresses the variety of ways in which policy intentions can be distorted in the process of implementation. As a result there has been a tendency to reject the rational model as a basis for understanding or prescribing policy processes as they occur in practice (Pressman and Wildavsky, 1973, pp. xii–xvii; Schon, 1973, p. 56; Lewis and Flynn, 1979, pp. 124–6).

These three themes – impracticability because of technical complexity, undesirability because of naivety about values and inapplicability because of inability to deal with the problem of implementation – are not, of course, mutually exclusive. Elements of the other two types of criticism are frequently found in the one that is being stressed, and may often be used as supporting evidence. However, it is felt that there is a clear enough distinction in principle between the three types of criticism to make it worthwhile discussing them separately, at least initially. The next sections discuss each type of criticism in turn, and the arguments are then brought together in the closing section.

RATIONALITY AND TECHNICAL COMPLEXITY

Possibly the most potentially damaging type of criticism of the rational model is that it is so technically complex and information-hungry as to be totally impracticable as a basis for public policy-making. A link is almost always made in such arrangements between rationality and comprehensiveness. It is assumed that the two concepts are intertwined and that any attempt at rationality must necessarily also be comprehensive in scope. However, as other writers have shown (see Stewart, 1971, p. 31; Skelcher, 1980a, p. 162), there is no *necessary* link in policy-making between rationality and comprehensiveness. Once the comprehensive/rationality link is broken, and the idea of *selective rationality* directed at particular, identifiable problem areas is admitted, then rationality begins to look more feasible than when bound up with the notion of comprehensiveness.

The second assumption made by Lindblom and his followers is that rationality must always involve the most demanding form of the rational model available. Dror's model of perfect rationality has recently become the one most frequently cited. Dror's rational model is open to criticism because of the mind-blowing demands it makes on the policy analyst. It is extremely difficult, if not impossible, to 'establish a complete set of operational goals, with relative weights allocated to the different degrees to which each may be achieved', or 'to prepare a complete set of the alternative policies open to the policy maker', or 'to prepare a complete set of valid predictions of the costs and benefits of each alternative'. If what rationality did involve was all the above requirements (and more) there might be good reason to dismiss the whole concept. Fortunately it does not necessarily do so.

Just as the link between rationality and comprehensiveness has to be broken to take the argument further, so also does the link between rationality and the perfect rationality model epitomised by what Dror has put forward. Rationality and the perfect rationality are not the same. The unattainability of the latter should not be taken as an excuse not to continue to explore ways of using the former in public policy-making (Faludi, 1973a, pp. 123–4). One response to the unattainability of perfect rationality is to dismiss any prospect of applying some form of rationality to policy-making as, in effect, Lindblom does. This response is not sensible. The problem is one of developing *alternative ways* of applying rationality in public policy-making. This standpoint is implicit in the approaches to policy-making which have sketched out some kind of middle way in policy-making. Etzioni's (1967) 'mixed-scanning' approach, and Hart's concept of 'jointed incrementalism' (Hart, 1976, ch. 6), are cases in point.

The third quality attributed to rationality by critics of its impracticability is a *static* quality. The rational model is portrayed as being a blueprint or end-state kind of activity with the need for review elements either played down or absent altogether (Lindblom, 1959, pp. 164–5). This misconception again follows from the form of rationality selected for criticism. There *are* versions of the rational model available which do indeed hardly mention the desirability of feedback, monitoring and review, or appear only to pay lip-service to such concepts. But there is nothing intrinsic about the rational model or the concept of rationality which precludes the inclusion of feedback, monitoring and review stages. Many enthusiastic proponents of rationality in policy-making emphasise these elements (see, for example, Stewart, 1971, pp. 142ff.; Eddison, 1973, p. 79; Wedgwood-Oppenheim *et al.*, 1976, pp. 9ff.). They would agree with Lindblom that 'policy should be made and remade endlessly'.

What, then, should be the role of rationality in public policy-making? A number of suggestions will be outlined here. However desirable pure rationality is in principle, it is hard to dispute the view that it is, in practice, unattainable. Thus any attempt to apply rational methods to the development and application of public policy must of necessity be a bounded one. The demanding requirements of Dror's model of perfect rationality can be set aside (except perhaps in the kind of limiting conditions of perfect administration set out by Hood, (1976, p. 67). However, the fact that a complete set of alternatives for a policy issue can rarely be identified is no reason for not trying to widen the range of alternatives considered (Stewart, 1971, p. 32). The difficulty of developing a policy from a set of objectives may be partly overcome by seeking to identify what goals are met, as implied by an existing policy (Gutch, 1972, p. 25). And the impossibility of 'carrying out a complete set of valid predictions of costs and benefits' should not preclude more modest attempts at evaluating and comparing alternatives. The general conclusion implied by all these more detailed observations is that rationality is a relative concept. To apply it in practical situations demands an ability to understand the context surrounding its application and to interpret it in relation to this understanding. This process of understanding and interpretation is not compatible with any kind of off-the-shelf model. Deciding the bounds of rationality in any given situation, and designing the most appropriate form of rationality to fit these constraints, are demanding and creative skills.

It follows from this that there will inevitably need to be a variety of approaches to policy-making appropriate to the range of different contexts in which the policy-maker operates. If this argument is accepted these different approaches will all be grounded in the rational model of policy-making, although this viewpoint does not, of course, preclude the use of 'extra-rational' methods at various points of the policy process (for example, at the generation of alternatives stage) so long as such methods can be rationally justified. Some policy contexts have a high degree of certainty while in others uncertainty is dominant. In some policy agencies responsibility for policy-making and implementation falls clearly within that agency, while in others co-operation with a number of other agencies is necessary to agree and implement a policy. Some policy issues are of direct political interest to an elected council; others are normally left in the hands of officers. All these kinds of variation are likely to imply a variety in appropriate methods of policy-making and implementation in the agency or agencies concerned.

A further role for rationality in public policy-making is that of providing a useful framework for the discussion of policy problems and an appropriate language for doing so. If one takes Stewart's 'common model of the process of management' (1971, p. 30) or Eddison's simple circular diagram of the 'policy process' (1973, p. 18) one has a framework which is useful in three ways. It is useful as an ideal for public policy-making which is more realistic and feasible than Dror's, and hence a more useful starting point for prescription in public policy-making. However, as both authors acknowledge, even these simplified versions of the rational model can normally only be used partially and selectively. Its second use is as a framework for understanding and evaluating what is taking place in a particular policy context. It is surely pertinent to ask of any given policy what objectives it is trying to achieve, what alternatives to it have been considered, or on what basis the existing policy can be shown to be preferable to a particular alternative. The basis for such questions lies in the framework provided by such models of bounded rationality. They thus act as a vehicle for analysing, criticising and justifying particular policies. Without such a framework, ways of opening up a debate about particular policies would arguably be much less coherent. In a similar way the concepts invariably used in the various models of rationality, perfect or otherwise, give us a very useful language with which to make sense of policy processes. Whether or not a policy has been evoked by developing and evaluating alternatives against a set of objectives, it is always pertinent to analyse those processes in terms of concepts such as 'objectives', 'alternatives', 'evaluation', 'implementation and review'. Although other concepts will also be useful, it is hard to see how the conceptual framework provided by the rational model could be excluded if one of the aims of analysis is to improve the quality of public policy-making.

The rational model is therefore useful as a framework for discussing, criticising and justifying policy-making; but prescriptively it should be treated in a much more *flexible* way than has often been the case. In particular, the process involved should be *continuous* or at least regularly reviewed (that is, there is no blueprint assumption); the cycle may be broken into *a number of different points* (that is, there is no assumption of linearity); and the policy-making process will normally be *selective* rather than comprehensive. Finally, it is accepted that there is no one best form of rational policy-making; but rather there should be a variety of different, rationally based approaches appropriate to different contexts. It is important to examine the constraints on and opportunities for the use of rationality in a variety of different contexts, and to probe in more detail how objectives, alternatives, monitoring, and so on, might be differentially handled.

RATIONALITY AND THE TREATMENT OF VALUES

> The prime requirement of the rational model is the ability to set a series of internally consistent objectives which represent *society's* values and priorities. Given the plurality of competing interests and values active (and latent) in society, the assumption of a consensual political environment clearly does not hold. (Hart *et al*, 1978, p. 37)

A similar perceived correspondence between the rational model and value consensus is implicit in the work of Benington (1976, p. 19) and Macdougall (1972, pp. 39ff.). A more familiar criticism of the rational model's treatment of values is to be found in Lindblom's assertion that it is impossible to state values and priorities between them in advance of the policies which embody them, from which he concludes that any model which relies on means/ends analysis is inappropriate in public policy-making. My response to this point has been covered in the emphasis in the previous section on the flexibility of the rational model. Lindblom also, however, shares the view that the rational-comprehensive model requires 'agreement' over values.

It is clearly Self's third view of rationality (1975, p. 196)[7] that Lindblom and Hart *et al.* are assuming in their 'consensus' criticism. An assumed consensus may indeed have been the view of certain proponents of *comprehensive* rationality (see, for example, McLoughlin, 1969; Chadwick, 1971). It is certainly not my view. It has already been emphasised how the rational model does not necessarily carry with it any assumptions of a unified public interest, or any spurious attempts to generate harmony between conflicting interests. There is no way a rational approach can say what values *should* be inserted into a particular piece of policy-making. Nor can it say on what value criteria alternative policies *should* be analysed. Nor can it say directly when the time has come for a policy to be reviewed. It can inform all these tasks: but ultimately the problem of value input into the policy process is conceptually separate. Any policy developed rationally from a socially insensitive set of values will be a socially insensitive policy.

It is an oversimplification to argue that some stages of the rational model of policy-making are political (for example, to be carried out, in principle, by the council, at local government level), while others are primarily technical. Scope for the intrusion of values which affect policy choice or impact is present at even the most seemingly value-free stages, such as the generation of alternatives, the collection of information, the implementation of the chosen policy and the interpretation of feedback. However, a distinction can still usefully be made between stages which are intrinsically of value choice (and hence, it is assumed, a political responsibility) and stages which are, in principle at least, technical (and hence, it is assumed, departmental responsibility). Identification of problems, generation of objectives and choice of policy would seem to fit into the former category; the remainder, with certain qualifications, into the latter. In a local government system where the implications of the distinction between politicians as representatives and officers as technical support are accepted, any attempt at applying rationality will necessarily be an instrumental one which takes as given the input of political values at the appropriate stages. The identification of such values is seen as an integral but conceptually separate part of the policy-making process which intrinsically involves elements of extra-rational political choice.

There are a number of objections to this position. The arguments about the unrepresentativeness, in practice, of councillors are well known (see Gyford, 1976, pp. 25–36, for a summary of the evidence). The reluctance of councillors to commit themselves in advance to goals or objectives has also been noted (for example, Muchnick, 1971, pp. 20ff.). The ability of a department to fix the selection of alternatives or to distort a policy through implementation has been described in a number of studies (J. G. Davies, 1972; Newton, 1976; Muchnick, 1971; Dennis, 1968). However, none of these issues detracts from the view that it is possible to make a conceptual distinction between the extra-rational value input stages of the policy process and those which do not require a specific value input. Neither do they demonstrate that a rational approach must necessarily have something to say about what, or whose, values should be incorporated.

There are a number of ways in which a rational approach to policy-making can usefully draw out the implications of the value choices made. It can do so by showing to what extent (within the limits of knowledge and predictability) various alternatives meet the objectives set out for the policy. Thus any political choice which obviously overruled a demonstrably preferable alternative would have to be justified in political value terms. In a similar way, by pointing out the implications of different policies for different affected interests, either at the policy evaluation stage or as an agreed policy is monitored, the policy analyst can broaden the information on which the political level makes a choice to select or review a policy and he can, with perhaps more difficulty, make publicly available such evidence. It was argued in the previous section that rationality could usefully be used in the justification or criticism of various policies. There is no reason why this facility should not be made use of by politician, officer, interest group, or member of the public.

Whereas the insertion of values into the policy-making process and the application of rationality in working through those values are conceptually separate, though interrelated, activities, and these separate identities and the different responsibilities they entail should be explicitly recognised, there is much that a rational approach to policy-making can do to expose the implications of the value judgements which are inserted and to inform the choices which must be made on the basis of them.

RATIONALITY AND THE PROBLEM OF IMPLEMENTATION

The concept of implementation has long presented difficulties. The phrase 'the problem of implementation' is frequently encountered nowadays in academic discussion about policy-making. What the problem of implementation actually is, is less easy to identify. Two different types of problem may perhaps be identified. First, there is the conceptual problem of distinguishing between policy formulation and implementation. Secondly, there is the problem experienced by policy formulators of their inability to exercise adequate control over those who implement the policy, or the environment upon which it impinges, to ensure its successful implementation.

The problem of distinguishing policy-making and policy implementation or administration is well known. B. Smith (1976, p. 14) writes, 'the distinction between policy and administration at most reflects nothing more than an artificial dividing-line between the broader or narrower, and the general, or more detailed aspects of government decisions'. Anderson comments 'policy is being made as it is being administered and administered as it is being made' (1975, p. 98). These difficulties have led a recent research group to set out a framework for studying implementation which eschews altogether the policy-making/implementation distinction and argues for the understanding of implementation as 'action'.

> The focus for this project has been on behaviour and observable action, and implementation has been taken in its descriptive sense to mean concern about 'how things get done' . . . we are concerned to understand action rather than attempt constantly to relate action back to its possible source in some reified 'policy'. Thus we offer a framework for understanding implementation as action. (Lewis and Flynn, 1979, p. 125)

The difficulty with this approach is that, useful though it may be for understanding the internal operations of organisation, it turns the study of policy-making into the study of organisational behaviour and offers little possibility of any kind of prescriptive content which attempts to improve the quality of public policy-making. We prefer to retain the conceptual distinction between policy-making on the one hand and the implementation process on the other, on the basis that in many policy situations it is possible to 'identify a point where policy-making can be said to be primarily completed' (Hill, 1978, p. 11). Even in those situations where the policy/implementation distinction is blurred, it may still be useful to employ these terms as an aid to understanding what is going on. It is readily accepted that the existence of 'organisational' activity does not require the existence of an explicit policy. But it may in this case be relevant to ask what values the activity is, in effect, furthering. Similarly the existence of an explicit policy may not be coupled with the existence of any kind of implementation process. Many see regional planning in this light. Again, however, the policy/implementation distinction is useful as a basis for asking why implementation is not proceeding and what needs to be done to set it in motion. What we would wish to stress, therefore, is that although it may well be that there are some activities performed by public bodies which may most appropriately be described as 'actions', there are many others that may more usefully be seen as 'implementation'. If our main concern is to prescribe improvements in public policy-making, rather than merely to understand it, it is hard to conceive of a conceptual framework other than the rational model (with the policy formulation/implementation distinction this involves) which could form the basis of such prescriptions. This model should, of course, be supplemented by other aids to understanding, such as the analysis of organisational behaviour.

The second sense in which 'the problem of implementation' is commonly used appears to reflect a growing concern that policies *formulated* by a policy-making agency often, in the process of their implementation, turn out very differently from what is intended. Three broad reasons may be posited for this phenomenon.

(1) *Problems of Organisational Control*
It may be that the assumptive worlds of those actors at the periphery of the organisation who implement the policies developed at the centre differ from those of the policy formulators (K. Young, 1978, p. 7). If this is the case, it is likely that the policy implementors at the periphery will attempt to use the discretion which is invariably available to them in one form or another to distort the official policy in the direction of their own perception of the problem. This aspect of control difficulties is compounded if the actors involved are located in different organisations from the actors involved in policy formulation.

(2) *Problems of Environmental Control*
Even in situations where there is a happy coincidence of assumptive worlds and problem perceptions between formulators and implemen-

tors, the policy implementation process may still produce results which are out of line with the intentions embodied in the policy. One possible explanation for this discrepancy is that the behaviour of those at whom the policy is directed cannot adequately be controlled, and they may fail to play the part that had been anticipated. Some policies can be implemented through coercion, whether the recipients like it or not (for example, a council housing improvement programme). However, the majority rely on some form of co-operation or positive response from those at whom it is directed (for example, a general improvement area; a campaign to improve the take-up of supplementary benefit). This co-operation or positive response may not, in part or in whole, be forthcoming.

(3) *Problems of Environmental Understanding*

All explicit policies are based on assumptions about the relationship between an activity undertaken by an agency and the impact of that activity on the environment. The fluid, socially constructed and often ill-understood nature of social behaviour should lead us to recognise that such assumptions may often be inaccurate, or, even if accurate for a time, may gradually cease to be so. It is often extremely difficult to anticipate the chain of effects which may result from a particular policy. So even where formulators and implementors act in accord, and the take-up of opportunities at the policy implementation stage is as anticipated, the *unintended consequences* of the implementation of the policy may again lead to results very different from what had been intended. The gentrification of areas of working-class housing in London improved under GIA schemes may be seen as an example of this kind of process.

The conditions under which a policy is implemented vary considerably, and the design of any policy process should reflect the particular set of implementation conditions which is pertinent. Several writers have attempted to develop useful classifications of implementation conditions. Hood (1976) devotes much of his useful and stimulating study of the limits of administration to this problem. Lewis and Flynn (1979, p. 134) in a DoE research feasibility study set out an eightfold classification of what they call 'modes of action' (for example, judicial control, procedural control, hiving-off, and so on). Stewart (1980, p. 302) has identified four major types of policy activity: a maintenance role; a solution-imposing role; a responsive change role; and a directed change role; and argues that these might imply very different models for analysis. Webster's first contribution to this book makes a useful distinction between types of service delivery (global/specific-locational/individual) and scope (area-specific/client group-specific/whole population). Thus a variety of policy implementation conditions exists.

If any policy is to be advocated it must be one that seems feasible in terms of its implementation conditions. It is accepted that this assessment can often only be made on a trial-and-error basis. Implementation problems cannot always be predicted in advance.

Often they are discovered in action. However, if a policy requires for its successful implementation controls which do not exist, or requires a large and non-recoverable outlay of resources to meet a complex urban problem which is by no means fully understood, or implies the co-operation of other agencies whose policies are incompatible with it, then it is not a rational policy. In other words, implementation situations can usefully be seen as a *constraint* on the process of policy-making and the scope of solutions considered. Such constraints can also act as opportunities for other policies (for example, the use of a sympathetic 'voluntary group', or the availability of finance on a 'payment by results' basis).

It is worthwhile standing the problem of implementation on its head, and suggesting that 'factors which pose problems for implementation may be viewed rather differently as contributing to flexibility and innovation' (K. Young, 1978, pp. 9–10). This idea, which is a useful reworking of the theme developed by Schon (1973, pp. 102–8) in his discussion of centre-periphery relationships, is one which is very much in accord with the idea of rationality presented here. It sees rational policy-making very much as a learning process, where the problem may not be to overcome the obstacles in the way of implementing a policy, but rather to recognise in the light of the problems of implementation that the policy may have been inappropriate, or, if once appropriate, may now require change in response to changing environmental circumstances. As Young puts it (Young, 1978, p. 9):

> the way in which policies are mediated by local managers and street level bureaucrats, operating with interpretative space, is the key question for implementation studies. But this perspective . . . inevitably shifts the focus away from a centre-periphery model, of policy application in which control loss or 'leakage' is deplored, towards a model in which peripheral actors mediate – and thus enhance policy in the light of its appropriateness or feasibility.

This interpretation underpins the comments in Chapter 2 on the 'measurement of effectiveness' and 'understanding achievement'. Part of what is involved in understanding achievement may well be a realisation that the criteria of achievement identified are inappropriate. A sensitive and flexible application of rationality to policy-making does not see implementation just as a control problem but rather, in part at least, as a learning device.

Our conclusions about implementation would, therefore, accept the difficulties of distinguishing policy formulation from implementation and sometimes of even identifying a policy that is being implemented. We would, however, wish to retain the conceptual distinction between policy and implementation as an analytical tool, and as a prescriptive device, and stress that the differing conditions of implementation and the constraints and learning opportunities embodied in them should be incorporated into the design of policy processes.

CONCLUSION: THE ROLE OF THE POLICY ANALYST

Public policy-making and implementation take place within a context. This context, and the constraints and opportunities which are part of it, have to be understood before a realistic attempt to apply rationality to the process of policy-making can be developed. This context can usefully be seen as consisting of the intra- and inter-organisational structures of the agencies involved; the political and organisational (for example, professional) values, interests and assumptions which are brought by relevant actors to the policy-making arena; the different kinds of resources which are available to make and implement policy; and the type of knowledge that the agencies involved have about the issues which they are tackling.

This kind of framework cannot be progressively developed by ever more detailed empirical work and ever more refined measurement until it reaches the status of an explanatory model. The reality of organisational policy-making is not that kind of reality. Policies and approaches to policy-making are social constructions which change as views of social reality and the powers to impose them change. Thus the most that could reasonably be claimed for the framework suggested is that it 'aids an awareness of the shape of the policy space' (Friend, Power and Yewlett, 1974, ch. 2) and acts as a structured checklist of relevant topics for anyone involved in the design of policy systems.

In most public organisations there is an actual or potential group of policy analysts with an interest in the development of more rational systems of policy-making and implementation. Such initiatives do not, of course, just develop themselves; they need a constituency of support. If such a constituency exists, rationality provides a useful resource as a language of *justification* from which the affairs of the organisation can be influenced. Rationality can, indeed, usefully be analysed as a resource in policy-making situations. It is in some individuals' or groups' interests to employ it; and in others' interests to ignore or subvert it. Any attempt to introduce more rational approaches into existing institutions should be made with a full awareness of the arena of structured interests upon which they impinge. Thus the skill of the policy analyst involves a skill in opening up the policy process at vulnerable points. It involves a skill in balancing the desirable with the feasible. It involves an ability to recognise the way in which it is possible and appropriate to apply the rational model. As Wildavsky (1969, p. 198) puts it:

> Policy-oriented executives will want to get better analysis. Executives wishing to increase their resource base will be interested in independent sources of information and advice. Those who would exert power need objectives to fight for. It is neither fashionable nor efficient to appear to seek power for its own sake. In polite society the desire is masked and given a noble face when it can be attached to grand policy concerns that bring benefits to others as well as to power seekers.

NOTES: CHAPTER 1

1 Aristotle, 1941: 'First, have a definitive clear functional ideal – a goal or objective – second have the necessary means to achieve your ends – wisdom money materials and methods – third adjust your means to that end.'

2 In the run-up to the 1974 reorganisation, the conventional wisdom, underlined by a series of official reports (for example, Committee on the Management of Local Government, 1967; Royal Commission on Local Government in England, 1969; Department of the Environment, 1972), advocated the use of some kind of rational policy-making model.

3 By 'extra-rational' we are referring to those aspects of the policy process that cannot be logically deduced from a previous stage, for example, generation of alternatives, choice of policy to be reviewed, and so on.

4 For a discussion of this term see Dearlove, 1973, p. 3.

5 See, for example, the various area approaches to policy-making in Newcastle, Sunderland and Middlesbrough (Harrop *et al.*, 1978).

6 See, for example, the approaches in Lewisham, Sheffield and Bradford (Skelcher, 1980).

7 See discussion in earlier part of this chapter.

2

Guidelines to Policy Derivation

JOHN STEWART

I THE DOMAINS OF POLICY-MAKING

Thought about policy-making takes place in different domains. Dependent on the domains involved, different rules of behaviour operate and different modes of thought have to be applied. It is critical, therefore, to the development of thought about policy and policy-making that the domain to which that thought is applied be understood.

Three domains are distinguished in this chapter:

- the domain of policy derivation
- the domain of policy adoption
- the domain of policy justification.

The domain of policy derivation centres on the working out of new policies or of changes in policy. It is concerned with the processes by which policy alternatives are worked out. It involves both discovery and exploration of what is discovered. The domain of policy adoption centres on the processes by which a policy moves to acceptance. It involves both formal procedures and the politics of bargaining. The domain of policy justification centres on the processes by which a policy is treated, by those who initiate, those who approve and those who are governed by it. It involves both the rules and the standards by which policies are justified.

It is common to distinguish between different phases of the policy-making process – between the setting of objectives and the analysis of alternatives or between the evaluation of alternatives and the monitoring of results. Differences in domains do not correspond to these phases in the processes of policy-making. Thus the same phase of policy-making is present or can be present in each domain. The same phase has, however, to be viewed from a different perspective and thought about in a different way depending on the domain. For this reason certain elements in the processes of policy-making may have a special importance in a particular domain. Objectives may have a role in the domain of derivation – they may assist discovery and exploration. They may have a role in the domain of policy adoption – they may assist or confuse the bargaining process. They have a special role in the domain of justification – since justification often relates policy to objectives.

Domains are not logically or actually separated from each other. The domains should not be thought of as separate and independent, delineated by clear boundaries. They are all domains in the study of policy-making, but they have their own points of focus within it. Each domain can have a role in other domains. Justification has its impact in the domains of adoption and derivation. Bargaining too can have a role in the domain of derivation and can set tasks for the domain of justification.

The study of public policy-making has no single or simple purpose. Its purpose will vary with the domain. Each domain has different roles which are performed and hence different frameworks for study are appropriate. In the domain of policy derivation the framework needs to encompass discovery and explanation. In the domain of policy adoption the framework should help the understanding of bargaining processes. In the domain of justification the framework must show the rules and standards involved. Each domain requires a different framework for study.[1]

II THE RATIONAL MODEL AND THE DOMAIN OF JUSTIFICATION

The rational model is certainly not a descriptive model.[2] Time and again it is shown that decisions are not made and policies are not determined in accordance with the model. But even as a normative model it is under attack as a model impossible of attainment. It is contended not merely that decisions are not made in terms of the rational model, but that they cannot be made or should not be made. Man is an animal of limited rationality; policies emerge from a bargaining process and it is better so (see Lindblom, 1959, pp. 79–88).

Yet the rational model still survives, although recognised to be impossible to apply in any pure form and impractical to apply even in a more limited form in many actual working situations. It more than survives. It underlies much writing. It is in effect appealed to by practical men in practical situations (in the domain of adoption) who attempt to show that they are making rational decisions in a rational way. Practical men disregard the impracticability of the rational model in their discourse if not in their practice. They justify their policies by reference to objectives. The rational model is pervasive in discussion of policies and policy-making. It is almost as if it is impossible to escape from. Shown to be impossible or impractical, argued to be undesirable, it remains ever-present in discussion.

The explanation of the paradox is that to show that it is impossible to make decisions in accordance with the rational model does not mean it is impossible to justify decisions in accordance with the rational model. The making of decisions belongs to the domain of policy derivation and policy adoption. To show that the rational model is not and cannot be fully applied in those domains is not to show that it is not and cannot be applied in the domain of justification. A distinction has to be made between the rational model as a method of policy-making and the rational model as a method of justification. It is the distinction between the domain of justification and the other domains of policy-making.

In the domain of policy derivation, policy-making may involve the imaginative design and the accidental discovery as well as systematic method. The policy analyst needs intuition and accident as much as he needs systematic method. In one real sense 'anything goes' in breaking out of the constraints of past thinking (see Feyeraband, 1975). But after the accident, the intuition, or the breakthrough, the analyst needs justification. That which has been done must be justified – to himself as much as to others.

Although the rational model belongs to the domain of policy justification, it has a relationship to other domains because the domain of justification has a relationship to those domains. It influences how policies are presented – for checking in the context of derivation and for debate in the context of adoption. It provides a framework for the discussion of policy whenever policy has to be justified.

Because the domain of justification sets certain requirements for the way policy is described and the way it is argued, it influences policy in its making. If policy is not originally derived through or adopted because of the rational model, the fact that the model is relevant to the justification of policy cannot be disregarded. The rational model has a role in providing a framework that can be used to present, argue about and check upon policies derived and bargained for through a variety of ways, precisely because of its role in the domain of justification.

It will be abnormal indeed for policy to be derived and bargained for (domains of derivation and adoption) in terms of the rational model. It will be common for it to be justified in terms of the rational model (domains of justification). That is description, but prescription is also possible. Justification can be improved as can derivation (and indeed as can bargaining).

III HEURISTICS FOR POLICY DERIVATION

The domain of policy derivation focuses on the processes by which new policy is worked out. It is concerned with the discovery and exploration of such policies. The domain does not focus on how the need for new policy or for policy change arises. There is a further domain for study in the process of agenda-setting. For the purpose of this study of the domain of policy derivation we assume a situation in which the need for policy review has been recognised. We assume what we shall call a policy dilemma, where the adequacy of existing policy or the need for new policy is on the agenda. The domain of policy derivation starts from a policy dilemma.

There is no method whose application guarantees the finding of adequate policy. Policy derivation is not based on the simple relationship input–process–output. In the domain of policy derivation any method can be used, if it works. The contexts in which policies have to be worked out vary. Policy dilemmas vary. They vary in complexity and certainty. The degree of knowledge and understanding that can be brought to bear varies. They vary in the degree of intransigence – the degree to which satisfactory policy appears far from discovery.

There is a case for variety in method in approaching any difficult policy dilemma. That case grows, the greater the intransigence of the policy dilemma. If a search for a solution by established policy-seeking methods proves abortive, the case for a variety of policy-seeking methods grows. There would be no such case if there were indeed a simple relationship between method of policy derivation and policy. All that would be required would be efforts to improve the performance of the correct method, by extending the data used, or increasing the rigour of the method. Yet if we do not know the correct method, improving the method used may be significantly less important than extending the range of methods used.

There is a further reason for variety in method in the domain of derivation. Any policy dilemma is set in a certain policy area. A policy area can be defined as the environment, activities, beliefs and actors which are deemed relevant to the policy dilemma. Policy areas are normally defined by the substantive area of concern which may itself be defined narrowly or broadly, namely, pollution policy, rents policy, town centre development. Different policy areas require different policy-making methods. A high degree of certainty may require different policy-making methods from one in which uncertainty is dominant. In a particular complex policy area with many different policy characteristics a variety of methods may be required to understand and analyse the policy area and to derive policies. Many complex policy areas are impermeable if approached by only one broad policy-seeking strategy. Advance has to be made where advance can be made and that requires a variety of methods.

What is required is variety in approaches to policy derivation. One needs heuristics that will suggest such variety in approaches. The rational model can be regarded in the context of policy derivation as one heuristic. It is, however, limited. It suggests a certain approach but not others. It leads not to variety but to a single approach. What is wanted is heuristics that extend variety in policy derivation. Thus:

- know the shape of the policy area;
- new alternatives require a change in the framework of thought;
- a new policy requires new stories;
- judgement knows no rules, but it can be encouraged;
- policy achievement can be understood even if it cannot be measured.

These aphorisms lack the sharpness of the rational model, but they may serve better as heuristics for policy derivation. Their role is to start processes of thought. These processes should help the understanding and exploration of the policy dilemma, generate alternative policies and deepen the judgement of them. What follows is written as befits suggestions rather than as required by rules.

IV KNOW THE SHAPE OF THE POLICY AREA

Most statements of the rational model begin with either the setting of objectives or the identification of needs and problems. There is a prior and an important stage. It can be described as 'know the shape of the policy area', 'map the understanding of the policy area', or 'get the feel of the policy area', but the implication is that one does not merely assume one knows the shape, has the understanding, or has the feel of the policy area. The implication is that one learns by challenge and questioning that will generate a new understanding of the policy area. Challenge and questioning can centre on

- constraints and opportunities
- dominant assumptions
- conflict and consensus
- patternings of behaviour
- dimensions of time.

Challenge and questioning are meant to deepen understanding of the policy area. They provide the means for understanding. They do not predetermine its nature. Questions are posed not to be answered in full detail, but to start processes of thought.

Constraints and Opportunities

For policy analysis to make a relevant contribution it must be set in the web of policy constraints and opportunities – not merely the web that is reflected in the dominant myths, but in the web of policy constraints and opportunities that emerges when those myths are challenged.

In local government dominant myths stress the major constraints of statute. Challenge lies in the identification of the actual constraints:

- constraints of statute
- constraints of resources
- constraints of knowledge
- constraints of values.

The identification should be undertaken to find not merely constraints but also where opportunities are greatest. Policy areas vary. Sometimes the lawyer can find a path through the constraints of statute. He takes the path where opportunities are greatest. The lawyer has a role in policy analysis that this approach identifies. He is a geographer of policy space, identifying the gradients of statutory opportunity and statutory constraint. Other approaches can challenge other constraints.

There is a testing approach. It is the process of dissolving constraints. This can be done by testing whether and how the constraints can be dissolved over time. Given time, resources can be built up or adapted, statutes can be changed, knowledge accumulated, or values challenged. By projecting constraints over time the permeability of the constraints can be tested.

The policy area is marked by constraints but also by present opportunities and opportunities to be made. The mapping of those constraints and opportunities is part of the geography of the policy area.

Dominant Assumptions

In any policy area there are existing policies to be understood. All existing policy lies embedded in assumptions which are more important to its understanding than are objectives. If objectives have meaning in policy derivation they have meaning only within the framework of assumptions held by those who set them.

A policy at its simplest assumes:

x leads to *y*
y is wanted
x will have *v* other effects
x will have no other effects apart from *y* and *v*

– even where those assumptions are not stated.

Assumptions have to be exposed in order to be challenged. Challenge tests how firmly based assumptions are, how widely held they are and how susceptible they are to change – and at what point. Assumptions underlie not merely a policy but also a policy area so that they limit those who seek new policies. The firmness of the base on which assumptions are set is part of the shape of the policy area.

Conflict and Consensus

Policy areas are crossed by lines of conflict and co-operation deriving from the different interests affected by the policy area. The criss-crossing of the policy areas by lines of conflict and co-operation defines shared and conflicting interests. The policy area can be regarded as moulded by forces of conflict and consensus.

In understanding a policy area, conflict and consensus have to be understood, as have the sources of conflict and the bases of consensus. The questions are posed to aid the understanding. What are the main interests in the policy area? Are there latent interests that have not yet been recognised? Are there interests even though not articulated? What are the main lines of conflict in the policy area? Where and for whom is the consensus? What are the main values held? Are there dominant values? The questions will not and cannot all be answered. They are questions to deepen understanding.

Patternings of Behaviour

Policies must be based on an understanding of the main patternings of physical, social and economic behaviour that affect or are affected by the policy area. Patternings of behaviour are not fixed over time. They lie in a particular society at a particular moment in time. What are the main patternings of behaviour relevant to the policy area – social, economic, physical? Policy can be designed to work with the patterning, to guide it, to modify it, or bear with it.

Dimensions of Time
The policy area can be conceptualised in terms of relative stability or relative instability over time. It can be conceptualised in relative certainty and relative uncertainty. Questions can be posed. Is the policy area changing? Where is it changing? Where is it not changing? Is the rate of change increasing? Can one cast a future scenario for the policy area easily or with difficulty? Are eddies of certainty or uncertainty dominant?

Knowing the Policy Area
Challenge and questioning can be directed at the very boundaries of the policy area itself. A policy area has been defined by what is considered relevant to the policy dilemma. That definition can itself be challenged.

The shape of the policy area, however defined, cannot be known merely through a set of predetermined questions. That would imply its shape was already known. The heuristics have to be loosely formed – not with the sharp delineation of the rational model. They should start processes of thought and imagination – which will deepen understanding and reveal new aspects of the policy area in which the analyst has to work.

V A NEW FRAMEWORK OF THOUGHT FOR NEW ALTERNATIVES

There are different policy dilemmas in which different approaches to policy are required. What may be required is incremental adjustment to existing policy. In that situation existing policy is dominant in thinking about alternatives. With policy dilemmas in which the policy area is known and bounded and certain limited measurable factors are identified as influential, quantitative techniques may be used to derive alternative policy within the boundaries identified.

Both such policy dilemmas are dominated by the known and by clear boundaries of policy derivation. They are policy dilemmas in the solution of which thought is constrained. Many policy dilemmas are of this type. But not all are, or need be. There are policy dilemmas which call for policy thought that is not so constrained. The problem is then how to avoid constraint in the range of policy alternatives generated.

New alternatives that require a breakthrough in constraints on thought can only be derived by approaches aimed at transforming the framework of thought in which the constraints are set. To achieve such a breakthrough is not easy. What may be required may be hunch and intuition coupled with the good sense to recognise a viable suggestion, as scientific discovery can take place by accident, coupled with the ability to recognise a discovery, which requires a deep understanding of the scientific area concerned.

The problem is to create conditions that make a breakthrough possible. This requires the challenging of existing frameworks of thought leading to alternative frameworks. The mixture of modes of thought represented by the interdisciplinary group may be important as a basis for brainstorming in a policy area previously considered the prerogative of a particular discipline.

Any policy is based on a set of assumptions. If some of those assumptions are removed the support for that framework is destroyed. A conscious removal of assumptions can lead to the generation of new policy options, which may even survive the restoration of some of the assumptions.

Thought is often constrained by the apparent certainty of the present. In the apparent necessity of the present it may not always be possible to recognise the possibilities of the future. Constraints can be dissolved over time, but until they are dissolved they limit present thinking. Scenario-writing can help to break through such constraints on thought. If one starts from *x* it may not be possible to see *y*. Present constraints set it beyond the possible. However, if in a scenario *y* is seen as the goal, it may be possible to work out paths from *x*. Scenario-writing can play a role in changing the framework of thought.

In any policy area there are likely to be points of friction where policy fits, but uncomfortably. Many of these points will be felt by those who have to operate the policy at the point at which it touches the outside world. Knowledge of points of friction may not be readily transmitted in large-scale organisations. Administrative hierarchies rub off the friction contained in information as it flows up the hierarchy. Points of friction can suggest the need for new alternatives – if they can be identified.

These are all aids to generating alternative policies. Selection, sifting and analysis of alternatives are required in policy derivation, but there can be a prior stage. Constraints on thought have first to be broken so that new alternatives can be developed.

VI A NEW POLICY NEEDS A NEW STORY

A policy needs a setting. To be accepted it must be set in an accepted framework of ideas and experience. Otherwise it will not be seen as relevant by those called upon to adopt it. A policy must have anchorage in events and ideas that are accepted by the policy-makers. In this way the domain of policy adoption has an impact on the domain of policy derivation. A policy must also – if it involves a significant change – show a clear relationship to the frictions that have led to the recognition of the need for new policy. Policy change rests in the discomfort and friction between existing policy (or lack of policy) and the world on which the policy impacts. Policy comfort or well-fitted policies generate but little policy change.

Round any policy, and the events that it is supposed to encompass, a policy account (or story) is built up (see Rein, 1979, pp. 266–7). It is compounded of the assumptions made and the facts acknowledged. It explains and elaborates them. Such policy accounts underlie existing policies and serve, in so far as the account is accepted, to justify them. Such accounts may derive from major reports or academic works, as the accounts of Keynes and Beveridge underlie much social and economic policy in postwar Britain. Actual policy may be far from the account as the policy of high-rise flats was far from the original account of Corbusier.

Policies can be disturbed by new and uncomfortable events that do not fit the patterns of behaviour expected in the policy accounts. The event may be a symbol that focuses discontent as Ronan Point focused the public discontent with high-rise flats. Such uncomfortable events destroy the framework of existing assumptions and expectations that underlie existing policy. That destruction eliminates the existing policy story.

A new policy story has to be found. A policy story links events, assumptions and expectations in a way that is satisfying to the main decision-makers and perhaps to the main actors. It requires inventiveness and that inventiveness can itself generate new policy. Policy slogans, which are after all simplified policy stories, can be important in persuasion as politicians have long recognised. They can also generate ideas.

In establishing a new policy, the policy story is critical. The creation of the high-rise flats and their demise was the replacement of one story by another. The crisis of the inner city destroyed old stories and new policies for the inner city were based on new stories. The inner area research studies were a means of developing those new policy stories.

The derivation of policy when significant change is required needs the inventiveness of the storyteller in linking together experience and values in ways that can lead to new policies.

VII JUDGEMENT IS A DELICATE FLOWER, IT CAN BE KILLED BY THE HARSHNESS OF EVALUATION

The judgement of a policy is not made by evaluation as described in the rational model. Such evaluation belongs to the domain of policy justification. It has its rules. Judgement belongs to the domain of policy derivation and cannot be so simply rule-bounded.

Judgement demands an understanding of the shape of the policy area to be judged. It demands an understanding of the shape of the policy to be judged. 'Shape' is the phrase used because concern is for gradients of possibility, the robustness of assumptions, the thickness of constraint, the gaps of opportunity and the mapping of interests. Judgement can be assisted. It cannot be made by substitution of rules for judgement, but questions as heuristics can be used that will deepen the basis on which policy judgement is made. The answers to questions provide the background to judgement, not a means of making the judgement. Who gains and who loses? And by how much? These after all are key questions of politics and hence critical to the judgement of public policy. What values are sustained by the emerging policy and what undermined? This question is related to, but not the same as, the first question, recognising that interests are sustained and are undermined by policy change, but also that ideology can extend or contract the sphere of interests.

On what assumption does the policy depend? How robust is the policy against change in assumptions? Each policy rests on a bed of assumptions. A judgement has to be made on their reliability. How many points of decision does the policy involve? What actors are involved in role change? How critical are the role changes? The policy has to be feasible. Feasibility may be endangered by obstacles to be overcome. The extent of those obstacles must be judged. Does the policy follow, guide, modify, challenge, block existing patterns of social behaviour? And of economic behaviour? Does it change or maintain existing behaviour? The relation of the policy to the world in which it is set has to be plotted. How near to present policy, philosophically and politically, is the policy suggested? Are any of the alternatives considered derived from different philosophies of government? How wide has been the search? And what would be the cost of further search? The relationship of the proposed policy to past search and potential search needs to be understood. Has the policy followed the easiest path as plotted by gradients of constraint and opportunity? It is not that easier paths must always be sought, but that the fact that they exist should be known.

Answers to these questions do not constitute judgement, but they are a basis for judgement. Judgement follows and is not made by analysis. To expect more is to expect judgement to be rule-bound – as if it were evaluation. The purpose in asking them is to gain the understanding necessary to informed judgement even if the questions prove unanswerable. It is asking them that is important.

VIII THE UNDERSTANDING OF ACHIEVEMENT IS NEARER REALITY THAN THE MEASUREMENT OF OUTPUT

The phrase deliberately chosen is ‘understanding of achievement’. To ask an officer or politician to measure output can be self-defeating. The request will often be automatically refused – either in a straightforward denial of its possibility or in the subtly dangerous sterility of output measures so limited that they have no credibility in any real process of policy-making.

The request will be denied in reality, if not in form. It runs contrary to the ideology of the service. That ideology is part of the service. The service cannot be understood without an understanding of the ideology. To request of the service that which is contrary to the ideology is not therefore to assist understanding of the service but to deny the means of understanding. A service that does not aim at measurable outputs – or believes that it does not – cannot be understood through measurable outputs, or at least not through measurable outputs directly sought and directly obtained. Thus the search to measure outputs in local authority social services can be seen as an attack upon their ideology. This is no retreat because output measurement is itself only a surrogate. It is a way to meet a particular need – the need to understand achievement.

Yet the barriers that are created by the phrase 'output measurement' are not necessarily created by the phrase 'understanding achievement'. Few professionals (including those engaged in local authority social services) would deny the need to understand achievement and most would believe that there are achievements to be understood. They might even go further and in soft and varying language start to describe that achievement. There is a rich vein to be tapped in understanding achievement. The routinisation of output measures does not tap that vein. Rather it blocks it up. It not only challenges the ideology of the service, but denies much knowledge. What is required is a means of approaching that knowledge and that understanding that is concerned to reap its richness and not to reduce the richness to a routine.

Processes can be devised that fit the circumstances of particular policies. To seek processes that bring out and characterise the sense of achievement or its lack is to open to review that which cannot be reviewed by routinised output measures.

IX WHERE WE HAVE REACHED

The heuristics put forward are for the domain of policy derivation. They are for the policy analyst who seeks a richer guide than the rational model for the derivation of policy. The heuristics are not for the domain of policy adoption, although they reflect the need to anticipate both constraint and opportunity in that domain. The heuristics are certainly not for the domain of justification. They are exploratory. They do not have the finality appropriate to the domain of justification. They belong to the domain of policy derivation. They guide. They do not enforce. They are appropriate to their domain. Too often the rational model with its rules for justification has been seen as a heuristic for the domain of policy derivation. That model leads to one approach but not others. Policy derivation requires many approaches.

This chapter has sought heuristics that go beyond the rational model:

- know the shape of the policy area;
- new alternatives require new frameworks of thought;
- a new policy needs a new story;
- judgement is deepened by many questions;
- policy achievement can be understood even if it cannot be measured.

They are a starting point for policy derivation. Once derived then the rational model has a special role. Policy has also to be justified.

NOTES: CHAPTER 2

1 Allison, 1971, shows how different frameworks of thought can be used in the study of the same event. He describes three models: the rational actor; organisational process; government process. The argument of this chapter would be that the first model is appropriate to the domain of policy justification, while the other two models are appropriate to the domain of policy adoption. Models for the understanding of policy derivation are imperfectly developed. Hence the focus of this chapter.

2 See Chapter 1 for a discussion of the rational model.

3

Corporate Planning in Local Government

CHRIS SKELCHER

In the period of local government reorganisation during the early 1970s the corporate approach was advocated as a central feature of the new authorities' operation.[1] Since then the application of the interrelated concepts of corporate planning and corporate management have been criticised as inefficient, bureaucratic and time-wasting (see, for example, *Corporate Planning Journal*, 1977; Butcher and Dawkins, 1978; Haynes, 1978) or technocratic, counter-democratic and business-oriented (see, for example, Benington, 1976; Cockburn, 1977) depending on the political perspective of the commentator. The aim of this chapter is to explore one particular facet of the corporate approach – the annual policy planning and budgetary cycle – as it has evolved in a variety of authorities during the past six years. After setting the background to the corporate approach, the chapter will review the structure of the annual cycle and the main lines of development which different local authorities have pursued. On this basis the final section raises a number of questions about the form and sequence of the process and its relationship to policy outcomes.

THE RISE OF THE CORPORATE APPROACH

Some local authorities began to experiment with elements of a corporate approach in the late 1960s, introducing the PPBS (planning programme budgeting system) methodology which had originally been pioneered by the US Department of Defense. Often drawing on the advice of private sector business consultants, London boroughs such as Greenwich and Lambeth developed the variously titled corporate, community, or programme planning systems, as did a small number of authorities in other parts of the country, notably Coventry, Stockport and Gloucestershire (Merrington, 1974; Greenwood and Stewart, 1974; Stewart, 1973). In most authorities, however, the impetus of local government reorganisation in 1974 (1975 in Scotland) provided the opportunity to apply the concept of ordering the activities of the authority as a whole in relation to needs and issues in the community.

For adherents the corporate approach provided three things – a set of ideas, an organisational structure and a process of operation

(Stewart, 1971; Earwicker, 1976). Central were the ideas, the philosophy informing both the structure and process of the local authority. In summary, these were that there should be a unity of purpose in the affairs of the local authority, with activities and resources geared explicitly to meeting changing needs and issues in the community. Such ideas rested on a set of beliefs about the nature of the environment and the role of the local authority in relation to its environment. The environment was perceived as complex and dynamic and containing issues such as urban decay, poverty and unemployment which local government could not ignore yet which were outside its traditional areas of concern and expertise. In a number of cases problems facing the community could be laid directly at the door of local government (J. G. Davies, 1972; Department of the Environment, 1977d), but even where this was not so – the closure of a major industrial plant, for instance – there was an expectation that the local authority would respond. This new image of the local authority as an active body striving alone or with others to tackle pressing issues in the community (Stewart, 1975) contrasted strongly with the traditional view of the local authority as a set of separate departments providing services largely independent of each other.

The philosophy of the corporate approach was given substance in proposals relating to both organisational structures and planning and decision-making processes. The structures were enshrined in the Bains Report for England and Wales (Department of the Environment, 1972) and the Paterson Report for Scotland (Paterson Committee, 1972), both of which suggested on the officer side the appointment of a chief executive to manage the authority as a whole, supported by a management team of the heads of departments, and on the member side a policy and resources committee of leading councillors to discuss and decide on major policy matters. At a general level these structures were adopted by virtually all the new authorities, although in some cases with different terms used to label the elements. While the post of chief executive was abolished in two or three authorities (in Birmingham, for instance, the position was deleted from the establishment and the city treasurer was redesignated principal chief officer and city treasurer), there has been a high degree of uniformity and stability in corporate structures throughout British local government (see, for instance, Greenwood, Hinings and Ranson, 1975; Midwinter, 1978). By contrast, wide differences are revealed in the policy and resource-planning processes of local authorities.

The rational model of decision-making underlay proposals for the corporate planning process (Meyerson and Banfield, 1955; Hambleton, 1978; Stewart, 1971), which contained five main stages. First, the analysis of needs, issues and problems in the community (the *community* or *environmental review*) which were matched against the existing activities and programmes of the authority (the *position statement*) to identify unmet needs or gaps in provision; secondly, the definition of objectives and setting of priorities; thirdly, the development of alternative programmes to meet objectives and tackle priority issues or gaps in provision; fourthly, the selection of that option going furthest towards the achievement of objectives and priorities, mobilising resources and establishing procedures of implementation; and fifthly, monitoring and reviewing the activities of the local authority and changes in the environment as a means of assessing the achievement and continuing appropriateness of objectives and programmes, an activity overlapping with stage one to form a cycle. A relatively small proportion of local authorities have adopted a formal cycle of activities based on the rational model, and those which have tended to be inner London boroughs, metropolitan districts or non-metropolitan counties; a handful of non-metropolitan districts have recently introduced or are now introducing formal planning processes (Skelcher, 1979a, 1979b). Those authorities which have developed an annual policy planning and budgetary cycle are the subject of this chapter.

POLICY PLANNING AND RESOURCE ALLOCATION

The annual process of resource allocation is a central activity for each local authority, since decisions here influence the development or maintenance of services and the realisation of political objectives. Consequently the relationship of policy planning to resource allocation has become a crucial issue in both the theory and application of the corporate approach.

The question of resources was seen as particularly important in the critique of the traditional management style of local authorities. In part because of the way in which local government had evolved from a series of fragmented local boards, there was a tendency for local authority departments to perceive resources as 'theirs' rather than belonging to the authority as a whole. An extreme but not untypical example was the case of the 'ransom strips' in Birmingham. Because the Housing Acts were used in clearance areas, the housing committee regarded the land so required as belonging to them. Having provided the highways committee with land for a road, the housing committee would retain a two-foot-wide 'ransom strip' on either side, thus enabling it to control the development of adjacent sites by other committees through the potential to refuse access over 'its' land (*Corporate Planning Journal*, 1977). Applying the corporate approach meant liberating resources from permanent departmental control explicitly in order to make authority-wide decisions on resource levels and allocation in relation to community needs and political priorities. There was to be a relationship between resource allocation decisions and the policy planning process of the authority as a whole. Thus 'the annual budget . . . should flow from the longer term corporate plans of the local authority [but] it should not be a separate and totally distinct exercise' (Hepworth, 1978, p. 212). As Stewart has shown, the traditional budget could not be regarded as adequate for planning purposes, in terms of either its internal structuring and presentation or the type of information it contained, since it was geared to a financial control role (Stewart, 1971).

While at a theoretical, prescriptive level the connection was made between policy planning and resource allocation, and those concerned with corporate planning in local government came to see the budget as a crucial means of realising corporate objectives and avoiding paper plans, in practice the relationship was slow to develop. Greenwood *et al.*, writing on the experience of a sample of authorities in the two years after reorganisation, comment (1976, pp. 87–8):

> One of the significant features of some local government authorities is the juxtaposition of traditional budgetary procedures alongside rather more novel policy [corporate] planning procedures. In these authorities the problem is one of bringing these systems together, causing them to lock. In some cases the impression is of corporate systems becoming more and more refined (even if still relatively crude) but having rather little or only peripheral impact upon the budgetary process. The preparation of issue analysis reports can be carried on, yet in the final analysis resources are allocated via a Spanish Inquisition.

It was, however, the pressures and challenges of constraint in local authorities' resource environment, starting with the publication of DoE Circular 171/74, that provided the impetus to relate formally the policy and resource processes. With zero or severely limited growth in financial resources, traditional forms of incremental budgeting were perceived as inappropriate. There was a desire to relate changes in levels of expenditure to priorities and to look for redistribution from less important budget heads. The corporate approach provided the means.

Because developments in practice were strongly influenced by the need to rationalise allocation procedures as a means of increasing control over the distribution and levels of resources, there is a validity in the assertions of Cockburn and others that the corporate approach was introduced to strengthen financial control in local authorities (Cockburn, 1977). But this view is only partially correct. As Paris and Blackaby note (1979, pp. 216–17):

> Budgetary control can be exercised within any management structure. Our experience in Birmingham was that budgetary constraint was imposed in spite of a corporate approach, certainly not because of it, and that the admittedly embryonic overall corporate process was not more likely to obscure and mystify cuts in public expenditure that any other framework of administration.

If financial control were the only concern, then the traditional attitude to resources and budgeting would suit equally well if not better than an annual cycle incorporating policy reviews, option exploration and priority setting. While the techniques employed in this corporate process may be based on questionable concepts (Benington, 1976), the very fact that authorities explicitly identify priorities for growth or cuts, rather than taking the existing pattern of expenditure as given, opens up a political debate around the process and the choices raised. On this basis the introduction of annual policy and resource planning cycles can be seen as meeting more than purely financial control objectives.

THE ANNUAL PLANNING CYCLE

In general the policy planning and budgetary process is built around an annual cycle ending in March with the agreement of estimates for the following financial year and declaration of the rate, but starting some twelve or even fifteen months beforehand. This annual cycle extends the budget exercise which lasts from September/October through to March, as well as reordering the sequence of events in that process. The traditional budgeting system is the *committee bid* approach. Claims for extra resources by individual committees are aggregated and, taking into account estimated rate support grant (RSG), other income and movements in pay and prices, give the rate levy required to finance the bids. The central finance committee would then take a decision on the politically acceptable rate levy and the size of bids would be revised accordingly. As public expenditure cuts began to bite, many local authorities adopted the alternative *resource rationing* system in which, on the basis of an estimate of RSG, inflation, and so on, early on in the process, a target rate levy and priorities are decided and guidance is given to committees for the preparation of their estimates (Hepworth, 1978). This guidance can take the form of reduction targets or growth limits expressed in percentage or volume terms. Some authorities, for instance, Cleveland, have asked committees to work to a series of test levels of growth or reduction before making a final decision on the rate target and consequent committee expenditure guidelines (Barras and Geary, 1979). The policy planning element of the annual cycle prefaces this budgetary stage, and is intended to review the authority's activities, identify changes in the environment and explore options for change.

A typical annual policy and budgetary cycle is that employed by Clwyd, lasting fifteen months and having four main stages. The process starts in January with the preparation by individual committees of *position statements* describing activities, issues, resources available and development priorities. Following their completion in April, the *county programme* is formulated centrally, outlining resource forecasts, expenditure guidelines and key objectives, and is presented in July to the main committee, policy finance and resources. Taking into account the guidelines contained in the agreed county programme, committees draw up *programme option statements* which identify alternative ways of meeting needs set out in the position statements, together with the finance and manpower implications of each option. Individual committees select preferred options in September, which are then presented to Policy Finance and Resources in October. This provides the input to the budget estimates procedure where, on the basis of existing commitments and activities and the agreed reduction or growth options, draft estimates are prepared and presented to committees in December and, following last-minute tactical changes to take account of the RSG announcement, to Policy Finance and Resources in February for the declaration of the rate.

While this description of Clwyd's annual cycle is very much simplified, it illustrates the underlying logic of the integrated policy planning and budgetary process employed in a number of authorities (*Corporate Planning Journal*, 1978). Across the country, however, there has been a considerable variety in the development and application of annual cycles. In some cases this is due to relative experience; Middlesbrough and Bradford, for example, were able to draw on the development work undertaken by their predecessor authorities while the majority of post-reorganisation authorities were starting from scratch. The attitude of key individuals in the authority is also significant, particularly the treasurer, chief executive and political leadership. In authorities such as Arun and Central Regional Council the treasurer and director of finance respectively supported the development of an integrated policy planning and budgeting process, while in some other authorities a different disposition has prevailed. There are, however, an increasing number of local authorities who have introduced or are in the process of evolving such a systematic process. The former class includes Berkshire, Bolton, Coventry, Arun and Waltham Forest, while such authorities as Lancaster have only recently taken the decision to establish a system of corporate planning and as a first step are exploring the form of the budget process. A few authorities, such as Kingston upon Thames, having experimented with a systematic process in earlier years, are now reassessing and modifying their approach. In the following pages four aspects of the policy planning and budgetary process are explored, drawing on the experience of a range of local authorities. These are the question of priority setting, the introduction of greater selectivity, the development of longer-term planning horizons and moves to counteract centralist tendencies.

PRIORITY SETTING

As the form and substance of the annual decision-making process in local authorities has become more explicit, and as public expenditure constraint has challenged the convention of automatic incremental growth in committee and authority resources, so a formal priority setting element has been introduced. Two general approaches to priority setting in local government can be identified. The first is *activity-based*, starting from the existing services and activities of the authority and aiming to identify their relative priority. Berkshire employs such an approach early in its annual cycle when, following the publication of the Black Book (a series of position statements supplemented with a commentary on financial resources and changes in the authority's environment), all members are surveyed and asked to rank activities according to their preference for marginal expenditure changes in the following budget. In the 1979/80 process, for example, highest priority was accorded to police authority staff, followed by fire operations, highway services and maintenance, and primary and secondary teaching staff, while the lowest priorities in descending order were planning, trading standards and school meals and milk (Gash, 1979; Berkshire County Council, 1979).

The second method of priority setting can broadly be termed the *issue-based* approach. Rather than starting from the detailed services and activities of the authority, this system focuses on issues facing the authority, often expressed in the form of policy statements. In the process leading to Lewisham's 1978/9 budget, guidance was issued that highest priority for committee developments, if necessary at the expense of other services, should be afforded to measures aimed at alleviating community stress – identified as housing, community activity provision, the needs of ethnic minority groups and employment. A related approach is used in Arun, where as part of the annual cycle members rank a set of agreed policy guidelines which are then applied to committee developments in the budget process.

While elected members are the focus of priority setting exercises, some authorities also undertake priority surveys of senior officers. Thus in Central Region the management team, as well as members, were asked as part of the 1979/80 process to state which of the 1978/9 issues and policies were still relevant and to rank those selected. The explicit introduction of public or community priorities is as yet underdeveloped in local authorities.

INTRODUCING SELECTIVITY

In many authorities which have developed an annual cycle the exercise is comprehensive in the sense that it covers the whole spectrum of activities and services. As priority begins to be given to particular issues or policy areas, however, so there is a natural progression towards complementary selective in-depth analysis. Such key issue work has rapidly developed in local authorities in recent years, in part because of the interdepartmental or non-departmental nature of such priority concerns as rural deprivation, the elderly, or the local economy. Key issues such as these would be covered at best in a partial and organisationally disjointed manner within the main committee-based policy review and budget development process. Three main ways in which selectivity can be introduced are by topic, client group and geographical area. Arun provides an example of the role of a topic study in informing policy considerations, since a detailed study of the impact of tourism on the district clarified the basis for policy formulation and decision-making and enabled an appropriate policy guideline to be established. A similar case is evident in

Lancaster, where a study of population and housing had a major impact on the development priorities of the authority, again by clarifying the basis for policy-making. Client group studies provide a second approach to selectivity, and many authorities have undertaken policy studies on provision for the under-5s and the elderly. Some local authorities have set up special subcommittees comprising both members and representatives of client groups, as in the case of Lewisham Policy Committee's women's rights working party which has had a considerable effect in raising issues related to council policy and practice (Coote, 1979, p. 891). A third way of introducing selectivity is by geographical area, such as Thamesdown's study of the issues facing and resources available in the villages surrounding Swindon (Thamesdown Borough Council, 1978). While these are the three main ways of introducing selectivity into corporate policy studies, other ways have also been used: for instance, Clwyd has undertaken policy studies on each of the authority's four key objectives.

The major problem for selective policy studies is in developing effective links with the main decision processes in the authority. The cases cited above may well be the exception to a general rule that policy studies, as with much research activity, will tend to languish in obscurity because no means have been identified to bring them into the practical decision arena. Bradford provides an example of an authority which is exploring the link between policy studies and the main decision processes in the authority. Key issues for further investigation, either by interdepartmental key issue teams of officers or by individual departments, are identified each autumn by members as part of Metplan (the annual cycle) and reports are fed back early in the following year's cycle. Recommendations with financial implications may be funded from specially earmarked budgets created by base-searching and redistribution from low-priority expenditure heads. In a period of financial constraint, however, difficulties can arise in funding action on corporate priorities where such projects must compete for resources with established committee spending programmes. This is illustrated in the case of rural community development in Hereford and Worcester. In response to concern by the public and councillors from Herefordshire that resources were being redistributed from their area in favour of the urban centres in Worcestershire. Hereford and Worcester County Council together with the appropriate district councils and the rural community council jointly sponsored the Rural Community Development Project (RCDP). The RCDP consisted of a small inter-authority project team whose brief was to explore the issues facing a sample of parishes in rural Herefordshire and develop 'trial projects' aimed at meeting identified needs. The team requested a block allocation of £50,000, arguing that schemes crossed committee responsibilities and that such an arrangement would prevent delay while each separate trial project was argued through individual committees. The sum of £25,000 was eventually allocated, but not in a block form. Schemes were thus required to compete with individual committee priorities for funding, and because the authority at this time was facing financial constraint the projects proposed by the RCDP team met with limited success in attracting county council expenditure (Hereford and Worcester County Council, 1978).

The move to selectivity is occurring also in the form of the policy planning and budgetary cycle. There are indications that while selectivity is occurring *within* the cycle, as described above, authorities are exploring the possibility of applying the process *itself* in a selective way with a full run every two or three years rather than annually. In the development of their regional report and budget process Central Region considered as one option the undertaking of a full cycle of activity and policy review, problem identification and priority setting (prior to the estimates procedure) every fourth year, to coincide with the election of the new council. In practice, however, a full cycle is undertaken biennially, with a review in the intervening year (*Corporate Planning Journal*, 1979). A number of other authorities are now also beginning to develop similar selective processes.

EXTENDING PLANNING HORIZONS

Proposals for a four-yearly full cycle, such as that investigated by Central Region, are important for two reasons. The first is that it provides the new council with the opportunity to undertake a wide-ranging review of issues and activities and hence to apply an appropriate strategy based on political priorities. The difficulties of applying such a system in England, however, are that metropolitan districts (and a considerable number of non-metropolitan districts) have elections by thirds, thus providing no regular opportunity for full policy review and strategy development related to the political cycle in those authorities.

The second point is that it raises the concept of a longer-term strategy for the authority and hence of extended planning horizons. Multi-year budgets and financial programmes are gaining acceptability in local government, especially in relation to capital projects where starts need to be programmed ahead and investment is spread over several years. This process has been expedited through the introduction of five-year rolling programmes in transport (transport policies and programmes) and housing (housing strategy and investment programmes) and in Scotland additionally the financial plan covering all capital expenditure by a local authority over a five-year rolling period. On the revenue side, medium-term budgets have been slower in appearing often because the concept is seen as implying a degree of certainty unrealistic when RSG is announced only for one year and inflation and interests rates are dynamic. Despite these constraints multi-year budgets have been introduced by a number of local authorities, since decisions on whether to increase, reduce, or significantly alter the level or distribution of financial resources need to be viewed and planned over several years. The annual rolling forward of multi-year revenue budgets provides the opportunity to take account of changes in the resource environment, and further elaboration such as the application of probabilities to a range of expenditure levels and the development of contingency plans can also aid the management of uncertainty (Public Finance and Accountancy, 1979).

Extending budget horizons is only one part of the picture, since decisions on resource allocation need to be set within a broader policy strategy for the authority as a whole. Longer-term policy planning takes a somewhat different perspective, being concerned with strategic rather than tactical planning and with 'anticipating events, making diagnoses and shaping appropriate courses of action, so that the organisation can be in the best position, ready and capable, to respond effectively to contingencies' (Mottley, 1978, p. 127). Such strategy development by local authorities, then, would be concerned with identifying and exploring desirable images of the future, and on this basis providing a direction for policy. However, as Firth has argued, 'there is precious little evidence of authorities really trying to think about the sort of community they are trying to create . . . Part of this is due to the lack of priority given to the study of future options' (Firth, 1979, p. 300). This reflects the tendency for short-term considerations to predominate, particularly in the current resource environment, and yet there is a need for local authorities to think about the future not only to help shape existing programmes but also as an aid to the development of contingency plans. A range of techniques are available and are increasingly used in corporate forward planning in the private sector; in local government,

> futurology and simulation would both play an important part in considering policy impacts and future environments. Futurology and gaming would both give systematic treatment to the extra-rational component of policy-making, where only a few . . . documents touch at present. (Earwicker, 1976, p. 6)

Some local authorities are developing approaches to longer-term policy and resource planning. For several years Coventry has produced the ten-year City Policy Guide, updated in the February–November period of the annual cycle and with Year One subsequently progressing through the detailed estimates procedure. This document outlines the main geographical and programme priorities and lines of development and provides a picture of planned revenue expenditure for the first four years and the last year of the plan period together with year-by-year capital starts and costs (Coventry City Council, 1978). Cambridgeshire has recently introduced a three-year rolling medium-term plan, which is approved by council in July, Year One being the basis for the subsequent estimates (Cambridgeshire County Council, 1979).

In the earlier stages of the annual cycle, when issues are identified, policies reviewed and options developed, a broader and longer-term look at the authority and its relationship to its environment could most appropriately be undertaken. Here there is an opportunity for freer and unconstrained thinking on policy direction and strategy before the immediate financial questions of the following year's budget present themselves. Contextual studies, such as the 'ten years ahead' work on particular issues undertaken in Cheshire, provide an example.

COUNTERING CENTRALIST TENDENCIES

A frequently voiced criticism of the corporate approach in practice is that it is associated with the centralisation of power in the authority both *horizontally*, in the sense that the traditionally autonomous service departments have become subject to increasing direction by the policy and resources committee, and *vertically* as the hierarchy of decision-making is reinforced through the leader–chief executive nexus. While the *structure* of power may have changed through the introduction of new central committees, departments and officer posts, it is debatable whether the *degree* of centralisation has significantly altered, given the dominance of one or two key figures – often the clerk to the council and an established politician – in pre-reorganisation local authorities (see, for example, Jones and Norton, 1978).

However, access to the policy planning and budgetary process in local authorities is in many cases 'closed' in the sense that it focuses on and involves a small group of senior officers and leading members. In one sense, then, corporate planning is not conducted 'corporately': many groups both inside and outside the authority are excluded or have only a marginal involvement in, and impact on, the process. A few local authorities are beginning to widen access to corporate planning and hence to temper centralist control, or at least provide opportunities for debate and the input of alternatives. Three groups in particular are being involved. The first is the councillor, both in his role as a ward member, drawing on his knowledge about local affairs and needs, and also as a backbencher. Secondly, there is the 'field-worker', an omnibus term covering a wide range of public sector employees: the health visitor, social worker, environmental health officer, youth worker, teacher, policeman, educational welfare officer, counter clerk in the housing or DHSS office, and so on, a group referred to in the United States as 'street-level bureaucrats' (M. Lipsky, 1976). These individuals, because of their structural position in the public agency and their task of delivering services direct to the consumer, often have a detailed and unique store of knowledge about issues facing groups in the community and the individual and cumulative impact of the operation of public and private organisations. Like the ward member they can hold a store of knowledge about corporate and intercorporate impact at the grassroots. And the third group is the public, either in general or in terms of individuals concerned with particular issues or areas and who are ultimately at the receiving end of local authority actions. Involvement with political parties and local councillors provides one means of input into local authority decision-making, but some authorities are also seeking more regular and structured means of contact on corporate policy and resource issues.

Lewisham is one of the local authorities which has experimented with arrangements to bring one or more of these groups into the policy process. In autumn 1975 a *ward report* system was introduced with the explicit aim of introducing the ward member's perspective into the central planning and decision process of the authority, and this has subsequently been repeated in 1977 and 1979. Ward members themselves produce the ward report on local issues which are considered together with the comments of officers by the corporate planning subcommittee of the appropriate main committees, who decide what further action to take. The ward reports also form an input to the policy committee's review of corporate priorities in July. The second element of Lewisham's approach is the ward seminars, held experimentally in two wards in November/December 1976 and offered to all members in autumn 1978 when they were taken up in fourteen of the sixteen Labour wards, in the two wards where control was split, but in none of the eight Tory-controlled wards. The seminars provided an opportunity for ward members, fieldworkers and representatives of voluntary groups working in each ward to come together to explore issues facing the area and possible changes in the policies or practices of public agencies.

Sunderland has employed a similar style of approach in its Wardwatch system, involving the preparation of ward profiles, member–fieldworker meetings, public meetings and 'ward walkabouts'. Such developments present a major challenge to the established pattern of hierarchical organisation and professional boundaries in local authorities. Peter Kershaw, commenting on area teams in Sunderland, illustrates this point: area terms 'were not convinced that there was a strong commitment to them at either political or professional level; they were naturally hesitant therefore to say anything which might arouse the wrath of either councillors or senior officers' (Kershaw, 1978, p. 50). Clearly the climate within the authority has to be amenable to such experimental, counter-hierarchical activity. A more limited approach was adopted by Sheffield during spring 1978 when, as part of the process of preparing its inner area programme, a 'grassroots survey' was undertaken to get the perceptions and views of individuals working at field level on the problems facing different areas of the city. Questionnaires were distributed to service departments of the local authority, the police, probation service, area health authority and council for voluntary service, and to city councillors, the results being used to compile area profiles (City of Sheffield, 1978).

A different method now being used by several local authorities is to establish joint member–officer groups, providing the opportunity for the sharing of views and development of policy which can draw on the experience and expertise of both parties. Strathclyde Regional Council has experimented with such groups set up to explore certain corporate issues and reporting to policy committee. These groups have involved backbenchers from majority and opposition parties as well as junior officers and fieldworkers in the policy review/policy development process (Young and Jay, 1979). Other authorities set up member–officer panels to undertake particular tasks within the annual cycle.

An alternative method of countering centralism is to introduce an areal dimension into the decision-making processes of the authority, although this has been criticised as a 'divide and rule' strategy and the 'tender' aspect of the local state's management of the working class (Cockburn, 1977). Middlesbrough and Newcastle illustrate two different approaches to areal disaggregation of the authority's processes. Middlesbrough has established a system of permanent district policy committees which comprise two representatives from each ward included in the district together with majority and minority leaders, committee and working party chairman and a number of additional members. The district policy committees are fully integrated into the authority's annual cycle, and their task is to formulate corporate policies for their area (taking into account authority-wide policies), which are included as chapters in the annual Middlesbrough Policy Plan (Harrop *et al.*, 1978, ch. 8; Middlesbrough Borough Council, 1979). Newcastle's 'top priority' scheme is somewhat different in character. A block priority area budget of £100,000 in 1976/7 rising to £860,000 in 1978/9 was set aside, and local area teams comprising junior officers and ward members have delegated spending powers of up to £5,000 on individual projects. The major impact of this approach on resource allocation processes is through the intention that revenue implications of priority area projects will be incorporated into service budgets in subsequent years, and consequently the main spending programme of the authority will be shifted in response to decisions made at a local level. Although the amounts involved are small in relation to total service budgets, 'individual services are being committed to certain expenditures by the decisions of the Priority Area Programme, which are made in accordance with area rather than service priorities and which are outside [service departments'] control' (Harrop *et al.*, 1978, p. 174). There is then a certain 'free' budget element which can reflect local priorities.

Area approaches have been applied in a number of local authorities (for a review see Harrop *et al.*, 1978; Hambleton, 1978; see also Chapter 9 of this book), but West Norfolk has probably gone furthest in spatially disaggregating its management and decision-making structure. At reorganisation the authority introduced a system in which housing, recreation and tourism, and certain technical services functions were decentralised to three areas each having an area consultative committee of local members and an area manager who sits on the central management team (Simkins, 1975).

LINKING POLICY WITH RESOURCES

Earlier it was noted that the annual cycle, as applied in local authorities, has as its concluding stage the preparation of estimates and declaration of the rate. The relationship of policy planning and resource allocation is therefore through their unification into an integrated sequence of activities. The budgetary process is reordered, largely in response to external financial imperatives, and is prefaced by a policy planning stage. There is a tension inherent in such a process since while resources are an important factor to be taken into account in policy review and development, the fact that the budgetary stage is the focal point can, especially in the current economic climate, result in immediate, short-term financial considerations driving out broader, longer-term policy questions. The difficulty local authorities face is to avoid producing 'paper plans' having no regard for resources without making the policy planning and budgetary process little more than an exercise in financial programming. In their review of the process leading to Cleveland's County Plan 1978/81, for instance, Barras and Geary (1979, p. 48) have commented that 'to the outsider the most immediate characteristic of the Plan is that it resembles a revenue budget document in a different guise'.

Honey (1978) has noted that annual cycles have tended to centre on rate-making and budgetary activity, but he questions whether it is 'necessary for corporate planning to become involved in the detail of the budgetary process in order to make its contribution'. He continues:

> The budget has many disadvantages for this purpose. It focuses people's minds on short-term tactical considerations and efforts to think further ahead founder on the uncertainty surrounding the future rate support grant levels . . . Officers are too busy working on estimates, and committee deadlines leave no time for plans to be re-considered.

The conclusion he reaches is that 'the budget should be considered as a means for deciding on the speed with which a corporate plan can be implemented rather than the process which reaches decisions on the plan itself' (p. 8). As Hepworth notes, 'the annual budget-making process is not, or should not be, a time for the making of major policy decisions about services' (Hepworth, 1978, p. 212).

This line of argument suggests a view of the budget as a means of realising those aspects of corporate policy or strategy having financial implications. This general point can be further illuminated when we consider that not all policies have direct financial expenditure implications for the authority. For instance in the mid-1970s town planners began to argue that enforcing a policy of separating 'non-conforming uses' was having a significant detrimental effect on the local economy. When small firms relying on cheap back-street premises in residential areas were encouraged to move to new flatted factories or industrial estates, the theory suggested, they would be forced out of business because of increased overheads. Changing such a policy does not require reallocation of, or additions to, finance, but commitment to a different way of doing things. Similarly rural authorities may pursue a policy of encouraging local employment provision by releasing development constraints on agricultural land, while the application of an equal opportunity policy will influence an authority's service provision and employment practices. Thus the budget becomes *one* device for releasing corporate objectives. The danger is, however, that reallocating expenditure in the 'budget' process – because it is the focal point of the annual cycle – can be seen as sufficient. Within their budget format, for example, some authorities isolate changes in expenditure between activities and label them 'policy changes'. Yet not only does this beg the question of the consequences of financial reallocations in terms of desired outcomes, but because they are visible, quantifiable changes they may distract from the need to focus attention on the less clear practices, behaviours and rules which shape the impact of the authority in any particular area – the 'deep structures' within the organisation or department (Clegg, 1975): for example, the way in which structures of decision-making may act to exclude certain interests or favour certain outcomes because of their design characteristics.

THE EVALUATION OF OUTCOME

Barras and Geary (1979, p. 40) have argued that

> the proponents of the corporate approach have tended to concentrate on 'structures' and 'processes' rather than 'effects', in terms of the actual policy or resource changes being made in the process. But policy effectiveness should be the main criteria against which the utility of the planning process should be judged.

Changes in policy or resource allocation do not by themselves indicate the success of a corporate approach any more than continuity or incremental changes represent its failure. The central feature of the corporate philosophy is the mobilisation of the authority's activities and resources in relation to needs and problems in the community, and thus its evaluation rests on the extent to which it can aid an authority's interventionist role. The study of the outcome of public policies is relatively underdeveloped;[2] however, an assessment of the difference that a policy and resource planning process can make at present rests on a belief in the superiority of this to any other form of decision-making. Such a belief is grounded in Lindblom's (1959) 'test of a good policy'. For incrementalists the test of a good policy is that it gains wide acceptability and hence stands a fair chance of implementation, while from the perspective of the rational model, and by implication the corporate approach, it is that decisions are made in a certain way – by identifying objectives, exploring alternatives and selecting the optimum solution.

Monitoring of policy outcomes has been slow to develop, both conceptually and in practical experiments. Work on performance indicators and comparative inter-authority statistics has so far tended to focus on *inputs* such as expenditure per head of client population or *outputs* such as the number of meals-on-wheels served, rather than the consequences or *outcomes* for different groups or areas, at least at the formal level. Informal assessments of outcome will be received by councillors or officers as part of their contact with individuals or groups in the community, yet because they are informal and haphazard there is no necessary indication of the extent of desirable or undesirable consequences and no guarantee that such intelligence as is received in various parts of the authority will lead to compensatory changes in policy, practices, or resource allocation. The reasons why outcome monitoring of particular policies or methods of working (the annual cycle, area approaches) is underdeveloped in local government are many, but of particular significance is that it can raise uncomfortable questions for particular groups in the authority who have an interest in a given policy or way of working because it is associated with either individual status or wider class interests.

NOTES: CHAPTER 3

This chapter first appeared as an article in *Public Administration*, vol. 59, Summer 1980. I am grateful for the agreement of the editor to reproduce it here.

1 For a review of contemporary literature see Dearlove, 1979.
2 For a general discussion see Chapter 4.

4

The Distributional Effects of Local Government Services

BARBARA A. WEBSTER

The importance of public sector policies and services in determining the life chances of different groups in society is now widely recognised. Pahl (1971) argued that 'the orthodox view that life chances are directly related to income gained from the work situation alone is too limited' and that 'those provisions which are administered by local or national government are critical determinants of life chances'. Many of the welfare services administered at the local level, such as education, housing and social services, can be seen as a means of redistributing income, and Townsend's (1979) study of poverty in the United Kingdom emphasised that the value of social services in kind makes an important contribution to family resources and hence to standards of living.

It has been emphasised, however, that it is not only those services which have an explicit welfare element that affect life chances. All public services and decisions can have distributional, if unintended, effects, so that the only really equitable concept of income would be one which 'embraces all receipts which increase an individual's command over society's scarce resources' (Harvey, 1973, p. 53, quoting R. M. Titmuss, 1962). Harvey has argued that there exist 'hidden mechanisms' which affect the distribution of real income, pointing particularly to decisions about the spatial form of the city. Such decisions affect the accessibility of both public and private resources to different groups in society and can also redistribute real income through externality effects on the value of property rights (Harvey, 1973). The general tenor of these arguments has been that the services administered and decisions made by local governments often serve to increase inequalities rather than redress them.

> One strand in the ideology of the Welfare State as a type of society was that need should be a more important criterion than wealth to determine access to facilities. If this ideology had been comprehensively pursued and supported, we might have expected a considerable redistribution of real income within and between localities . . . We could expect to find a positive correlation between the need for public services and their provision . . . However, it is a commonplace to observe that this does not happen, although detailed documentation presents many complicated methodological problems. The provision of public services and facilities has its own pattern of inequalities. (Pahl, 1971, p. 134)

The significance of local authority policies and services has also been recognised in the development of policies in the field of urban deprivation. The Inner Area Studies identified a number of ways in which the policies, activities and procedures of the local authority tended to exacerbate problems of deprivation (Department of the Environment, 1977a). An area analysis of resources undertaken in the Liverpool study area lent some support to the argument that deprived inner areas receive less than a fair share of local authority resources. Although the analysis suffered from the lack of comparable data for other areas of the city and from the lack of specific information relating to spatial variations in need, it did show that District D received less than city average resources in relation to population, despite the fact that it would generally be regarded as exhibiting greater needs than other areas (Liverpool Inner Area Study, 1976). The recent Policy for the Inner Cities reflected the findings of these studies and other research (Stewart, Spencer and Webster, 1976) in emphasising that dealing with the problems of inner cities could not be divorced from the existing policies and resource allocations of central and local government.

> One of the lessons of recent studies is that the main policies and programmes of central and local government must be used to the full in order to tackle the problems of the inner areas effectively. These include . . . the whole range of policies for education, health, personal social services, housing, transport and planning, together with the provision of a wide range of environmental services and improvements . . . Local authorities for their part can do a great deal to redirect their policies to give greater assistance to inner areas and to bring about a more co-ordinated approach. There is scope for making better use of resources and for pursuing policies of positive discrimination. (HMSO, 1977, pp. 10–11)

In this respect the new policy represented a marked change in emphasis from the view, evident in earlier initiatives such as Urban Aid and the Community Development Projects, that deprivation was a distinct problem requiring special programmes on the part of government.

In view of the significance attached to local authority activities in both academic and policy contexts, it is perhaps surprising to find that we still know relatively little about the effects of local authority policies on the real income of different groups in society. In particular, there are few empirical studies of how services provided by local authorities are actually distributed. This issue has been neglected in the field of public policy studies in Britain.

One reason for the neglect may be that much emphasis has been placed on describing and explaining the way in which policy and resource allocation decisions are made. A number of writers have examined the politics of policy-making at the local level, and sought to identify the access to, and influence on, decisions by interest groups external to the local authority (see Newton, 1976; P. Saunders, 1979;

Dearlove, 1973). Others have focused more specifically on internal decision-making processes, examining local authority policy planning systems and organisational arrangements and the way these are shaped by the power, interests and values of different groups within the authority (see Hinings *et al.*, 1980; Ranson *et al.*, 1980). What both types of study have in common is that they are primarily interested in the *process* by which policy and resource allocation decisions are arrived at, rather than the effects of those decisions on the local environment. Some case studies, notably those by P. Saunders (1979) and Dunleavy (1977), have also considered the substantive content of policy, being concerned to identify whose interests are served by the decisions or non-decisions made. However, they have not generally traced through the actual incidence of costs and benefits which flow from changes in policy. Moreover they have tended to focus on major identifiable, and often controversial, policy issues or decisions, such as city centre redevelopment, Green Belt policy, or the introduction of comprehensive education, rather than the ongoing provision of local services, such as schools, cleansing services, environmental health, or recreation.

Growing recognition of the fact that policy decisions are not always put into practice and do not necessarily have the consequences intended, has led to renewed interest in the operations of administrative systems as implementing agencies. The issue of implementation does direct attention to service provision and delivery, rather than the process of policy formulation. However, the interest in such systems is primarily in what they contribute to an understanding of the process by which policy decisions are translated into action on the ground, and the implications for the extent to which, and the way in which, that process can be controlled (see Dunsire, 1978; Hood, 1976; Pressman and Wildavsky, 1973). Again little attention has been given to the substantive effects of that translation process in terms of the goods and services provided to the local community. A concern with such issues is more apparent within the tradition of social administration, where the relationship between the client and the administrative system has been the focus of study (see Hill, 1976; B. Davies, 1978; Rees, 1978).

There is, however, one strand of work which focuses specifically on substantive variations in the policies and provisions of local governments, and this has been referred to as the 'local output studies' (Newton and Sharpe, 1977). These have often taken levels of expenditure as indicative of 'output' (see Boaden, 1971; Nicholson and Topham, 1971; Alt, 1971; Oliver and Stanyer, 1969) although some have employed more direct measures of service provision (B. Davies, 1968; Pinch, 1980). Although such studies have been seen as directing attention to issues of distribution and territorial justice, and away from decision-making itself (Newton and Sharpe, 1977), they have generally been concerned to identify and explain variations between local authorities, and at this scale of analysis it is difficult to draw conclusions about which groups in society are actually benefiting from the resources or services provided. Issues of distribution are much more amenable to analysis *within* a particular local authority, but relatively little comparable work has so far been undertaken at that scale.

The distribution of local authority services within local government jurisdictions has been the subject of greater research effort in the United States. Investigations have been undertaken for education, the enforcement of health and housing regulations, recreation and library facilities and services concerned with the cleanliness and maintenance of the physical environment.[1] The level of interest in this question is undoubtedly related to the special legal significance of inequalities between racial and class groups in the delivery of municipal services, which may be regarded as contravening the Fourteenth Amendment (Lineberry, 1977, ch. 2).

The absence of a similar legal provision in Britain may help to explain not only the lack of academic interest but also the fact that local authorities themselves have paid little attention to the distributional effects of policy and service provision decisions. Although one or two authorities have expressed an interest in the area analysis of resources (Randall, Lomas and Newton, 1973; Liverpool Inner Area Study, 1976; Allen, 1979), generally there is a lack of practical policy analysis which confronts distributional questions. Perhaps of more direct significance is the way in which policy planning has developed within local government, and in particular the influence of ideas concerning the need for a corporate approach to managing the affairs of the authority.[2] In practice, the ideology of corporate planning led to an emphasis on authority-wide objectives (Stewart, 1975), and it has been argued that its development resulted in distributional questions being obscured (see Benington and Skelton, 1972; and also Chapter 9 of this book). However, Stewart has pointed out that the theory of corporate planning is not necessarily antithetical to the consideration of such issues, and local authorities may not in any event be anxious to explore them. Both officers and elected members are often reticent to provide information which shows clearly what different groups or areas receive in terms of expenditure or services because of the way that information might be used, and Bovaird (1979) has noted the reluctance of local authorities to state explicitly what their distributional objectives are. He suggests that councillors are unwilling to 'declare their hand because of the great danger of losing votes' (ibid., p. 37) and the relatively low levels of interest and activism in local politics by the public may provide little external incentive for questions concerning who get what to be examined.

More attention may be paid to distributional issues in the future. The recent cutbacks in public expenditure bring the question of who benefits from local authority policies and services more sharply into focus. As part of the process of deciding priorities for expenditure and where any cuts will occur, local authorities have begun to appraise existing policies and the use of resources more thoroughly. Assessing the distributional implications of existing services may be one aspect of such an appraisal, and some authorities have given explicit priority to the protection of particular disadvantaged sections of the community, such as those living in inner city areas (Greenwood *et al.*, 1976).

The intention in this chapter, therefore, is to consider how the distributive effects of local government policy can be analysed at the intra-authority scale. It focuses particularly on the ongoing services and facilities provided for the local community. Many local authority services may appear routine and insignificant, even banal, when compared with major policies, for example, on urban development or redevelopment, but these services are none the less essential to everyday life and are often regarded as important by the public (see Antunes and Mladenka, 1976; Birmingham Inner Area Study, 1975; Lambeth Inner Area Study, 1974). Any distributional analysis implies the definition of what it is that is being distributed and to whom, and the debates surrounding these two issues are discussed. The clarification of concepts such as resource input, output and outcome, and of arguments concerning the appropriate basis for the analysis of local authority services, is fundamental to any attempt to identify empirically who gets what or who benefits from local government. While answering these questions is a prior task, it is equally important, from both academic and policy perspectives, to develop an understanding of how those distributions come about. The latter part of the chapter explores a number of mechanisms which are likely to have a direct influence on the distribution of services, illustrating how they may operate by reference to existing studies of particular local authority services.

DISTRIBUTION OF WHAT?

Fundamental to the study of the distributional effects of public policies is the question of what it is that is being distributed. How are the benefits of public sector activity to be defined? On this issue the literature is very confused. Policy outputs, resource inputs, levels of provision, outputs, outcomes and impacts have all been the subject of scrutiny, and different writers have interpreted particular concepts in different ways. As B. D. Jones (1977) observes, part of the confusion arises from lack of consistency in the way particular terms are used, and this is due to the fact that those interested in distributional questions come from two quite distinct academic traditions.

The tradition of 'local outputs' research in political science has its origins in the model of the political system developed by Easton (1965), in which the inputs to the system are demands and supports from the environment, and the outputs are public policies or the 'authoritative allocation of values'. Although there may be debates about alternative methodologies for examining this system (Dearlove, 1973, pt 1), the political process is the main focus of study and the 'outputs' of this process in terms of policy or resource allocation decisions are the variables to be explained. The terms 'outcome' and 'impact' are generally used in political science to refer to the effect those decisions have on the environment (King, 1975). By contrast, the traditional concern in economics, particularly welfare economics, is with public sector organisations as systems for producing a particular level and mix of goods or services designed to achieve policy goals. The term 'output' therefore normally refers to the changes in social or environmental conditions which result from these activities and services, and 'output measurement' in the public sector is concerned with the 'measurement of the degree of achievement of the objectives set for a service or activity' (Bovaird, 1979).

Taking account of these terminological conventions can help to dispel some of the confusion, because different terms are being used to define broadly comparable concepts. Resource allocation or expenditure patterns which the political scientists refer to as 'outputs' the economists regard as 'resource inputs'. What the economists call 'outputs' (that is, changes in social and economic conditions) is similar to the political science notion of 'outcome', in that it relates primarily to the intended consequences of government activities (Rich, 1979). The term 'impact' generally has a wider meaning, encompassing the unintended, and perhaps undesirable, consequences of policy decisions as well as their intended effects (King, 1975).

Recognition of these differences of focus between the two disciplines does not, however, enable a common and unambiguous conceptual framework to be identified. An examination of existing studies of the distributional effects of public policies and services reveals important differences in the measures used, and it is not always clear whether similar measures are intended to represent similar concepts since the concepts themselves may not be well defined. In particular, the nature of the distinctions between governmental activities or services and resource inputs, on the one hand, and their effects on social conditions, on the other hand, need further clarification.

This is illustrated by the approach adopted by Lineberry and Welch (1974, p. 704) who, in the economic tradition, suggest that

> . . . the only feasible approach to the problem is to define the output of a public agency in terms of the *contribution of its service activities (resource inputs) to its objective(s)*, or in other words, in terms of the *effect of its service activities on selected community conditions*.

Because of the constraints on directly measuring public service 'output', they argue that indicators of the quantity and quality of 'resource inputs', that is, staff, equipment, and so on, and of service delivery quality should be used as substitute or proxy measures of 'output'. Major problems with this approach are that it denies the independent significance of the activities and services themselves and fails to distinguish between resource inputs and service provision. The importance of differentiating conceptually indicators of output and indicators of service provision has been well illustrated by Culyer, Lavers and Williams (1972) in the context of health care. If indicators of health provision, such as hospital beds or doctors per 1,000 population, are not separated from indicators of the state or level of health in the population, then it becomes impossible to ask important questions about the effects of alternative forms and combinations of health care on health. B. D. Jones (1977) makes the same point when he suggests that the governmental production process should be conceived as involving two stages – the first in which resources or expenditure are used to produce a certain level of services, or government–community contacts, and a second in which that governmental effort has more or less effect on social conditions. Since governments only have real control over the first stage, indicators of the nature and intensity of government–community contacts can therefore be regarded as what government produces.

Such a framework still leaves open the questions of what is the nature of the service that government provides and how are these government–community contacts to be measured. Moreover other writers have not adopted the same definition of 'resource inputs' as Jones, extending the term beyond expenditure to encompass measures of staff and equipment levels, for example, and have often left unanswered the question of whether, and how, service provision differs from such resource inputs. For example, is the teacher/pupil ratio a measure of the education service itself or simply a measure of the resources invested by an education authority in order to provide 'education'? As demonstrated by the quotation above, Lineberry and Welch treat service activities and resource inputs as synonymous, and in their study of Oakland Levy, Meltsner and Wildavsky variously use expenditure data, staff resources, and measures of service delivery as indicators of what they call 'urban outcomes'.[3] A further issue on which there is no obvious consensus concerns who it is that benefits from the provision of a service or governmental activity. Do only those residents who choose to use the local library or park receive or benefit from the service, or should such facilities be assumed to benefit all those who live in the vicinity irrespective of whether they do or do not actually utilise it?

Some of these difficulties arise, I believe, because of the tendency to conceive of local authority services and activities as what *government produces* rather than in terms of what *consumers receive*. Where distributional issues are the focus of concern it is what different groups of consumers receive, in terms of the quantity and quality of goods and services, that is important, rather than the resources which the authority combines in various ways to create those services. What is important about library provision is how accessible the local library is, how long and how convenient the opening times are, what type of facilities are available, how easy it is to obtain books and assistance, and whether the book stock meets consumer interests, rather than the number of staff and number of books *per se*. Similarly it is the speed and effectiveness of response to a call from the fire brigade which is of immediate relevance to the individual citizen, rather than the existence of a fire substation and its level of staffing, although decisions on the building and closure of such stations and manning levels obviously have an important bearing on response times.

Viewing services from the perspective of the consumer emphasises a point which often goes unrecognised, namely, that specific types of measures of service provision will not necessarily have the same significance for all services. Lineberry and Welch provide, for example, a list of input quantity measures, such as police patrolmen/population, teacher/pupil ratios, and maintenance personnel/park and recreational acreage. In services where professional staff, such as teachers or social workers, have a central role in the provision of the service, such measures are likely to be key indicators of the service received by consumers. However, in services which involve manual labour, such as refuse collection, road maintenance, or meals services, direct measures of service received, for example, the frequency of refuse collections, response times on pothole complaints or the regularity of the meals-on-wheels service, are more appropriate than measures of staffing. Obviously the desirable direct measures of service received will not always be available, and measures relating to staff and equipment may have to be regarded as indicative of the level and nature of the service. For instance, the quality of teaching in individual schools could only properly be discerned by direct assessments of the teacher–pupil interaction, but in practice indicators of the qualifications and experience of teachers would probably have to suffice. The important point is that once the concept to be analysed has been clearly defined, that is, services as received by the consumer, the way particular indicators relate to that concept can be clarified and whether they are appropriate measures of it can be assessed.

The issue of utilisation of services and who benefits can also be resolved, since it becomes clear that an important aspect of the service from the consumer's point of view is simply the *opportunity* to use particular services and facilities. What governmental agencies often provide is the capacity or potential to supply services which the consumer must opt to use (Rothenberg, 1976). The significance of such opportunities is highlighted in those services, such as hospitals, where it is important to the consumer to know that the facility is there should a need arise, even though he or she may not actually want to use it. Thus in considering the distribution of certain services, differentials in the accessibility and availability of facilities to different groups and the range of services offered should be examined, as well as the actual use made of the facilities by those groups. This generally applies where the service is provided at a limited number of locations, as opposed to where it is delivered directly to the individual consumer at his place of residence.

To summarise the discussion, I find it useful to distinguish between four main concepts[4] defined in the following way.

Resource inputs: the financial resources or expenditure, both capital and revenue, allocated to secure the provision of services and facilities.

Services received: the goods and services rendered to, or received by, individuals or groups in the community; it has a quantitative aspect, the level or amount of service received, and a qualitative aspect.

Outputs: the intended effects of services received on community conditions, that is, outputs are defined in relation to the objectives set for a service; they may include both objective changes in social, economic and environmental conditions, and changes in the subjective attitudes and satisfactions of consumers.

Impacts: the longer-term effects and unintended consequences of the provision of services and other local authority actions; these consequences may be either positive or negative, that is, providing benefits to or imposing costs on the consumer or citizen.

This terminology broadly follows the economic tradition, and is compatible with the use of the phrase 'output measurement' in British local government (CIPFA, 1972). Given these distinctions, it is now possible to consider how appropriate these different concepts are for the study of the distributional effects of local government services. Are they best examined in terms of resource inputs, services received, outputs, or impacts?

The main emphasis in existing studies of distribution at the intra-authority level in the British context has been on resource inputs or expenditure (see Webster and Stewart, 1974; Randall, Lomas and Newton, 1973; Liverpool Inner Area Study, 1976; Allen, 1979; Tunley, Travers and Pratt, 1979). Yet the use of expenditure data has been criticised because it may be a very crude indicator of services received (Newton and Sharpe, 1977). The implicit assumption that the benefits derived by consumers from governmental activity are equivalent, or at least closely related to, their costs is difficult to sustain. Variations in expenditure may arise because the cost of provision varies in different physical or social circumstances, the efficiency with which services are provided varies, or because of variations in the nature and age of the physical stock (Webster and Stewart, 1974). Perhaps more important, changes in policy or the type of service provided may not always be reflected in expenditure patterns. For example, the type of book stock provided at a library could be changed without changing expenditure, and the same salary bill in two different schools could hide variations in the number and quality of teaching staff. Expenditure, then, has little direct meaning for consumers; what they experience are variations in the amount and quality of service. It therefore seems preferable to use direct measures of service received or output in the analysis of distributional questions. As Lineberry (1977, p. 7) says, 'There is more to urban policy than a budget. Behind the budget lurks the people who spend it and the people who receive its purchases of goods and services.' This is not to say that resource allocation decisions are insignificant in determining the distribution of services, or that the relationship between resources expended and services received, that is, issues of efficiency, are unimportant. Rather it suggests that resource inputs should not be the primary focus of study.

Ideally it would be desirable to identify the distribution of services received, outputs and impacts, and to examine the relationships between them. Such an approach would focus attention on the benefits and costs derived from public sector activity and would help to answer questions about what difference local authority policies and services make to the real income, or life chances, of different groups in society. However, tracing the externality effects and unintended consequences of local authority actions is recognised as a particularly difficult research task (King, 1975; Harvey, 1973). Even gauging the extent to which local authority services are achieving the intended changes in community conditions is problematic. Although in some fields, notably health and education, considerable effort has been invested in the development of output measures, appropriate indicators of this type are often lacking. Local government has generally been slow in developing performance measurement, and those authorities which have embarked on the collection of information for this purpose have tended to concentrate on measures of levels of activity or throughput of clients rather than true measures of 'output' (Bovaird, 1979).

The expense of data collection and the measurement problems involved should not be underestimated. For example, citizen or consumer satisfaction may be an important aspect of output (ibid., and Hatry, 1976), yet the assessment of consumer valuations of services is likely to involve either attitude surveys or extensive information on consumer behaviour from which inferences about such valuations can be drawn (Bovaird, 1979). But the lack of output indicators may also be due to the difficulties involved in specifying appropriate measures in the first place. The vagueness or ambiguity of official objectives may provide little guidance on what sort of changes in community conditions are intended. Where efforts have been made to specify objectives in local government they have often been defined in terms of the activities of the organisation rather than in terms of social conditions and have not always been specified in an operational way which allows the degree of attainment to be measured (ibid.).

A further problem in analysing outputs lies in the difficulty of assessing how far any changes in community conditions are in fact attributable to local authority actions. Outputs may also be influenced by external or environmental factors, which are largely outside the local authority's control. The continuing debate about the causes of educational attainment exemplifies this problem well. Some have argued that home background and parental attitudes are the predominant influence on attainment and that school provision itself has a relatively minor role (Jencks, 1973; Douglas, 1964). Others have argued that the nature of the educational system itself does have a significant effect on attainment, whether in terms of the priority given to education and the overall nature of provision in different authorities (Byrne, Williamson and Fletcher, 1975), in terms of the social organisation of individual schools (Rutter, Maugham, Mortimore and Ouston, 1979), or in terms of the qualities, attitudes and expectations of individual teachers. As long as it remains difficult to isolate the contribution of public policies and services then only limited progress is likely to be made in assessing distributional effects in output terms.

Increased efforts in developing output indicators for local government services are therefore essential, but until this work has advanced the only feasible approach in many services may be to examine distributional issues in terms of service received. In any event this pattern is worthy of study in its own right. First, although the precise nature of the relationship between services received and outputs may not be known it seems reasonable to assume that most services do have a significant effect on social and environmental conditions. For example, the frequency of street cleansing is likely to affect the cleanliness of the environment, and the provision and maintenance of public housing does influence housing conditions. The distribution of these services between different groups is thus an important issue, which can be distinguished from questions concerning the effectiveness of current services in meeting the objectives set for them.

Secondly, services received from the local authority can affect the morale, attitudes and satisfaction of consumers. There are two aspects to this. On the one hand the consumer may derive satisfaction from some aspect of the service which is not part of its specific objectives; for example, the elderly may value the delivery of a meal and the human contact associated with it, even though the frequency of its provision may make it of dubious nutritional value. On the other hand the receipt of a service may have a symbolic effect. What government is seen to be providing may be important to the citizen or consumer as well as how those services are meeting needs or demands, that is, the very act of provision may be of value in its own right (B. D. Jones, 1977).

Finally, it can be argued that the pattern of services received will reflect the distributional principles followed, explicitly or implicitly, by local authorities in providing and allocating services. How far the actual distribution accords with the underlying principle, whether it is one based on uniformity of service or one based on some notion of need or equity, is an important policy question.[5] If there are significant disparities then a case can be made that the authority should attempt to remove them. Inequalities or inequities in services received are likely to be much more amenable to direct change through local authority decisions than inequalities or inequities in output. In addition, the former are likely to be compounded in the latter, for disadvantaged groups, and those from lower socioeconomic groups in general, are not only unable to purchase comparable goods and services in the private sector, but are often least able to take advantage of the public sector services which are provided (Lister, 1974; F. Williams, 1977).

In a reflective review of research on the distribution of urban services in America, Rich recently put forward a contrary view. Pointing to the previous concentration on measures of service provision, he suggested that 'outcomes' (that is, 'outputs' in the terminology used here) should be given research priority. Since the same level of service can have different effects depending on the needs and social conditions of different groups, Rich (1979) argues that the equality of benefits from municipal services enjoyed by those groups cannot be evaluated properly unless output indicators are examined. His argument can be questioned on the ground that it seems to confuse the issue of which is the appropriate distribution to examine, services received or output, with the separate question of what is the appropriate criterion for evaluation. It is certainly true that American research has been preoccupied with the question of whether different income or racial groups receive equal services, with little attention being given to the notion of equity and variations in needs, but both types of distribution can be assessed against an equity standard. As Rich observes, if the concern is with equity then some indicators of output are necessary for evaluation purposes, since the definition of needs is intimately bound up with the objectives underlying service provision. However, given the paucity and relatively crude nature of such indicators, and the absence of comparable research on service provision, it seems appropriate in the British context to attach some priority to analysing the distribution of services received. This distribution therefore forms the main focus of the rest of this chapter.

DISTRIBUTION TO WHOM?

When issues of distribution are being examined a key decision that has to be taken prior to any analysis is which are the appropriate groups to consider. Along what type of societal divisions or dimensions are variations in services received likely to occur? Four main types of defining characteristic can be identified:

(1) social class, socioeconomic status or income;
(2) race;
(3) characteristics which define particular client groups, for example the elderly, the under-5s or the handicapped;
(4) place of residence, that is, geographically defined areas or neighbourhoods.

Most studies of the distribution of resource inputs or services received at the intra-authority level have been based on the last of these, geographical areas. This is despite the fact that the main focus of attention for American researchers has been socioeconomic/income and racial groups, because of the legal significance of discrimination on these grounds. Such variations, however, have had to be studied indirectly by examining variations in service between geographical areas and assessing how far these correspond to areal variations in socioeconomic status, income or racial composition (see Lineberry, 1977; Jones, Greenberg, Kaufman and Drew, 1978). The reason for this approach is that the most comprehensive sources of information on social characteristics are national censuses, and they provide summary information for small geographical areas which does not allow the identification of individual consumers or households.

The use of geographical areas is thus often based on an assumption that the areas are in fact homogeneous with respect to the relevant social characteristics.

> . . . the delivery of services is intimately bound up with the geographic dispersion of the population composing a particular metropolitan region. One basic fact of urban geography makes this the case: diverse urban populations are not distributed randomly across the metropolitan landscape. Rather, individuals similar in class, race, religion, or ethnicity cluster together, and the region is composed of a diversity of clusters rather than a diversity of discrete individuals. Not only is each municipality of a metropolitan region composed of a population generally distinct from other municipalities, but populations are segmented within municipalities by neighbourhoods . . . Since urban neighbourhoods are distinctive in their composition, by distributing services unequally to neighbourhoods governments are distributing services unequally to categories of citizens. (Jones and Kaufman, 1974, pp. 337–8)

Obviously the validity of this assumption will depend to a considerable extent on the size of the areas and the boundaries chosen. While for the smallest unit, the enumeration district or census tract, there may exist a high degree of homogeneity with respect to socioeconomic and racial characteristics, services may be difficult to analyse at this scale and larger neighbourhoods have frequently been employed (Levy, Meltsner and Wildavsky, 1974; Nivola, 1978; Webster, Lambert and Penny, 1979). Research in the context of urban deprivation has argued that social problems are much less geographically concentrated than has often been supposed (Holtermann, 1976; Hatch and Sherrott, 1973) and particular doubts can be raised about the spatial concentration of specific client groups, such as the elderly or the mentally handicapped. For more general social status or racial characteristics, however, a reasonable degree of homogeneity is likely to exist, but this is not always the case and some areas of older housing, in particular, may exhibit very mixed social characteristics. Certainly ward boundaries, which are the second level of aggregation used in the British census, do not always correspond very closely to socioeconomic divisions (Webster, Lambert and Penny, 1979).

This problem emphasises the need for care in the initial selection and definition of areas and for awareness of where the assumption of homogeneity cannot really be sustained. Moreover the use of geographical areas has important implications for the type of inferences which can be drawn about the relationship between the distribution of services received and other social characteristics. As Lineberry (1977) notes, conclusions can only be drawn at the area level if the 'ecological fallacy' is to be avoided. Although, for example, comparatively high levels of service provision may be found in areas where there are concentrations of white people, and relatively low levels in areas where there are concentrations of immigrants, it cannot necessarily be assumed that immigrants, as individuals, are disadvantaged relative to whites, as individuals, in the services they receive.

Although data availability may necessitate the use of areas or neighbourhoods, there are two positive reasons why they may be appropriate units on which to base an analysis of service distributions. The first is that certain areas have special significance in the study of public services where, as in Britain, the local electoral system is based on geographically defined constituencies. Decisions on the provision of services might be made in such a way as to gain electoral advantage or to favour those areas which supported the political party in control. The vigour with which individual councillors advocate the needs of their constituencies might also be expected to be reflected in the pattern of services received, and local politicians themselves are likely to be most interested in information on service provision relating to wards. The second reason for the choice of geographical areas relates to the nature of local authority services themselves. Although some services, such as refuse collection, home helps and improvement grants, are provided to individual consumers and often delivered directly to their place of residence, other services are area-specific in that they are intended to serve particular neighbourhoods; schools and swimming baths are good examples. It has already been argued that the study of services received should include an analysis of service potential as well as service used in the case of the second type of service. That potential cannot be attributed to particular individuals and must be examined in an area context. Further, there are some services where it is simply not feasible to identify individual beneficiaries because the service does not involve any identifiable act of consumption. Such services, for example, street lighting, police patrols and pollution controls, are generally termed non-exclusionary (Peston, 1972; E. Ostrom, 1974; Webster *et al.*, 1979) and can only be attributed to geographical areas.

The use of census tracts and other 'arbitrary boundaries' has recently been criticised by Rich (1979) on the grounds that research had failed to identify 'whether these were also sociological neighbourhoods in that residents shared a sense of common interests or were bound together by local institutions' (p. 150). The extent to which neighbourhoods were or were not organised for collective action would, he argued, be an important factor in explaining service variations. Organised consumer demands may obviously have an important influence on the decisions of local authorities regarding service provision. But the call for this characteristic to be used as a basis for area definition seems to underestimate the significance of the long-standing debate about the validity of the neighbourhood community idea and the practical difficulties involved in the identification of such 'political' neighbourhoods. However the concept of 'community' is defined, the assumption that the term is synonymous with a defined geographical area has been seriously questioned (M. Stacey, 1969; Bell and Newby, 1976). Those who share a common location do not necessarily share common interests, and although residents of a particular area may organise around a specific issue, that organisation may not prove self-sustaining and there may not exist any consciousness of mutual interest and involvement (Bell and Newby, 1976).

What is important to recognise is that the choice of areal units is ultimately bound up with the purposes of the analysis, and that different purposes may impose different requirements. Studies of service distributions reveal three primary aims: a descriptive one, which seeks to identify the distribution of services and to discern whether any patterned variations exist between geographical, social or racial groups; an explanatory one, which is concerned to identify the determinants of service patterns; and an evaluative one, which involves making judgements about distributions based on normative criteria. Thus the definition of the groups in society which are the subject of descriptive analysis, the areas for which information on services is available or meaningful, the areas relevant to the variables used as explanatory factors and the areas for which measures of evaluation criteria, such as indicators of need, are available may all have a bearing on the units selected. To argue, as Rich does, that areas should be defined on the basis of neighbourhood communities, emphasises the explanatory aspect and perhaps pre-empts conclusions about the relative importance of community organisation compared with, say, political representation or administrative decisions on service provision. The point is that no one set of areas is likely to satisfy all the demands of analysis, with areas suitable on one criterion failing to meet another criterion.[6] The choice of areas for the study of service distributions inevitably involves compromise, and the most appropriate units will depend on the specific hypotheses which it is concerned to test and the policy purposes to which it will be put.

MECHANISMS UNDERLYING SERVICE DISTRIBUTIONS

The mapping and evaluation of service distributions are important tasks which will enable conclusions to be drawn about the distributive effects of local government policy and provision. But it is also important to explain how those distributions come about. Such an explanation is not only desirable from an academic standpoint, for it may be difficult to identify what actions are necessary to bring about changes in existing patterns if the mechanisms underlying them are ill-understood. Knowledge of those patterns may not in itself be a sufficient basis for policy formulation. If, as has been suggested, the distribution of real income in the urban system is often the result of 'hidden mechanisms' (Harvey, 1973) and decisions which are not overtly distributional, then attempts at redistribution through direct allocation decisions may well prove ineffectual.

Studies which seek to explain the distribution of resource inputs or services between areas at the intra-authority level can be divided into two broad types. The first approach is an ecological one which attempts to relate data on service provision to the social, economic or demographic characteristics of the areas under scrutiny. The alternative approach focuses specifically on the processes of decision-making within local authorities, seeking to understand how they actually affect such distributions and whether these effects are intentional or unintentional. A parallel can be drawn between studies at this level and studies which are concerned to explain inter-authority variations, where a similar distinction has been identified (Dearlove, 1973). Many of the 'local output' studies have been of the ecological type (Newton and Sharpe, 1977), and have been criticised for their failure to examine the way in which social and environmental characteristics are translated into policy and resource allocation by governmental institutions (Dearlove, 1973). The two different approaches have generally been allied with different methodologies, the ecological approach being based on statistical analysis using correlation or regression, and the processual study often employing non-quantitative methods such as in-depth interviews. But it is important to recognise that there is no necessary correspondence, as some decision processes can be formulated in such a way as to allow the statistical testing of explanatory hypotheses through regression analysis.[7]

Social and demographic characteristics, for example, the population in certain client groups such as children or the elderly, have frequently been employed as explanatory variables in inter-authority analysis, for variations in these characteristics are assumed to create varying needs for services (Boaden, 1971). This argument can similarly be applied to the distribution of services between neighbourhoods. Socioeconomic characteristics could, in addition, give rise to variations between areas in the propensity to use services and facilities, and in the extent to which the public and consumers articulate demands for services (Jones and Kaufman, 1974; Rich, 1979). But the importance of ecological variables has also been seen to lie in the way certain social groups are consciously discriminated against by those who control policy-making and resource allocation in governmental institutions.

Much of the literature on urban politics has argued that not only do low-income and minority groups, and more generally lower-class groups, have little bargaining power and ability to influence decision-making, but their interests are systematically excluded from consideration through various forms of non-decision-making (Bachrach and Baratz, 1970; P. Saunders, 1979). In his study of San Antonio Lineberry sought to test the hypothesis that service distributions could be explained in terms of discrimination against the 'urban underclass' using the ecological approach. He argued that if this did in fact occur, we might expect the quantity and/or quality of services received to be positively related to the proportion of the population which were of higher socioeconomic status, to the proportion which were Anglos and to the presence of those who occupied positions of power in urban government. None of these hypotheses was strongly supported by the data. To the extent that an explanation of the inequalities in services between neighbourhoods could be found in the attributes of those neighbourhoods, age and density of population were the most important variables. But all four factors taken together could not account for a major proportion of the variation in inter-neighbourhood servicing.

An important reason why ecological analyses may offer a poor explanation of service distribution is that they assume a direct relationship between the social and political characteristics of neighbourhoods and the pattern of service distribution, when the influence of those variables is in fact mediated through the policy-making or decision-making processes of local authorities. In Lineberry's (1977, p. 61) analysis, for example, the political power of a neighbourhood was measured by the number of formal and informal public offices held by neighbourhood residents, the assumption being that those 'heavily populated by influentials may have more clout in securing urban services'. Clearly the nature of the decision-making process is much more complex than this notion of neighbourhood power implies, with decisions about provisions often involving service administration rather than conscious political choice. The same argument applies to other ecological variables, since both needs and organised political demands are mediated through the decision processes of the authority. It is the recognition and definition of needs by politicians and bureaucrats, and the way that public sector organisations respond to neighbourhood pressures or demands, that are of direct significance in determining the distribution of services received, rather than the needs and demands themselves.

The significance of this mediation lies in the fact that the relevant decisions may not involve any overt discrimination or conscious allocation between areas. Decisions which appear neutral in that they do not seem to favour any particular area or group, and decisions ostensibly made in the interest of the community as a whole, the 'public interest', may none the less have spatially distributive effects. In the context of town planning, for example, Simmie (1974) has argued that decisions are often influenced by professional or personal values reflecting particular class interests, yet which are assumed by those concerned to reflect the interests of society as a whole. Hence it may be fruitless to search for spatially defined factors to explain the distribution of services if the decision processes which determine them are aspatial in character.

The approach of Levy, Meltsner and Wildavsky (1974) in their study of schools, streets and libraries in Oakland thus drew attention to the importance of examining directly and in depth the decision-making and resource allocation processes of local government. They forcefully made the point not only that this form of analysis could lead to a more satisfactory explanation of 'outcomes', but also that it was a question of identifying factors which had policy relevance. Aggregative ecological analyses, they felt, say

> . . . little about the allocation process itself and, therefore, do not identify particular levers which might be used to alter policy outcomes . . . This is not to suggest that demographic variables are unimportant in determining municipal outcomes, or that it is not

> essential to learn about the constraints that bind. Rather we say that, for purposes of policy it is important to focus on those variables which are under the agency's (or at least someone's) control. (Levy, Meltsner and Wildavsky, 1974, pp. 10–11)

Their findings, and much subsequent American work, point to the overriding importance of service bureaucracies and the decision rules they employ. Lineberry argued that such decisional rules and premises provided the missing link in the analysis of allocative processes and the 'outcomes' (services received) of urban government, although he did not supply any systematic evidence on the way such rules operated or their effects on service distributions. The perceived strength of their influence, compared with the motives and the decisions of the elected representatives, led Rich (1979, p. 146) to suggest that:

> . . . the study of urban bureaucracy becomes more important than the study of local politics. If the patterns found in Detroit, Houston, Oakland and San Antonio can be generalized, community power structure is less important in determining the authoritative allocation of values through city government that is the organization of public service delivery systems.

While it is probably the case that the different structure of local government in America affords local bureaucrats greater control than is the case in Britain, this may overstate their role in determining the allocation of resources and the provision of services. Certainly research in English local government reveals a varied and complex pattern of relationships between elected representatives and officials (Dearlove, 1973), which makes distinctions between them on the basis of their role in policy-making and service administration difficult (Lewis, 1975). Moreover 'service delivery rules' have been interpreted widely so as to refer to the basis of almost any decision, from a decision concerning the location of new recreational facilities to the immediate response to individual police calls. Illuminating though many of the studies of individual services are, they have not differentiated between the different types of mechanism or offered any systematic evidence as to whether different mechanisms vary in their significance for different types of service. The intention in the remainder of this chapter is therefore to discuss the nature of these mechanisms and how they relate to service characteristics. How far such mechanisms are influenced by formal policy-makers, the elected representatives, and how far they are shaped by professional service administrators are questions for empirical research.

Service distributions, I would argue, can be *directly* explained as the outcome of local authority decisions to supply services, on the one hand, and the nature and pattern of consumer demands for services, on the other hand. It is therefore important to understand how those supply decisions are made, how and why the pattern of demand varies, and how decisions to supply services interact with consumer demands.

Decisions on the supply of services include general decisions to provide certain facilities and services and decisions about the allocation of those services to individual consumers or clients. They encompass all decisions which affect the quality or nature of the service, as well as those concerning the level or quantity of provision. They will therefore be made by various bodies and individuals, at different levels within the local authority organisation. Some may be taken by committees or individual elected representatives, some may be taken by senior departmental officers, and yet others are left to lower-tier officers, field-workers, or even clerical staff. It is useful to distinguish between four main types of influence on the supply of services; the framework of policy and resource allocation within the authority; departmental rules and guidelines; the organisation of service provision; and the nature and use of discretion by those involved in the provision of services.

The Policy and Resource Allocation Framework

Local authority policies regarding the provision of services and statements of resource allocation, in particular the annual budget, provide the overall framework within which specific decisions to supply services are made. Policies are generic in character, providing guidelines which define how future decisions relating to particular classes or types of situation are to be taken (Friend and Jessop, 1969, p. 105). Since elected representatives are formally responsible for policy decisions the term is perhaps best confined to those guidelines which have been endorsed or established by formal decision-making bodies. In some instances explicit policy statements may exist, but in other cases policy will be implicit, in that although decisions of a similar type may be consistently made in the same way the basis of those decisions has never been formally stated.

Some policies will be explicitly distributional in defining that services are to be provided or resources allocated so as to benefit different neighbourhoods or social groups in a particular way. In the case of parks and recreation provision in Detroit, for example, it was found that the city consciously chose to concentrate the provision of playlots in the inner city areas (Jones, Greenberg, Kaufman and Drew, 1978). Policies of positive discrimination in education in Britain might similarly be expected to be reflected in the pattern of services received by different areas. It has been suggested, however, that public sector organisations often tend to adopt a principle of uniformity, providing the same level and type of service to all areas. In their study of refuse collection, for example, Jones *et al.* found the provision of the service was guided by a policy that refuse should be collected with the same frequency, once a week, in all parts of the city (ibid.). Uniformity may not, however, always reflect a principle of equal treatment but may arise through the adoption of nationally or professionally defined standards of provision (Stewart, 1980). Such standards may take little account of variations in need for services and hence lead to inequitable distributions (Stewart, 1973; Rich, 1977).

Some policies may not be overtly distributional in intent but may none the less have distributional consequences. A policy of achieving high standards in recreation facilities, for example, could lead to a concentration of the service in a few central facilities rather than a more dispersed pattern of less well-equipped facilities. This concentration may well have distributional implications. As Levy *et al.* (1974) showed in their analysis of library provision in Oakland, a large proportion of the resources available were devoted to the establishment of a specialised central collection which was disproportionately used by upper-income groups.

Although policies may indicate what services the authority believes should be provided or aims to provide, the resources actually required to put them into practice may not always be available. Resource allocation decisions, by contrast, do indicate the services the authority specifically intends to provide over a given time period. They indicate the authority's priorities and are thus likely to be important in determining the services received in different areas at a particular point in time. Again, although resource allocation may be explicitly distributional this is often not the case. The allocation of library resources has, for example, been argued to discriminate against more deprived areas, because it is based on the previous year's book issues and libraries tend to be utilised less by people from low-income or deprived neighbourhoods (ibid.; and Stewart, Spencer and Webster, 1976). Levy, Meltsner and Wildavsky have also demonstrated how the use of criteria such as safety and ease of traffic circulation in determining the street construction programme in Oakland emphasised the major arterials and tended to benefit those who resided in high-income areas (ibid.).

Departmental Rules and Conventions

Local authority policies vary in the degree to which they provide guidance for departments in putting them into effect through individual decisions on the supply of services. In some cases, for example, housing allocation points systems, a policy may be well codified and specify exactly how decisions on the allocation of the service to individual consumers are to be made. In other instances only broad policies or objectives may have been established, and it is left to the department, often through delegation to the chief officer, to interpret what the policy implies in terms of the day-to-day work of the department. Departmental guidance to individual officers on how particular types of decision are to be made and their work carried out may therefore be important in determining the pattern of service received.

That guidance may take the form of explicit rules or codes of practice which lay down the circumstances in which a service is to be provided and what type of service is appropriate. Social security payments provide a good example where the eligibility of different types of individual is well codified. Similarly the work required in order for an applicant to be eligible for a house improvement grant is often clearly stated in the guidance provided to environmental health officers on property inspection and the specification of necessary work

(Lambert, Penny and Webster, 1980). Where such formal rules do not exist there may none the less be conventions or regularised procedures which have been built up informally within the department, and which lead to a tendency for all those responsible for a particular area of work to behave in a similar fashion and to act consistently in the way decisions are made. There is often a tendency in environmental services, for example, to provide them in response to demand. This applies to environmental enforcement in Detroit (Jones *et al.*, 1978), with environmental health and shop inspections (Stewart, Spencer and Webster, 1976) and for road repairs (Levy *et al.*, 1974). Such conventions can lead to the provision of the service being biased towards middle- and upper-income areas where the residents have a greater propensity to complain.

As Jones *et al.* point out, departmental rules and conventions are often related to the norms and practices of individual professions and are more concerned with achieving the overall goals of the service and the efficient allocation of organisational resources than with questions of distribution.

> These rules are formulated, consciously or unconsciously, in an environment which favors the view of service as product and discourages inquiry into the distributional consequences of the rules . . . Professional public administrators often focus on services as products which are subject to quality control standards, rather than on services as scarce commodities to be divided up by groups who disagree, at least implicitly, about who ought to receive what level of service. (Jones *et al.*, 1978, pp. 339–40)

The Organisation of Service Delivery

The way that service delivery is organised within individual departments may also implicitly channel services to specific groups or areas, or affect the nature of the service received. The management of the work of the department on a day-to-day basis often requires the establishment of a number of smaller divisions or work units, and that division is frequently geographical. Hence the definition of area boundaries can be important in determining the level of service received. The use of a set of districts which are unrelated to the need or demand for the service can lead to an uneven distribution of workload, which inevitably affects the level and quality of service. This occurred in environmental enforcement in Detroit where, for purposes of compatibility, the districts established by a different department, the sanitation department, were adopted (Jones *et al.*, 1978). Similarly, the definition of school catchment areas and changes in their boundaries can influence the nature of the education service received by children residing in different neighbourhoods through its effect on staff/student ratios and on access to schools of different quality. In the United States, where local residents have an important role in the management of schools through school boards, catchments have even more significance since they affect the racial composition of schools in different neighbourhoods and hence the ability of different local groups to control their children's education (Bunge *et al.*, 1972).

Another aspect of service organisation is the extent to which the service is decentralised and responsibility for decision-making delegated to those in charge of the service in a particular area and to individual officers. The structure of decision-making is significant because it is indicative of the discretion formally allowed to officers in making decisions on the provision of services.

Discretionary Freedom and Individual Service Decisions

Decisions on when a service should be provided and what type of service is appropriate are in many cases controlled by individual officers. Headteachers have considerable freedom in determining what happens in individual schools; social workers have discretion over whether to take an individual child into care; environmental health officers often have discretion in deciding whether or not to take action on a health complaint; and librarians use their discretion in making choices about book stocks. These officers operate at the interface between the local authority and the consumers of the service, and have been referred to as 'street-level bureaucrats' (M. Lipsky, 1976) and 'social gate keepers' (Pahl, 1971). Their discretion arises not only from the explicit delegation of responsibility, but from the absence, vagueness or ambiguity of departmental rules and conventions. The way it is used may have a bearing on the pattern of services received.

As Hill (1976) has emphasised, such discretion is important in avoiding rigid responses and in allowing those most closely in touch with localised or individual needs to determine the most appropriate course of action. Moreover some degree of individual freedom is inevitable because it is impossible for the agency to enumerate all the possible problems or circumstances which may arise, because the individual officer has to determine what the clients' problems or circumstances are (Hood, 1976), or because the clear specification or enforcement of the rules could lead to demands on the service which could not be coped with. Indeed, even where clear standards are laid down, the goals of the service may be more effectively met by disregarding them in certain circumstances rather than applying them rigidly (Nivola, 1978).

In offering an explanation of why policy decisions or departmental rules fail to be implemented or are distorted in practice, Dunsire focuses on the cognitive aspects of administrative systems. The capacity of officers to understand policy statements and to translate generalised rules into implications for their own behaviour in particular circumstances often, he argues, provides a better explanation than deliberate recalcitrance (Dunsire, 1978). However, it is the affective aspects of the decisions of individual officers which may be more important in understanding their distributional consequences. The existence of discretion may result in decisions regarding the provision of services being shaped by professional and personal attitudes and values as much as by the circumstances, needs, or preferences of particular consumers or neighbourhoods.

Individual officers within a particular service may subscribe to quite different professional ideologies concerning the role of the service, the best means of achieving its goals, or the relationship between providers and consumers. The attitudes of headteachers can, therefore, lead to marked variations in curriculum and social organisation (Rutter *et al.*, 1979) between schools, and the frequency of arrests can vary between police patrol areas (J. R. Lambert, 1970). Similarly, social workers hold different conceptions of the value of undertaking work with particular types of client (Rees, 1978), which could lead to variations in the nature of the service provided by social work teams.

More personal beliefs and assumptions may also influence decisions made about individual consumers or areas, and stereotypes built up of particular groups may lead to conscious or unconscious discrimination in service provision. The distinction between the deserving and undeserving poor is evident in the field of welfare services (Lewis, 1975), and studies have shown how the recommendations of housing visitors on housing allocation may be influenced by the visitors' own assessments of housekeeping standards (Lambert, Paris and Blackaby, 1978) or other personal characteristics (Gray, 1976). A similar form of bias has been noted in the context of housing inspection in Boston, where officers were predisposed towards complainants who were more 'co-operative' by making efforts to keep their property in good order and only using the department when really necessary (Nivola, 1978). Further, the effects of personal self-interest should not be ignored. Environmental health officers, for example, may arrange their own work so as to spend disproportionate amounts of time in those parts of their district which are more pleasant or lucrative in expenses (Puffitt, 1977), and housing inspectors who work in difficult or hazardous areas are likely to become somewhat apathetic about enforcing repairs (Nivola, 1978).

Consumer Demand

Many local authority services are made available to the whole population, or particular sections of it, yet receipt of the service relies on the consumer or member of the public voluntarily expressing a demand for it. The term 'demand' is here used to refer to the explicit actions taken by an individual or group of consumers, or by a third party such as a councillor or officer acting on their behalf, in order to obtain a service. This action may take the form of a personal request or application for a service, for example, for a council house or a special refuse collection, a complaint, for example, about footpath repair or an environmental nuisance, or the direct use of a facility such as a swimming pool or a park. It is this type of demand which will have an immediate and direct bearing on the receipt of services. More generalised pressures or demands on the local authority, in terms of representations from consumer groups, the length of waiting lists, or overcrowded facilities, may also affect service distributions. But their influence will be indirect, since they often require changes in policy or resource allocations which can only be brought about over a longer time period.

Systematic variations in the level of demand from different areas often result in a tendency for particular groups to benefit from the provision of a service. And frequently the more affluent neighbourhoods receive the greater share of services, because take-up is generally higher among middle- and upper-income groups. This applies both to services which are provided locally to meet the needs of specific neighbourhoods and those which are intended for the community as a whole and perhaps provided at a central location. Levy, Meltsner and Wildavsky (1974) demonstrated marked differences in the user patterns for library services, and showed that road maintenance services strongly favoured upper-income areas because of the number of complaints made by residents. Similarly, citizen-initiated contacts in environmental enforcement came from all over the city of Detroit but were disproportionately concentrated in neighbourhoods in the middle ranges of social well-being (Jones *et al.*, 1978). Consumer advice services are also likely to be utilised less by lower-income groups, because they rely on complaints or queries; yet these groups tend to live in areas where unscrupulous practices are particularly prevalent (Stewart, Spencer and Webster, 1976). Such variations become all the more important where, as is often the case, housing, environmental and other problems are concentrated in lower-income neighbourhoods.

It can be argued that variations in demand are simply a reflection of consumer choice or preference and that for many services this basis is the most appropriate on which to allocate them. Obviously personal attributes and attitudes, such as income, pride, or sociability, may influence decisions as to whether to make use of services and these characteristics will often be outside the local authority's control. However, patterns of demand are also influenced by the nature of service provision itself. Services may be physically more accessible to some neighbourhoods than others. Knox (1978), for example, found that the location of primary care facilities in Scotland tended to result in those areas with high levels of need, in terms of above-average rates of morbidity and high rates of infant and perinatal mortality, having lower accessibility to doctors. Other facets of access to services, such as knowledge of their availability, the procedures involved in applying for or using them and the attitudes of officials, particularly clerical staff who often represent the first point of contact with the authority, may also influence the ability or willingness of consumers to utilise the service (Lister, 1974; A. S. Hall, 1974). Finally, the nature or type of service or facility actually offered may not meet the needs or interests of particular groups of consumers as they perceive them. The way such factors can result in certain areas being relatively disadvantaged has been shown in the context of recreation provision for inner city areas (Department of the Environment, 1977e).

The Relationship between Supply Decisions and Consumer Demand

The significance of supply decisions, on the one hand, and consumer demand, on the other hand, in determining the pattern of services received is likely to vary according to the characteristics of individual services.[8] In some services, such as improvement grants, meals-on-wheels, home helps, housing repairs and environmental health inspections, consumer demand must be expressed before a decision is made whether or not to supply the service. Such demand is therefore likely to be an important determinant of the distribution of services. It will be all the more significant where, as has been shown, it becomes institutionalised in the policies or departmental rules governing supply decisions. In services made available for use at a limited number of specific locations, such as libraries, museums, recreation facilities, youth facilities and health centres, consumer demand will again be an important factor, although in this instance certain decisions regarding the level and nature of service will have already been made and demand is not a prerequisite for the receipt of the service. In other services, such as education, refuse collection and street cleansing, consumers have little or no choice as to whether they receive the service, and supply decisions will necessarily dominate the pattern of services.

Generally it might be expected that the greater the 'divisibility' of a service, that is, the extent to which it is possible to differentiate the level and nature of the service supplied, the greater the likelihood of inter-area variations in services. As Yates (1976b) points out, where services are highly divisible, 'urban administrators can make countless small adjustments and reallocations both in their deployment of street-level bureaucrats and in their definition of what service policies and procedures should be followed in a particular neighbourhood'. Departmental guidelines and the use of discretionary freedom by individual officers might be expected to be especially important in the case of services where demand exceeds supply and where some mechanism for rationing the service is required.

Not only will the relative importance of supply decisions and consumer demand vary between services, but the way these two interact may differ. The discussion of specific factors gave some indication of the interdependencies which exist, but a further example, from a study of the distribution of improvement grants in Walsall (Lambert, Penny and Webster, 1980) illustrates some of the complexities involved. In this case the expression of consumer demand, in the form of an inquiry, sets in motion an application process which culminates in decisions on whether or not to supply a grant and what level of grant should be approved. Inquiries are thus a primary determinant of who is likely to receive a grant. However, the policy on housing improvement, as reflected in eligibility criteria concerning the age and rateable value of the property, then acts to filter out certain inquiries. Eligible properties are then inspected so that environmental health officers can determine the work which will be required and send the formal application form, specifying these works, to the consumer. This stage of the procedure is predominantly shaped by written departmental rules which provide detailed guidance for inspectors on the standard of work required. The significance of these rules, however, lies not in any explicit intention to give preference to certain types of consumer or property in the allocation of grants, but in its effect on the subsequent expression of consumer demand, in terms of the decision to pursue the inquiry and submit the formal application. A variety of factors may influence such decisions (Kirwan and Martin, 1972) but the standards required by the authority are often far in excess of consumer expectations and imply significant financial commitment on the part of the applicant, and are therefore likely to be an important influence on the decision to proceed. The spatial distribution of grants is, in this case, dominated by the distribution of initial inquiries, but the example demonstrates how the pattern of service received can be shaped by a complex sequence of stages in which consumer demand interacts with a variety of factors influencing the supply of the service.

CONCLUSIONS

This chapter has argued for the systematic study of the distributional effects of the range of services and facilities for which local government is responsible. Not only is this a neglected line of analysis in the field of public policy studies but it has an important practical role in reviewing the performance of local authority policies and services and developing local strategies for dealing with problems of deprivation. Further, it has been suggested that such study should focus on the level and quality of the services received, and that for many services the analysis must necessarily relate to the distribution between areas or neighbourhoods. It is important, however, to recognise the limits of such an analysis.

In the first place, it tends to ignore questions of whether the services currently being provided are in fact the most appropriate. It may not be very encouraging to know that a particular service is equitably distributed if it is not very effective in meeting the needs it was designed to meet. This point emphasises the importance of the continued development of output measures for local government services and of research efforts concerned with understanding the role of local government provisions *vis-à-vis* other environmental influences in determining changes in social, economic and environmental conditions. Experimental projects and innovations in service provision can also play a significant role in this context.

Secondly, an analysis based on geographical areas may not capture all the differentials which exist in the distribution of local authority services. This chapter showed how various mechanisms, the framework of policy and resource allocation decisions, departmental guidelines, the organisation of service delivery and individual discretion and consumer demand can have spatially distributive effects, even if the mechanisms themselves are aspatial in character. But not all the distributional implications of such mechanisms may be expressed geographically. Housing allocation procedures, for example, may have important distributive effects, but it may not be particularly meaningful to analyse these on an area basis; the important differentials are more likely to exist between family types, income categories, or racial groups. An area-based analysis can be valuable since it allows comparisons between services and hence can help to identify whether the same areas are consistently advantaged or disadvantaged in terms of a whole range of services. But for some services it may be important to undertake a complementary analysis of service distribution based, say, on income, race, or social class.

Affecting changes in the distribution of services received depends on an understanding of the mechanisms which determine that distribution. This chapter has stressed the importance of studying the nature of local authority decision-making processes and suggested that attention needs to be given not only to policy-making but to the processes whereby services are provided and delivered to the public. The mechanisms which may have a significant influence on the pattern of services received extend beyond the conscious policy choices of the authority and encompass the whole gamut of professional and national standards, the priorities reflected in resource allocations, departmental customs regarding the allocation and organisation of service provision, individual attitudes and the use of discretion. Moreover they are bound up with the complex interaction between the provision of services and demands from consumers, that is, between the local authority organisation and its environment. Empirical research is needed to identify how these mechanisms operate; which are most important in the context of specific types of service; and to what extent they are shaped by elected members and professional service administrators.

Even if such mechanisms could be shown to result in an unequal or inequitable pattern of service distribution, it would not necessarily imply that they should be changed. For they may well be justifiable on other grounds: uniformity of provision could be argued to be justified politically on the grounds that all areas contribute to the rates and that the level of contribution is not related to the need for services; professional standards could be argued to be necessary if the service is to be effective in achieving its overall objectives; departmental practices relating to the allocation of staff workloads could be argued to be necessary in terms of staff morale and career progression; the discretionary freedom available to individual officers may be seen as essential in ensuring the most appropriate service response in dealing with the problems of different individuals or areas; and it could be argued that the take-up of services is a question of preference and motivation on the part of the individual consumer, and it is not the responsibility of the organisation to affect or change these. However, there is a strong case for suggesting that such arguments would be more acceptable if they were made in the light of knowledge about, and recognition of, their distributive effects. This is not generally the case.

Although emphasis has been placed here on understanding local authority decision-making processes, this does not deny the significance of other explanations based, for example, on power or class. It is recognised that inequalities or inequities in services may reflect more fundamental inequalities in society, which are unlikely to be altered through changes in the structure or operations of local government institutions. However, it can be argued that it is important to examine such institutional factors, because it is these which directly determine the distribution of specific services, even though they may in turn be shaped by wider power relationships or structural forces.[9] Moreover, the study of decision-making processes focuses specifically on factors which are often amenable to control by the local authority, and demonstrating their distributive effects might result in action designed to bring about a more equitable pattern of service provision. Even if no such action were initiated, at least more explicit consideration might be given to distributional issues in local authority decision-making. The lack of correlation between the need for public services and their provision, which for writers such as Pahl (1971) is a 'commonplace to observe' might not be quite so obvious to policy-makers and administrators in local government.

NOTES: CHAPTER 4

This chapter is based on a paper originally presented to the Urban Geography Study Group of the Institute of British Geographers in 1977. I would like to thank all those who commented on that earlier version, and in particular John Stewart, Rod Rhodes and Chris Skelcher, whose detailed and constructive criticisms led to a number of important revisions.

1 For useful reviews of the findings of these studies see Rich, 1979, and Burnett, 1980.
2 For a discussion of local authority management systems and the adoption of corporate approaches see Greenwood, Hinings, Ranson and Walsh, 1976, and for a discussion of the development of corporate planning see Chapter 3 in this volume.
3 Levy *et al.* use the term 'outcome' to refer to the evaluation of 'outputs', the latter being defined as the goods and services produced by governments (Levy, Meltsner and Wildavsky, 1974, pp. 7–8). I find it more helpful to separate clearly issues concerning what it is that governments produce from issues concerning evaluation, because it may be desirable to evaluate a number of different distributions.
4 In an earlier paper I distinguished between level of provision, as the service provided by the local authority, and outcome, as the service received or consumed by the population (Webster, 1977). However, in view of the argument discussed above concerning the importance of viewing services from the consumer's perspective, and the fact that this distinction is not meaningful for certain services because those who receive services are, by definition, those to whom it is provided (for example, home helps, housing maintenance), it seems more useful to consider only service received, yet recognising that the nature of that 'service' may vary.
5 Any evaluation of the distribution of service received requires the specification of some criterion or standard against which it can be judged. This issue cannot be discussed in detail here. For a review of alternative distributional principles see Harvey, 1973, D. M. Smith, 1977 and Lineberry, 1977, and for a discussion of the concept of need see Bradshaw, 1972, and Culyer, 1976.
6 For a discussion of the relative merits of wards, service administration areas and areas defined on the basis of socioeconomic characteristics see Webster, Lambert and Penny, 1979.
7 See, for example, the study by Jones *et al.* of the distribution of the environmental enforcement service in Detroit (Jones, Greenberg, Kaufman and Drew, 1978), and

the analysis of the distribution of improvement grants by Lambert, Penny and Webster, 1980.

8 For a discussion of the characteristics of different local authority services see Webster, Lambert and Penny, 1979, and for a more general discussion of the nature of public goods, see Peston, 1972, and E. Ostrom, 1974.

9 A similar line of argument has been developed by Batley, 1980, in a thought-provoking article which examines the place of organisational analysis in understanding the distribution of benefits in the urban system.

5

The Use of Information in Policy and Management Systems

STEVE ROGERS

INTRODUCTION

The increased availability and sophistication of electronic data processing equipment have made possible the provision of almost unlimited amounts of information within organisations and have resulted in immense benefits in improving management information systems. Such developments have also produced certain disbenefits. They have tended to lead to an excessively narrow and technology-dominated view of the design of information systems in general, which in turn has led to considerable human and organisational problems in the implementation of some information systems.

The purpose of this chapter is to explore some of those aspects of individual and organisational activity which have been ignored or given low priority by many information system designers. In particular attention is focused on the concept of *information need* as a major factor requiring consideration in the design of information systems. The chapter is thus intended to form a broad framework of ideas which may be used in analysing the information needs of an organisation. Three areas are identified for exploration and analysis; the organisational context, the nature of information and models of organisational activity, and their implications for the development of methodologies for analysing information needs are considered.

THE LIMITATIONS OF EXISTING APPROACHES TO INFORMATION SYSTEMS

Much of the work on information systems in recent years has displayed some of the following limitations.

Systems designers have been more concerned with the possibilities provided by, and the requirements of, developments in *information technology* than with the problems of implementing and applying those developments in organisations. Their apparent inability to take account of human factors stems in large part from the fact that early computers were expensive both to build and operate. As a result considerations of technological efficiency were consistently given high priority and despite the recent dramatic reduction in the cost of the technology itself, such considerations tend to retain their high priority.

Most approaches to information systems have been based on the *formal systems and structures* of organisations, thereby ignoring the informal aspects of organisation which may be important determinants of the way information is used in an organisation. An approach which attempts to include an analysis of informal systems is likely to achieve greater reality and therefore to be of potentially greater value to an organisation. At the same time, however, such an approach will be more difficult to handle from an analytical point of view and also may be perceived as threatening by some members of the organisation in that it implies making overt some behaviours and activities which formerly were covert.

Work on information systems has tended to assume either that managers and organisations are *purely rational* or that they want to become more rational. It may be hypothesised that the production of better information in a systematic way within an organisation will lead to greater rationality of the organisation. Depending upon one's point of view that may be a result to be applauded, or one to be feared and disliked, and therefore the assumption that all organisations (and individuals within those organisations) seek greater rationality has to be approached with some scepticism. While it may be agreed that organisations such as local authorities *should* act more rationally (a normative judgement) – and require better information and communication systems to do so – it must also be recognised that in practice they only do so to a limited degree – which may vary from one organisation to another and even within parts of the same organisation. Moreover attempts to *impose* rationality on organisations by, *inter alia*, setting up formal information systems may have limited results, and in some instances negative consequences. The introduction of formal information systems is often equated with consequential organisational changes which are perceived as undesirable by those who are affected by them. The lowering of line-management discretion, greater centralisation and increase in the power of information technologists are some of the effects which have been identified by researchers such as Mumford and Banks (1967) and Whistler (1970).

There are, perhaps, two reasons for this. First, formal systems are representations of a bounded rationality. For certain tightly defined functions these boundaries encompass all the significant factors which need to be taken into account. For other issues the boundaries are too narrow; the system can at best provide data which has to be qualified or added to by statements from less formalised sources. Secondly, the above argument still presupposes that organisations strive to optimise when taking decisions. From such a perspective many decisions would appear to be non-rational in that they are by no means optimal for the organisation as a whole. It is only when the boundaries are extended still further, to include the personal concerns of the interested parties, that some semblance of logic is restored. It appears probable therefore that where optimisation takes place it does so only within the boundaries imposed by the personal concerns of individuals and groups within an organisation. There are therefore limits to organisational rationality which cannot be 'overcome' just by producing more and better information. The approach to information system design should not therefore be to impose rationality but to seek to identify those situations where the use of more, or less, or better information is likely to assist in creating greater rationality.[1]

Information has been treated as an independent variable in the organisational context. Many designers of information systems have failed to recognise the interdependency of information with many other aspects of the organisation. To move beyond this unidimensional view it is necessary to link the concept of information (a piece of data) with that of communication so that a system is considered which involves (*a*) the transmission of meaning and meaningful symbols, (*b*) concepts of sharing and exchange and (*c*) the implied occurrence of some change in the receiver, be it a reduction or increase in the level of uncertainty, a greater degree of understanding, or an increased (or decreased) level of confidence in an existing viewpoint.

Relating these issues to the organisational context an information/communication system may be viewed as comprising a number of elements or variables.

(1) *PERSON(S) and GROUPS OF PEOPLE* (who are different in respect of their values, expertise, knowledge, interests and ability to use new information, in the degree to which they are analytical or emotional in taking decisions, and in terms of their basic psychology)

(2) . . . *who face PROBLEMS* (which differ; they may be wide-ranging or narrow, short- or long-term, affecting one or many people, relate to the past, present or future)

(3) . . . *which occur within an ORGANISATIONAL CONTEXT* (which may itself affect the problems which occur, how they are perceived, to whom they are presented, and so on)

(4) . . . *which require EVIDENCE* (the degree to which certain types of evidence are needed, that is, perceived by the individual or group, and are useful or usable, will depend on 1, 2 and 3 above)

(5) . . . *through some FORM OF PRESENTATION*

(6) . . . *which requires ANALYSIS* (the degree to which information can be formally analysed depends on the analytical tools available, the type of date/information available and the inclinations of the individuals/groups involved)

(7) . . . *in order to arrive at a DECISION/SOLUTION/REVIEW*

(8) . . . *which may lead to some course of ACTION/IMPLEMENTATION* (but may also result in inaction)

Such a listing of elements does not in itself constitute a framework of ideas for analysing information needs. It is only one limited way of expressing what the basic elements of an information/communication system might be. However, as Mason and Mitroff (1973) (from whom this taxonomy is in part derived) suggest, making explicit the basic elements of a system illustrates that each element contains within itself variables, or degrees of variability.

A complete analysis of information needs might seek both to derive a complete taxonomy of the variables within each basic element and to test the interactive effects of all possible combinations of these variables. Such an analysis, assuming it were possible, would be extremely lengthy and resource-consuming. My present approach is more limited, being an attempt to indicate aspects of three areas which are considered to be of key importance.

I THE ORGANISATIONAL CONTEXT

Individuals and Groups

In examining information need attention should be focused on those individual or group variables which might affect the way they perceive the need to use information, and the way they actually use information – what information is used and how it is used. Of these variables the following are likely to be of importance.

(*a*) *Cognitive Style and Psychological Type*. Individuals clearly differ in the ways they perceive the world and react to what they see. Different individuals placed in the same situation are likely to require and use different types and amounts of information. Numerous attempts have been made to classify different behaviour patterns, cognitive styles and perceptual abilities and to chart their effects on information-seeking behaviour and decision-making, using such categories as 'concrete' and 'abstract' (see Schroeder, Driver and Streufert, 1965), 'thinking', 'feeling', 'sensation' and 'intuition' (Mason and Mitroff, 1973). The problem of using such classifications of individual behaviour is that they are purely theoretical constructs. They are caricatures of how individuals behave in reality. In addition by taking individual differences as a primary focus of research there is a likelihood that the analysis will be more informative about the differences between individuals than about their commonalities. In attempting to improve information systems in an organisation there must be a trade-off between the degree to which individual needs can be met (where they differ) and the cost to the organisation of so doing. The acknowledgement that such differences exist has considerable implications for the type of methodology which might be used to identify and meet information needs. In particular it would appear important that it should incorporate an approach which seeks to present individuals with some choice as to both the presentation and content of information.

(*b*) *Values, Appreciative Systems and Organisational Roles*. All individuals have sets of values, or 'appreciative systems' (Mason and Mitroff, 1973) which lead them to view the world in certain ways and respond accordingly. In the context of local government two important processes by which individuals develop appreciative systems is through membership of and training for a particular profession, and through membership of a political party or group. The effect of membership of such groups is to enable individuals to select certain items of information from the totality which surround them. Of greater importance in this process of selection, however, is likely to be the role which an individual has in an organisation. There are certain situations where individual differences may create significant problems in the use and communication of information:

- where different professionals are involved in the same decision process;
- where conflict exists between the needs of superiors and subordinates. It may be argued that such conflict sometimes exists in social services departments where the needs of social work managers and those of social work practitioners may be very different. There is also evidence from research in other organisations that status hierarchies can affect the flow of information in an organisation (Read, 1962, pp. 3–16);
- where individuals value the person-to-person contact created by informal systems of communication and therefore resent the creation of formal information systems which will tend to replace such contact with system-to-person contacts. The identification of need and the formalisation of information systems which may flow from that identification must therefore encompass not only the content of information but also its format and the organisational context by which it is transmitted.

(*c*) *Information Overload*. Human beings are capable of using only limited amounts of information. As a result they adopt filtering devices which allow them to ignore aspects of the information they receive. One possible response to such devices is for organisations to shower individuals and groups with as much information as possible in the expectation that they will be able to extract from it those aspects which they require. Evidence suggests however that filtering devices cannot adequately cope with such a response and that information which is structured and summarised to meet the particular needs of a decision situation is likely to improve decision-making performance (see, for example, Chervany and Dickson, 1974). This problem is best approached by identifying the roles which individuals fulfil, using the organisational activity model presented later.

Organisations – Structures, Environment and Climate

The need to have a clear understanding of the nature of an organisation in order to appreciate the information needs of its members derives in large part from the fact that an *organisational structure* may itself be considered to be an information processing system. The very existence of an organisational structure is an indication that information/communications are expected to follow particular routes. Formal information systems and organisational structures are therefore interdependent when viewed from such a perspective. As a result an analysis of an organisation may be expected to identify situations where an expression of information need may be met either by improving the formal information system or by adapting the structure of the organisation. While knowledge of organisations and organisational behaviour is not such that rules or hypotheses may be stated which are both generally applicable and sufficiently detailed to aid choice in individual cases, it is possible to predict that the following aspects of organisational structure will be relevant to an analysis of information need and therefore require to be incorporated into any such analysis:

- degree of vertical and lateral structuring;
- complexity of structure in terms of the interrelationships between line functions and staff functions;
- effect of geographical location.

In the same way that information systems cannot be considered in isolation, so it is necessary to move beyond organisational structures themselves to consider their environment. The literature of organisational theorists (Lawrence and Lorsch, 1967) suggests that mechanistic, bureaucratic structures are more appropriate when the *organisational environment* is fairly stable, while more organic structures are suitable for turbulent environments. The same principle applies to information systems. In this context turbulence involves at least four elements:

(i) that the environment of the organisation is changing so rapidly that it becomes difficult or impossible to scan it effectively and to digest information about those changes and respond appropriately;
(ii) that the prescribed role of the organisation may be subject to change;
(iii) that the problems that an organisation is attempting to deal with are complex and ill-defined;
(iv) that the effects of services provided by the organisation are uncertain.

The presence of any of these aspects of turbulence leads to uncertainty about organisational activities. Organisations may react to uncertainty by using a number of strategies, only one of which is the creation of new formal information systems. The problem then becomes one of how to identify those instances where such a response is appropriate. In part this will be determined by the nature of the information required – in particular whether it is sufficiently capable of quantification and precision to be contained within a formal information system. If it is not so capable then other strategies may be considered such as the creation of teams or by changing the locus of decision-taking.

The aspects of an organisation's environment which are particularly important in the local government context are the complexity, extent and clarity of relationships which exist between an organisation and other organisations, and the extent to which such interrelationships give rise to the need for information to cross organisational boundaries. While the local authority may have little control over the information flows which result from inter-organisational relationships it is important to identify those areas where a local authority is dependent, or is likely to be dependent, on information generated externally, and to assess the predictability of its supply. Attempts to translate general considerations about the stability of a local authority's environment into a precise methodology for identifying information needs are likely to be problematic in that the state of knowledge about the effects of organisational environment is insufficient for precise indicators or measures of turbulence and stability to be put forward. In addition some environmental conditions will vary from one part of a local authority to another. For example, one department may be much more dependent on externally generated information than another. Tasks in one department may be much more predictable than in another. Awareness of these and other intra-organisational differences becomes of particular importance where an attempt is being made to design an information system which is authority-wide. Despite the difficulties involved, a methodology for analysing information needs must at least have regard to the following kinds of change which will effect the type of information system appropriate for a local authority as a whole and for particular departments within it:

(i) frequency of changes in statutory duties;
(ii) extent of, and changes in, the demand for information;
(iii) frequency of changes in the structure of the organisation;
(iv) predictability of tasks;
(v) rate of change in the size of the organisation;
(vi) changes in major stated policy objectives, budget allocations, and so on;
(vii) degree of dependency upon externally generated information and the predictability of its supply.

The exploration of the organisational context has so far made reference to several factors which are considered to be of importance in understanding the use of and need for information. Two of these – the organisational structure and individual characteristics – interact to produce what is generally referred to as *organisational climate*. Organisational climate 'describes the characteristic behavioural processes in a social system at one point in time' (Payne and Pugh, 1976). Numerous researchers have attempted to measure organisational climate using both objective and subjective measures.[2] While there is no clear direct evidence from this research about the relationship between organisational climate and the use of information within an organisation, there is considerable indirect evidence that organisational climate, as measured by subjective factors such as trust, individual autonomy, consideration, warmth and support, is likely to influence the degree to which individuals are willing to transfer reliable information within an organisation – especially when that information is being used for the purpose of control.

While it is not suggested that an analysis of information needs requires a detailed investigation of the climate of an organisation, it is necessary to obtain some indication of how an organisation is operating and of the possibility of introducing certain types of information system change. Such knowledge is a prerequisite to the design of any information system. Four areas have been suggested as being of particular importance, these being:

(i) individual characteristics – especially with respect to one individual's ability to process information;
(ii) the processes of selection which individuals operate in their use of certain types and sources of information;
(iii) the effect of organisational structure in creating needs for certain types of information;
(iv) the effect of organisational climate – especially in terms of the transfer of information, both horizontally and vertically within an organisation.

II THE NATURE OF INFORMATION

The second broad area of consideration focuses primarily on the nature of information and the use to which it is put in organisations. The question – 'What is information used for?' – arises as a direct result of the earlier arguments in this chapter in that a clear implication of those arguments is that information needs should be determined by an examination of what people do when filling their roles in an organisation. Studies of what people do (see Mintzberg, 1973) indicate that their use of information can be put into four main categories:

(*a*) operating a decision and control system;
(*b*) building a picture of the world for themselves and persuading others of the truth of this picture;
(*c*) negotiating – about plans, budgets, job content, and so on;
(*d*) stimulating action in others.

This classification is important because it highlights the significance of information that is only indirectly related to decision-making processes. A good deal of effort is spent by managers trying to form an opinion about people and situations, and much of this activity occurs in an apparently unstructured manner, during what superficially appear to be social exchanges and gossip. In the next section of this chapter this information search has been encompassed into a model of management processes, where it is referred to as 'scanning the relevant external world'.

The person's role as a negotiator and a stimulator has implications for the way information is selected, made available and duplicated. Information is used as a weapon, defensive or offensive, in negotiations at every level in the organisation, and only under limited conditions, and where there is a good deal of trust, will it be treated as a neutral, freely available commodity. Often it may only be obtained if an appropriate trade-off can be agreed. Similarly, an individual's managerial style in stimulating action will affect both the content of the information he requests and shares and the manner in which this is done.

Programmed and Unprogrammed Decisions

To say that a study of decisions fails to embrace all organisational activity is not to deny its crucial importance. But decisions are not all of one type; some have clearer precedents than others. Many information systems have been developed to serve a series of decisions which are of the same type and have to be repeated frequently. An example of these programmed decisions is the decision about when to reorder stocks and how much to order. Much of the thinking about information systems has been based on assumptions that all decisions are of this type. At the other extreme, however, many decisions for which information is needed are unprogrammed. That is, the decision is about a new issue and, once it has been made, there may be no need ever to repeat it.

Decisions may be unprogrammed for several reasons: they may be strategic, charting a new course for the organisation; the organisation may be evolving rapidly and facing sudden changes in the environment; it may not be very specialised, thus dealing with a wide range of issues, or, at the limit, each decision may take into account a unique set of factors; finally, there may be little agreement as to the factors which are relevant or the goals to be achieved.

Most decisions fall between these two extremes and individuals, as well as organisations as a whole, are likely to be involved with a mix of more or less programmed decisions. But the balance will vary, both within and between organisations. It is frequently claimed that people in social services departments have a high proportion of less programmed decisions. Certainly many of the problems they deal with have unique features, but the requisite variety of response may not always be available to reach an appropriately unique decision. A decision is made in terms of a model, implicit or explicit, about the way the relevant factors relate together and affect the choice to be made. *Where a decision is programmed* the information needs and the model of how they relate together become increasingly explicit, and ultimately a formal mathematical model may be built, designed to provide an optimal answer each time the decision is made. A formal model will determine completely what information is needed, how frequently, in what degree of detail and how accurate it has to be. Where there is no formal model the decision itself still determines what information is needed but in a less precise way.

So, information needs for programmed decisions can be determined by obtaining an understanding of the decisions themselves. This is the ideal situation since the information needs are so clearly specified. It should be noted, however, that even here other, less clearly specified, information is needed that will identify whether the model for a series of programmed decisions is still relevant or should be changed.

Where decisions are unprogrammed information needs are less likely to be exposed by examining decisions, since the set of factors relevant to any particular ones may not be relevant to others. Thus a backcloth of information is required which is relevant to the *sorts* of decisions necessary to carry out the responsibilities of the organisation. Such information will not always be used, nor will it precisely meet the needs of particular decisions. But it does provide a base from which informed judgements can be made – both about decisions themselves and about the further unique information necessary for them to be made. Given that it is an approximation, one needs both to allow for changes in its content over time and to provide the facility for further data collection. Much of the information is likely to be obtained by informal means, which should be supported by appropriate organisational structures.

One basis for deciding which information to collect will be some analysis of the functions and outputs of the organisation and the roles and tasks performed by those working in it. The ways in which this analysis might be structured are discussed below. But this analysis cannot be the sole basis – it will never be possible to provide, or assimilate, all the information that is potentially useful, so that there cannot be a uniquely correct answer.

Information Needs for Other Purposes

Information is also required to build a picture of the environment, to negotiate and to stimulate, and the importance of informal aspects of organisations have been noted in this respect. There is a danger in imposing formal systems which enhance the capacity to take appropriate decisions but drastically reduce face-to-face encounter. Yet formal information systems can also serve these wider purposes and many of the comments made about information needs for unprogrammed decisions apply here. In addition, individual preferences will clearly have an influence; the world which, for example, the social worker who sees herself as a community resource facilitator seeks to make sense of is different from that of the social worker who is more concerned with the psychodynamics of client situations. The housing manager who sees his role as the controller of the council's housing stock will seek out different information from the housing manager who sees the council's housing function as one element of the local housing market.

Methods of Meeting Information Needs

Finally, in considering the nature of information it is important to consider the different methods available for meeting information needs. These may briefly be classified as:

(*a*) collection, storage and retrieval systems for data of different types and in differing forms – quantitative, qualitative, bibliographic;
(*b*) organisational capacity to collect, analyse and distribute information as required;
(*c*) organisational structures and procedures (both formal and informal) that facilitate contact with appropriate sources of information;
(*d*) training and other means of increasing knowledge, awareness and understanding of certain classes of information and skills in handling them.

Although all these approaches are necessary, information scientists (as contrasted with organisation scientists) have concentrated on (*a*), with a recent growth in the recognition of the importance of the more formal aspects of (*b*). However, while in many organisational contexts the impact of *formal* organisational structures and procedures may be a key determinant of the availability of information, no organisation can operate without an *informal* system which will also have an impact on the availability and use of information. The informal system has the advantage that it is flexible although it may not always provide a sufficient structure for all people to benefit from it. It can readily respecify its own needs, find new sources and cope with information that is in a wide range of forms. It is therefore not always beneficial to attempt to formalise an existing informal system. Moreover it is probable that the informal systems will be more responsive to the fact that individuals within the organisation have only a limited capacity to absorb and use information. Informal systems may in part, therefore, act as filtering devices which attempt to overcome problems of information overload. Automated data systems can absorb large amounts of data and reduce the quantities to manageable proportions for particular decisions, or they can be used to select or summarise information for general background purposes. The problem is still not solved, however, because there is more information available than can be economically stored, and, as illustrated earlier, much information is unsuited for formal systems.

In summary:

- there are great problems in trying to introduce a comprehensive management information system;
- one has to be selective about determining which information needs will be met;
- one must regularly reconsider the information needs and be capable of altering the mix as the situation demands;
- where possible, systems should be designed to reduce the amount of information which individuals have to absorb.

III MODELS OF ORGANISATIONAL ACTIVITY

In this section a range of concepts concerning organisational activity are brought together to guide the examination of information needs. There are several relevant ways of describing organisation activity but the wide range of work in which local authorities are engaged and the variety of their organisational contexts mean that different descriptions (models) are more useful in different situations. These models are not mutually exclusive. Each describes an organisation from a different point of view. But in any one organisational context one model is likely to be predominantly useful. Before discussing these, however, it is necessary to define the elements of these models and their relationship to each other.

The Basic Element of the Models

Local authorities undertake a range of *activities* which are reflected in certain *outputs*. These may be external (for example, the provision of a home help service) or internal (for example, staff training). Explicit *objectives*, or at least implicit aims, exist for those activities in terms of the needs and problems which they are designed to meet. When fully articulated, objectives can be related to activities and outputs by means of *programme structures*. Activities are implemented by a *management process*. That process may be described by the use of a model comprised of a number of linked elements which indicate management *functions* (for example, planning, implementing, reviewing, controlling). These management process functions will be common to a number of activities.

The management process functions are reflected by the allocation of *roles* (specific to activities) to individuals and groups in the organisation. Each role embodies responsibility for a number of detailed *tasks* which contribute towards the aims of the organisational activity. *Task expectations* are negotiated among role incumbents within the organisation. *Information needs* relate to the fulfilment of those task expectations.

The particular models put forward are:

- a *systems* model, relating organisational inputs to outputs;
- a *programme structure* model, focusing on objectives;
- a *management processes* model, describing managerial functions.

In each, one or more of the above elements predominate as a means of structuring the analysis of information needs. Each breaks organisational activity down to a series of statements about roles and tasks, but the nature of those statements will differ according to which element is dominant.

The Relationship between the Models

It should be stressed that these models are complementary, though the relative importance given to each will vary considerably depending on the characteristics of the organisation being examined and on the level of management for which the information is required. Thus the programme structure model may be useful for examining information needs in organisations where there is a clear relation between the activities of the organisation and its overall goals, in particular for strategic decisions – what services should be provided, what should be the principal means of providing services, or what mix of resources should be employed.

The systems model, on the other hand, will be most useful in analysing situations which can be seen in information flow terms, and in particular for examining the information needs of the operational part of the organisation where the effects of the services provided by the organisation are clearly defined outputs.

The management processes model is the most general model. It can be used to examine both the organisation as a whole and the decision process at any level. It can be used to understand both highly formalised activities and relatively unstructured activities. Because of its general applicability it is described in the greatest detail. However, its generality can be misleading. It describes processes rather than the subject matter with which those processes are concerned. To use it questions have to be asked about the subject matter and the relevant organisational activity.

Similarly, it could be used at various levels in the organisation. If it is being used to analyse high-level activities, various elements (boxes) could be analysed further. For example, the analysis element clearly has its own detailed programming, operational and control elements contained within it. It may or may not be necessary to investigate these, depending on the level of the information problem posed. At the operational and operational control levels such expanded investigation could well be by means of a systems model, provided the links between inputs, conversion processes and outputs can be clearly shown.

The Systems Model

In many organisations, or parts of organisations, it is possible to understand the relationship between the activities by studying the flows of information through the organisation and relating them to a model of how organic systems maintain control over their activities in relation to their environment. Figure 5.1 shows a systems diagram as it might apply to a very simple process.

In using this approach a systems diagram would be built up by identifying the various activities (subsystems) and the flows of material (or energy, or people) and information between them. This diagram would then be analysed to see whether the existing information flows were adequate and necessary. The concepts of feedback and hierarchical levels of control are central to this analysis. Each subsystem has to be controlled by obtaining information about its outputs, checking whether these are within acceptable limits and if necessary modifying the inputs to bring about a correction. Control has

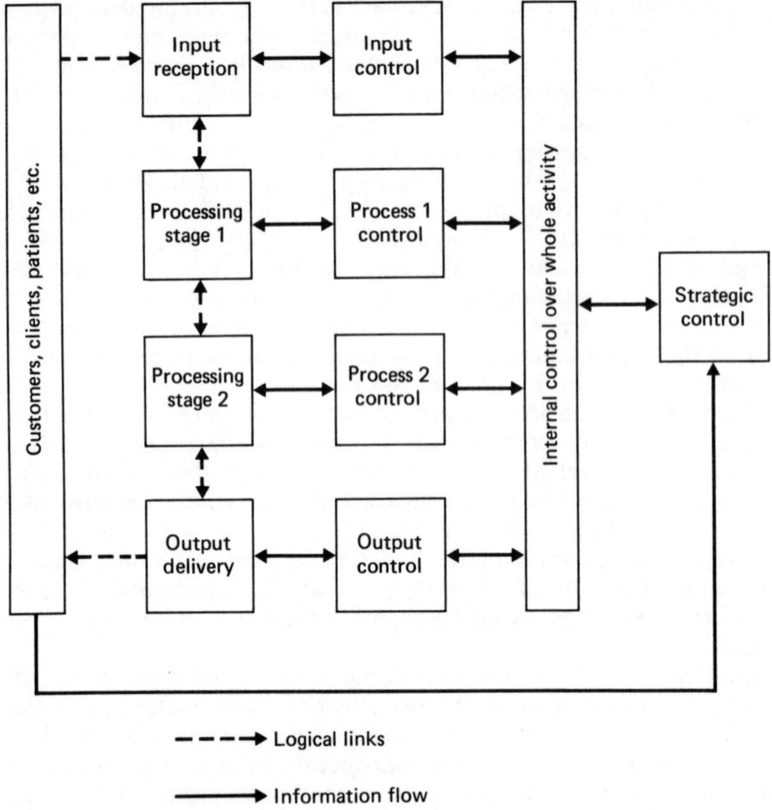

Figure 5.1 *A systems model.*

also to be exercised over the whole system, both to co-ordinate its subsystems and to ensure acceptable outputs of the system.

This model is a very powerful way of analysing information needs in contexts where material, or people, are processed in a limited number of defined ways. It could be usefully applied, for instance, in housing maintenance, building regulations control and many similar operations in local authorities. It should also be useful conceptually at the operational level in examining social services departments, though it may prove difficult to apply this approach rigorously in that context.[3]

The Programme Structure Model

Programme structures, a concept derived from the PPBS approach to corporate planning, have been used to help identify organisational information needs and priorities. A programme structure is a statement of the organisation's objectives and activities, showing how they relate. This is done by listing the principle objectives of the organisation and subdividing each of these into the necessary sub-objectives which have to be achieved in order to achieve the principal objectives. These are then further subdivided into the broad grouping of activities (programmes) which serve these sub-objectives, and so on down until the individual activities are listed and organised hierarchically under the principle objectives.

Information is needed to judge the size of each activity and the cost, efficiency and effectiveness of the organisation in pursuing each objective, and in principle the information should be structured in the same way as the programme structure. In fact programme structures do not have an objectively correct form. Information needs to be structured in different ways at different times and for different purposes. Nevertheless, where a programme structure can offer a clear picture of the principal objectives to be pursued, and the relationship between these and the activities, it may also be helpful in deciding on priorities for information development.

Programme structures are useful at a strategic level in showing the links between differing overall objectives. Similarly they are a useful means of demonstrating the relationships of activities to objectives. Problems arise, however, when an attempt is made to combine a horizontal with a vertical view of these relationships by developing an overall matrix of the links between various operational activities and various objectives. At an operational level objectives can act as constraints upon each other; in particular, those objectives concerned with maintaining the organisation in a healthy state – good public relations, good labour relations – frequently impact upon those concerned with service provision in a way which distorts service-providing priorities. Other complications also arise; a less important service may be more urgent, for example. Thus it becomes impossible to obtain a set of operational priorities in which the weight given to each remains stable. A stable set of informational priorities is equally impossible.

Such considerations may not be important in a stable organisation with relatively few objectives and operating in a stable environment. Unfortunately not many local authority departments are like that. A perhaps more telling criticism is that within many local authority activities our knowledge of the link between means and ends is extremely tenuous. In education, city planning, housing markets, traffic planning and many social services functions it is possible to say very little about the effectiveness of activities in meeting objectives.[4] As the complexity of the relationships unravels so the need for new sets of information becomes apparent – information as to the social costs of road construction or environmental pollution being two examples. The programme structure model thus shares some of the limitations of the systems model.

The Management Processes Model

The management processes model is shown diagrammatically in Figure 5.2. The model is intended to be a representation of all decision-making processes, be they the preparation of major plans or the making of small daily choices. However, in some cases the elements of the model will be clear explicit stages of the process, whereas in others

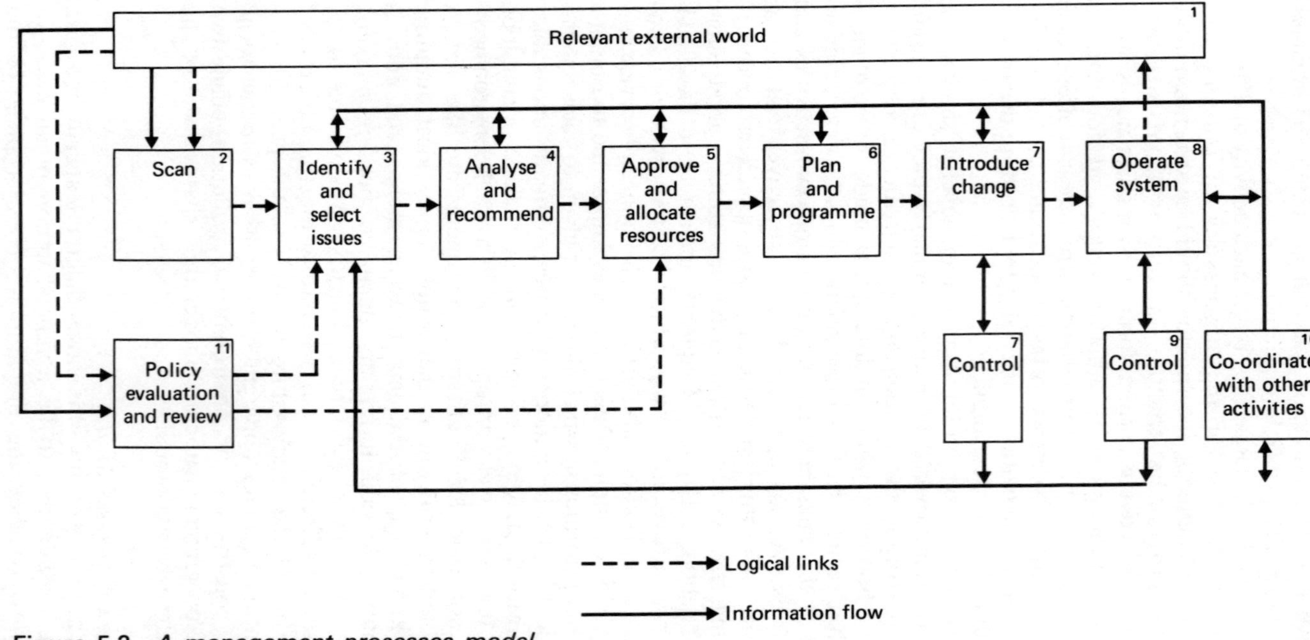

Figure 5.2 *A management processes model.*

they will be implicit and possibly inextricably combined with other elements. Particular elements may have to be elaborated in greater detail for the model to be useful in particular contexts. The elements of the model may be described as follows.

(1) *The relevant external world*. This concept refers not only to the particular aspects of the environment which are the responsibility of the organisation but also to those parts of the external world which may have an impact on the work of the organisation. So in the case of a social services department it would include not only the population of clients and potential clients but also other parts of the local authority, such as the housing department, and other agencies, such as DHSS and voluntary organisations.

(2) *Scan*. It is necessary not only to have a general background picture of the relevant external world but also to be aware of changes which may be of potential importance to the organisation. Much information gathering activity serves this purpose. Although routinely provided data series may contribute to this awareness, much relevant information is likely to arrive as discrete items, often in qualitative form and often through informal channels. Although some formalisation of information processes for scanning may be helpful, there will always have to be a heavy dependence on informal, human contact-based channels. Clearly the information scanned will be influenced by an appreciation of the goals of the organisation and of the nature of the relationships between these goals, the activities of the organisation, and other variables in the external world. However, the information scanned must not be completely determined by these factors, or newly relevant factors will not be discovered.[5]

(3) *Identification and selection of issues*. The scanning process and the review of existing policies will reveal future as well as current problems and opportunities. The selection of which issues to explore further may be made on the basis of political or professional judgements but may also involve the preliminary collection of information related to the issues. This activity is essentially a preliminary analysis and can be treated in the same way as the analysis element.

(4) *Analysis and recommendations*. This activity includes any process, however simple or complex, by which proposals for a change of activity might be derived. The information needed at this stage will be specific to each issue being analysed. It will include existing and predicted resources, statutory responsibilities, policies (including those of other organisations) and other constraints as well as descriptions of the problem and predictions of the consequences of different actions that might be taken. When unprogrammed decisions are being made it is common to find that the information required, though it may appear on initial description (for example, caseload statistics) to

be information already available for some other purpose, is in fact different because of the particular classification needed (for example, cases classified by housing conditions). Therefore existing data is very often not of direct use and special data collection exercises have to be mounted.

(5) *Approval and resources allocation*. The processes whereby approval is given to a proposal and resources allocated may be totally informal and involve no formalised transmission. However, it is likely that information about the recommendations will have to be transmitted to appropriate officers and committees, often fitting into a committee cycle or an annual cycle with highly formalised information flows. What may have been until now a process that has been concerned with a unique issue, requiring information specific to that issue, has to provide information in a form that will fit in with, and be timed to fit in with, a routinised system.

(6) *Programming and detailed planning*. A policy may have to go through several stages of planning of increasing specificity before it can be translated into action. The information requirements as plans become more detailed are likely to become more concerned with costs, manpower, staff attitudes and existing procedures, rather than with information from outside the department. The plans produced at this stage may contain detailed targets concerned with such items as costs and other resource usage, productivity, datelines, quality and quantity standards. They will determine much of the information needed from controlling the introduction of changes and the operating of the system (see 7 and 9, below).

(7) *Introducing and controlling change*. The period during which a new system or policy is being introduced has distinctive monitoring and control requirements concerned primarily with meeting time and cost targets, and with meeting unforeseen snags. For large changes information systems may be set up to provide regular, quantitative information as in the use of network analysis. In other contexts information will be exchanged by setting up appropriate meetings and reporting arrangements; that is, the information needs will be met by organisational rather than by information-technology means.

(8) *Operating the system*. The use of information is likely to be an essential part of the basic operational tasks of the organisation operation. Where these operations are programmed it may (but not necessarily) be possible to systematise the provision of the data needed. For other operations, as in the case of much social work, a good deal of the information is inevitably transmitted between individuals in a loosely structured manner and it would be difficult, if not counterproductive, to attempt to structure it. Even if the information is capable of being structured there are likely to be disadvantages to centralising the information processing, which is best kept close to where it is used and

where changes in its structure can be initiated by the users, provided the centre ensures their broader compatibility. If the information study is to concentrate on this aspect of the activities of a department it is appropriate to examine this area, including operational control (9) and co-ordination (10), referred to below, using the systems model presented earlier.

(9) *Controlling operations*. Many aspects of operational control are programmed, or capable of being programmed, and in these cases the information can be provided as determined by the nature of the control decisions that have to be made. Much of this information will be concerned with meeting predetermined operating targets. But the proportion of decisions which are programmed will vary. In many instances no targets exist, sometimes because it is inappropriate to set relatively simple quantifiable targets. In these cases much operational control will depend on unstructured information.

(10) *Co-ordination with other activities*. This activity may be seen as a higher level of control involving more than one type of operation, either within the organisation or between the organisation and other agencies. There may be several levels of co-ordination before reaching the organisation as a whole. The higher the level the less likely the decisions are to be programmed, and also the more likely it is that information from outside the organisation will be needed.

(11) *Policy evaluation and review*. The activities of the organisation have an impact on the external world. Some of these impacts are the reason for the activity. Others are by-products, good or bad, foreseen or unexpected. The policies have to be reviewed periodically to attempt to judge them in terms of the achievement of their original intentions, their relevance to current conditions and the desirability of their unexpected consequences. Where an organisation is capable of being quickly responsive to certain specific consequences, formal systems can be set up to monitor impacts. It is often the case, however, that the organisation is only capable of periodic adjustments in any one policy area, and also that there is no clear view about the critical variables to be monitored. In these cases the process of evaluation and review is analogous to the earlier process of analysis.

The three models in this section are not represented as being mutually exclusive. Any one of the models may be considered as being most appropriate in a particular situation. It has been suggested that problems may occur in attempting to utilise the systems model and the programme model in a local authority context and therefore greater reliance is placed on the management processes model as a useful framework for developing methodologies for the analysis of information needs.

CONCLUSIONS – TOWARDS A GENERAL STRATEGY FOR ANALYSING INFORMATION NEEDS

Identifying those issues and factors which are likely to have an impact on the need for, and use of, information in an organisation is only a preliminary step towards improvements in the design of information systems. A greater difficulty, in some respects, lies in making an awareness of these factors operational from an analytical point of view – that is, in translating a general knowledge and appreciation into specific tools for investigation and analysis. As already indicated, some of the factors which have been specified as of importance are unlikely to be capable of precise quantification (for example, organisational climate) – at least not without extensive research – and can therefore only be utilised in a subjective way by incorporating into the analysis the perception of the members of the organisation and the information analysts. In other cases a more precise and quantitative analysis will be possible.

In setting out to specify an appropriate methodology for analysing information needs it does not appear feasible to aim to be both universally applicable and sufficiently detailed to be of immediate and practical assistance to potential analysts. These concluding remarks, therefore, attempt to outline a generalised strategy.

The strategy depends fundamentally on a problem-solving approach. It assumes that organisations will only attempt to design or redesign their information systems if there is an awareness within the organisation of *an information problem*. The most probable starting point for any investigation of information systems will therefore be a statement of a problem at some point within the organisation.

The second stage of the strategy should then involve *a testing out of the problem definition with members of the organisation*. Organisation members, in this context, may often fall into two groups – those individuals who have perceived and stated the problem (most frequently being senior managers) and those whose work, responsibilities and roles may be affected by any solution to the problem as defined. Given that perception of the problem may differ between the two groups this stage of the analysis should be considered as *a process of analysis and negotiation*, leading to an agreed definition (or reformulation) of the problem. This stage is likely to involve considerable evaluation of the organisational context (section I of this chapter) and a less detailed evaluation of the nature of the information (section II) and the management processes and activities involved (section III).

The third stage of the strategy consists of a detailed analysis of the agreed problem definition, selecting those aspects of organisational context, information and management processes which were identified during the second stage as being of relevance to the particular problem. The precise methods of analysis will vary from one situation to another but may include: content analysis of existing documents and data system; examination of existing information flow patterns; direct observation and interviews; group discussion; questionnaires and time diaries.

The final stage of the strategy involves the presentation of the results of the analysis as *a set of detailed proposals*, which relate not just to changes in data systems but also to changes in organisation and management generally. Such proposals are likely to require negotiation within the organisation prior to their implementation.

In conclusion, it may be seen that the strategy adopted involves a combination of a 'hard' and, where possible, quantitative, analysis with a 'softer' process of evaluation and negotiation. It may be argued that such an approach is more likely to facilitate information system improvements which are incremental rather than comprehensive. While I would argue that this is not necessarily the case, it is considered that partial incremental changes will often meet the perceived needs of the organisation and of its individual members and will therefore be more liable to satisfactory implementation than more comprehensive, large-scale solutions.

NOTES: CHAPTER 5

This chapter is based on work carried out as part of a research project into information needs in social services departments, funded by the Department of the Environment. The author is greatly indebted to the following people for their contributions to the chapter: F. Wedgwood-Oppenheim, Institute of Local Government Studies, and N. Thomas and R. Bowl, Department of Social Administration, University of Birmingham.

1 For a development of the issues concerning rational policy-making see Chapters 1 and 2, above.

2 For a full review of the literature see Payne and Pugh, 1976.

3 The systems approach is well covered in the systems analysis literature. See, for example, Coleman and Riley, 1973; Churchman, Ackoff and Arnoff, 1964.

4 The difficulties in specifying policy-effectiveness are discussed in greater detail in Chapter 4, above.

5 An approach to the technology of scanning has been described by Wedgwood-Oppenheim, Hart and Cobley, 1976.

6

Monitoring and the Planning Cycle

FELIX WEDGWOOD-OPPENHEIM

The purpose of this chapter is to explore ways of improving the capacity of a public organisation to receive and use information about how effectively its policies or strategies are working. The problem which it attempts to tackle is complex. In general information is collected, indeed likely to be perceived, only if it is relevant to a model, or an *appreciation* in Vickers's terms, of a field with which someone is concerned. Most writing on information systems does not concern itself in great depth with the determination of what information to collect, but when it does it has nearly always been concerned to reflect accurately a well-defined appreciation of the system about which information is required. Most successful attempts at improving, formalising or automating information systems have involved formalising the model of the system in order to specify the information required. But policy-making is concerned not so much with managing well-understood situations as with responding to new appreciations of the situation. Policy monitoring is concerned with the capacity to become aware that policies need to be changed because old models are no longer adequate. We need to be able to receive information that is not determined by the existing models but which might cause them to be changed. However, if relevant information for this purpose cannot be determined by existing models, what criteria are there to direct our attention, or what approaches are there that can be open to new information and yet not allow us to be overwhelmed by the infinity of information available?

The problem is particularly acute in general-purpose public organisations, such as local authorities, which have a broad, generalised concern for a population area. In these organisations new appreciations of the situation not only may call into question existing policies but may require policies to be formulated in fields previously untouched. One example of this is the new concern of many local authorities in the last few years for policies to attract industry. Similarly the regional strategies of the 1970s had just such a generalised concern for their regions and offered a context in which to examine this problem. The regional planning context shows up the issue being considered here particularly strongly for two reasons. First, the regional planners were specifically charged with *strategic* concerns and so were not concerned with information to support ongoing practices. Secondly, there being no regional executive organisation with powers sufficient to implement the strategies, they were heavily dependent on the value of their information and the use to which they could put it.

The author was involved in a study for the Department of the Environment which advised on the setting-up of a unit to monitor the Strategic Plan for the North West and the rest of this chapter is based on that work (Wedgwood-Oppenheim, Hart and Cobley, 1976).

LEVELS OF MONITORING

Monitoring has to be considered as part of the planning and control system in which it is embedded. It appears that some of the confusion about the concept of monitoring relates to lack of clarity about the planning and control system which it serves, and in fact many of the beliefs about monitoring relate to models of planning and control that are only to a limited extent applicable to the strategic context.

It is useful to categorise planning and control into three levels referred to by Anthony (1965) in relation to business activities, as operational control, management control and strategic planning. The three approaches to monitoring which parallel these levels are referred to in this chapter as (*a*) *implementation monitoring*, (*b*) *impact monitoring* and (*c*) *strategic monitoring* respectively. The first part of this chapter considers briefly these three levels as they apply to public planning, relating the final level to the policy-making context. The necessary characteristics of strategic monitoring will then be highlighted by examining the limitations of the lower levels. Finally, a mixed scanning approach to the information-handling process of strategic monitoring is described.

Implementation Monitoring

The model of monitoring used here is appropriate to the context of a stable environment which is well understood and where there is a high degree of control over the situation planned. It is suitable where there is a task to be completed and where little account need be taken of changes external to that task. This model was held implicitly, though not always appropriately, by the early postwar physical planners, particularly in relation to new towns. The role of monitoring here is to see that implementation takes place according to plan.

Impact Monitoring

Impact monitoring is associated with Anthony's managerial control level and is the model widely held by those concerned with monitoring.

The assumptions here are that there is a fairly high level of control of the issues planned for and that, as in the previous model, the plan relates to a clearly demarcated field of interest. However, even where the plan is being successfully implemented the outcomes may not be as intended and the plan therefore allows for a variety of resource allocation choices. Impacts are monitored and if these deviate from planned targets there is sufficient understanding of the situation for resources to be reallocated – within pre-set limits – to bring the system back into line. Adjustments can also be made if the operational control system cannot ensure implementation as planned. Monitoring may also be concerned with checking the accuracy of forecasts on which the planned outcomes are dependent. Ideally mathematical models of the planned system exist which not only determine the information to be collected but can be used to inform, or even determine, the response.

This level of monitoring is extremely important and widely, though not universally, applicable. River pollution levels, traffic flows, incidence of lung cancer and levels of literacy and numeracy are obvious areas of applicability.

Strategic Monitoring

Strategic planning and control is concerned with coping with a dynamic, imperfectly understood and imperfectly controlled environment, with a broad or unrestricted definition of possible fields of interest. We are concerned here with the situation where management control is no longer sufficient because the actual contingencies are not allowed for and because the unintended consequences of existing policies require new ones. We are concerned with dealing with problems and opportunities, existing or predicted, arising out of current plans, or creating the need for new ones.

The need at this level is for a continuing planning activity, anticipating possible future developments, responding to current issues by developing new policies and reviewing past policies to establish their impact on current and possible future situations. The information required for this task is unlimited; there is not only a need to be concerned with information relevant to past policies but also for information relevant to possible new policies. If this is to be adequately carried out there will have to be an efficient process of information selection. The approach put forward here may be described as *mixed scanning*. It can be regarded as the information management dimension of the mixed scanning approach to policy making proposed by Etzioni (1967) and described by Stoten in Chapter 11 of this book, 'Planning Health Care Services'. Mixed scanning in the information context involves collecting specific information with high resolution of detail about issues that are known to be of importance to existing policy areas and analysing them in depth. At the same time this approach involves taking a very broad, low-resolution scan of a wide range of issues that could potentially affect the concerns of the organisation, and 'zooming in' on those matters which emerge as important. For the intensive analysis, information will need to be collected with specific reference to the problem and detailed quantification will be important. In the broad scan we want to increase awareness of as wide a range of information as possible. Depth gives way to breadth, and in seeking to absorb large quantities of information we will look for it in condensed forms such as articles, written reports, or diagrams, rather than as raw data. An approach to mixed scanning is developed later, but first it will be useful to examine why many existing approaches to monitoring based on the impact monitoring model are inadequate for the strategic context.

A CRITIQUE OF TRADITIONAL APPROACHES TO MONITORING

Monitoring has become a popular word amongst those concerned with planning, but there is a great deal of discussion about what monitoring should imply in practice. It appears that much of what has been written and discussed is based on the impact monitoring model referred to earlier. This model clearly applies to a wide range of planning contexts, where there are a limited number of clear objectives and a reasonably well-understood and demarcated subject area. However, when considering plans that are more strategic – implying a concern with change and with wide-ranging consequences, taking into account long-term considerations and often involving a number of organisational units – this model becomes insufficient. It is worth examining some of the assumptions of the model, if only to indicate some of its weaknesses for strategic planning and thus to highlight some of the requirements of a strategic planning and monitoring system. These assumptions relate to:

(1) the use of objectives and targets;
(2) the monitoring of planning assumptions;
(3) the relationship between planning and action;
(4) the role of the plan in defining information needs.

The Use of Objectives and Targets

It is widely held that monitoring reveals problems or issues for consideration by identifying gaps between planned outcomes (targets) and reality. On examination it appears, however, that for a number of reasons relatively few problems are actually revealed in this way in strategic planning situations.

First, if gaps between actual and planned outcomes are to be recognised, targets must be expressed in operational terms, that is, they must be precise statements of what is expected. The achievement of these targets is instrumental in fulfilling higher-level objectives, usually providing a general sense of direction without necessarily being operational themselves. Information can then be collected to measure the progress towards targets and objectives.

However, in many plans and policies operationally specified targets are few, and where they exist it is often difficult to establish the relationships between the stated general objectives and the targets specified. The widespread belief that setting operational targets is necessary for good planning is in marked contrast to strategic planning as distinct from programming practice and leads one to doubt whether in fact target-setting is appropriate at this level. Where targets do not exist it becomes immediately less clear what information it is crucial to monitor and it becomes much more a matter of judgement what can be regarded as being off course.

A second reason for doubting the general usefulness of monitoring the gap between reality and target is based on the experience of an important experiment in monitoring a subregional plan (Gillis, Brazier *et al.*, 1974). It was found that significant deviations from the strategy were rarely detected by the monitoring unit before they were pointed out by one of the local authorities in the subregion. Where there were divergences the determination of whether these were significant was never a technical activity. Rather the determination of significance depended on judgement and varied according to the viewpoint. What is more, issues to be dealt with tended to be thrown up not as a result of a divergence but rather as a problem arising independently of any measurement of achievement.

The third point is that when concerned with strategic planning in the context of uncertainty about economic, political and social changes, and where there is still a very imperfect understanding of the way these systems behave internally and interact with each other, there is a need to be not so much concerned with the *intended consequences* of plans as with the *unintended and unforeseen* consequences. To take the example of the house-building programme in Britain in the 1960s, whether or not the slum clearance and house-building targets were being met was, in the event, of considerably less interest than the discovery of the social consequences of breaking up traditional communities and of the problems caused by high-rise blocks of flats. Similarly with the building of roads, monitoring achievements in increasing road capacity revealed less useful information than the discovery of the effect on the total volume of traffic of greater road capacity. If one considers the important changes of policy that have taken place in the last decade it is evident that failure to achieve stated aims was secondary in motivating the changes to a concern with reducing the unpleasant, unintended consequences, or with capitalising on the beneficial consequences of past policies. One needs therefore to be concerned with increasing the responsiveness to these unintended consequences and not just measuring the achievement of intentions.

One can argue that to evaluate a current policy it is unhelpful to go back to the intention of the policy-makers. Rather one needs to evaluate the policy in terms of how it actually works, affecting the community in many more ways than the policy-makers were likely to take into account, and in terms of the *current* aims and understanding of needs.

One may conclude, therefore, that collecting statistical data which is directly determined by the planned targets should not be given undue emphasis. Instead the monitoring function needs to be more concerned with the ability to perceive changes in relevant factors more quickly, whether or not they had been considered during the planning stage.

The Monitoring of Planning Assumptions

Planning can be seen as a process whereby aims, factual evidence and assumptions are translated by a process of logical argument into appropriate policies which are intended to achieve aims. The fact that time proves many assumptions to be false has important consequences for the planning process and for the nature of monitoring. When the outcomes of a plan deviate from expectations it is because some of these assumptions were incorrect. One group of assumptions relates to the accuracy of estimates of relevant factors (that is, independent variables, for example, birth rates, industrial productivity, labour mobility), how they interact with each other and, in particular, the way they will change over time and affect the outcomes of the planned actions or policies. If these factors are monitored and projected into the future, whenever they are found to vary from the assumed levels the plan or the implementing actions can be adjusted in response. It is desirable therefore not only to monitor outcomes but to reduce their likelihood of deviating by monitoring factual assumptions and making appropriate adjustments. One should, however, take this process further and stress the need to monitor not only quantitative variables, as implied so far, but also qualitative variables; not only explicit but also implicit assumptions; not only 'hard' but also 'soft' information. These ideas are developed in the following paragraphs.

First, a large number of assumptions relate to the occurrence, or non-occurrence, of certain events, such as the possible liquidation of a major industrial firm, or a change in the EEC's regional fund policy. The logical distinction between *qualitative* changes of this sort and *quantitative* changes such as a sudden increase in the rate of inflation is not possible to maintain. However, the implications for monitoring systems of the distinction between modest changes in the value of a variable which do not alter the structural relationships of that variable to the system as a whole and radical, or step, changes which tend to be referred to as qualitative, is very important. Thus it is necessary not only to be concerned with the collection of statistical data but also to monitor events that could be of importance whether or not these events lie within the system to which existing policies relate.

Secondly, however well exposed are the assumptions on which the plan is based, the biggest assumption of all, and the one with the most far-reaching implications for the planning process, is that all factors not referred to in the plan are either irrelevant to the plan or will remain constant. This assumption is a catch-all for a multitude of implicit assumptions about factors which there was too little time, resources, or knowledge to take into account when the plan was formulated, or are essentially unpredictable. By their nature these assumptions cannot be monitored by collecting information specifically on each. An assumption usually becomes of interest only when it is falsified or when an unexpected event occurs. These assumptions may be revealed as a result of diagnosing the cause of a deviation from an unexpected outcome – by which time the damage has already been done – or they may be discovered by a generalised scanning activity.

Finally, one should stress the need for 'soft' information.[1] Many of the events that need to be monitored are the policies of public bodies which affect the region. 'Soft' information about policies still under consideration is clearly very useful in speeding up the response that can be made to emerging policies, and for enabling analyses to be carried out in the knowledge of the directions in which other government or non-government bodies are moving. The need for 'soft' information implies not only the scanning of written material, but also the need to be in personal touch with key members of the principal bodies affecting the region. This makes the problem of access to information particularly critical, which in turn is a consideration affecting the organisational arrangements for monitoring.

The Relationship between Planning and Action

The view in traditional monitoring models that planning leads to action and that monitoring is followed by corrective action bears little relationship to the conditions applicable in strategic planning situations. It is common that strategic plans are not directly implemented as a result of the plan. Rather they provide a context for the creation of more detailed plans, often by other agencies. An important implication of this is that as implementing the plan involves the adoption of plans and policies by other government agencies, there is a need to be concerned with monitoring these plans and policies, as well as external variables.

Additionally, as resources for monitoring are likely to be limited, if the best use of these limited resources is to be made careful consideration needs to be given to the balance of effort that is put into the three activities of information collection, analysis and the presentation of information and recommendations. Too often, in practice, relatively little thought and effort have been put into this vital final stage. Clearly there is little point in investing heavily in information collection systems if the information cannot be adequately analysed, and in particular if the chances of being able to influence action are slim. Great care has to be taken to ensure that information is well presented in a comprehensible manner to the right people at the right time.

The Role of the Plan in Defining Information Needs

The information to be collected for the impact monitoring model is determined by the targets set and the assumptions built into the plan. However, in examining that model and relating it to the strategic context it has been necessary repeatedly to widen the scope of the information with which monitoring would have to be concerned. There is a need to collect information generally relevant to organisational policies, not limited to predetermined targets and assumptions but concerned also with future contingencies and unintended consequences.

This widening has to be taken a stage further if it is taken into account that no strategic plan is *comprehensive*. This is not a criticism; comprehensiveness is an unattainable goal. Continuous planning, as well as evaluating the performance of existing policies, must be concerned with developing new policies to deal with new problems and opportunities as they emerge. The information-gathering function has to be concerned with all matters of potential concern even though the scanning process will be most intense in relation to matters that are believed to have a high probability of providing significant information.

MIXED SCANNING APPLIED TO THE REGIONAL CONTEXT

Regional planning has been particularly influenced by there being no regional executive or resource-allocating body responsible for implementing the plan. The task of monitoring is thus distinctive in that there is a more than usually tenuous link between the information collected and that information being put to use to influence policy development. Nevertheless the regional context has many similarities to other public planning contexts. There is a similarly weak relationship often between county structure planning and the county districts and even county council departments that are to be guided by the plan. Also the plans of central government departments are often much affected by the degree of freedom local authorities have to pull in different directions. Other characteristics of the regional structure which affect the strategic monitoring system required are widely shared with other policy-making and planning organisations. The general concern for a geographical area or population is widely shared, the concern with responding to change, problems, opportunities and unforeseen consequences are common to all agencies that are not merely executing policy developed elsewhere. So though this section is written with regional strategic monitoring in mind the ideas should be relevant to a wide range of policy-making contexts.

It has been shown earlier that a large range of information is of potential relevance, and it can be shown from theoretical considerations (see Stamper, 1973) that to increase the level of control it is in general more important (*a*) to increase the speed of response and (*b*) to increase the range of variables taken into account, than to increase the amount of detail on each variable. One of the most difficult problems to handle satisfactorily is the selection of information, for the problem in general is not one of obtaining enough information but rather of reducing the amount of irrelevant material so that the relevant information can be perceived and acted upon (see Ackoff, 1967) while the capacity to perceive the relevance of new information is maintained. It is necessary therefore also to consider the process by which a change in the intensity of scanning, or in the information scanned, is triggered. The next sections will look at this process in relation, first, to quantitative data series and then to qualitative information, before considering the relationship with analysis and distribution and the control of the whole mixed scanning process.

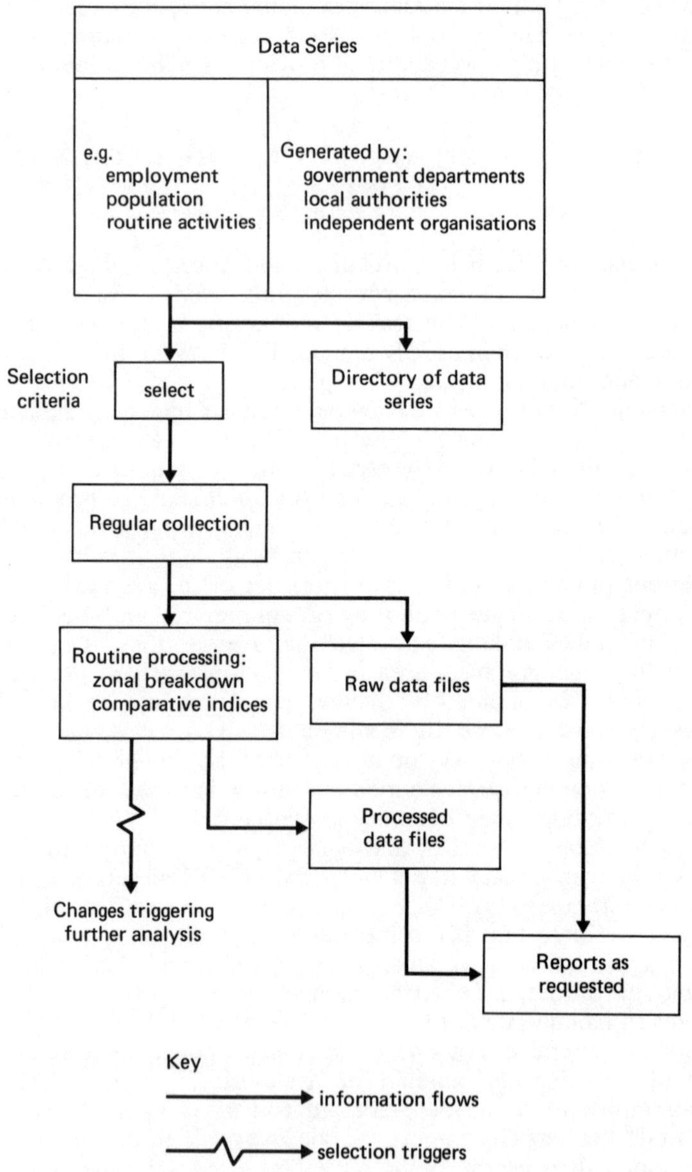

Figure 6.1 *Quantitative data series: collection and processing system.*

Quantitative Data Series

There is considerable experience of industrial management information systems, and some indication from local authorities, which show that the high hopes that accompanied the development of comprehensive information systems for planning and policy-making purposes have been disappointed. Such information systems are in fact much more applicable to implementation and impact monitoring, involving the control and short-term planning of current activities, than to strategic planning and monitoring. Strategic planning is concerned with changing situations and changing policies and has to respecify its information requirements according to the issues with which it is concerned. However, at any one time there are a few variables that have borne the test of time – variables which affect a wide range of current issues and which are likely to give a bearing on future issues. A limited number of such variables should be regularly collected. However, these should be decided upon only after careful consideration of likely continuing usefulness. Such information is likely to include, for instance, demographic distributions, employment characteristics, and so on.

In most public authorities where there are routine activities being executed there will be considerable amounts of data, some of them of potential strategic significance, available for processing as described below without any additional cost to the organisation.

Data series that are routinely collected should be processed as soon as they are received in order to reduce the quantity of data on the selected variables to proportions which are more readily absorbed and interpreted. It is always possible to go back to the original data where there is a desire to obtain a more detailed understanding of a particular item. Figure 6.1 shows how routine processing links into the data collection activities. How these activities relate to other parts of the mixed scanning system is shown later in Figure 6.5. Processing in this case involves such procedures as aggregating the data to parts of the region and to the region as a whole, and plotting trends for each of these areas. A further reduction in the information to be absorbed can be obtained by producing indices such as the ratio between a level for a part of the region and the average for the region as a whole, or similarly the ratio of the region to the average of all regions. These can be plotted and an exception-reporting system introduced. Computer program packages exist (for example, CYBERSTRIDE, see Beer, 1973) which for any number of variables will calculate indices on these lines and report automatically only those items where a significant change in level or in trend is established.

To back up the limited number of variables which can be regularly collected, and to provide assistance in finding data series as and when they are required, it may be useful to set up a directory of the data series that are collected by other bodies. The concern here is with all those data series which can be either aggregated to the regional level (because they are collected on a compatible basis) or which can be disaggregated to the regions. It has to be accepted that exact

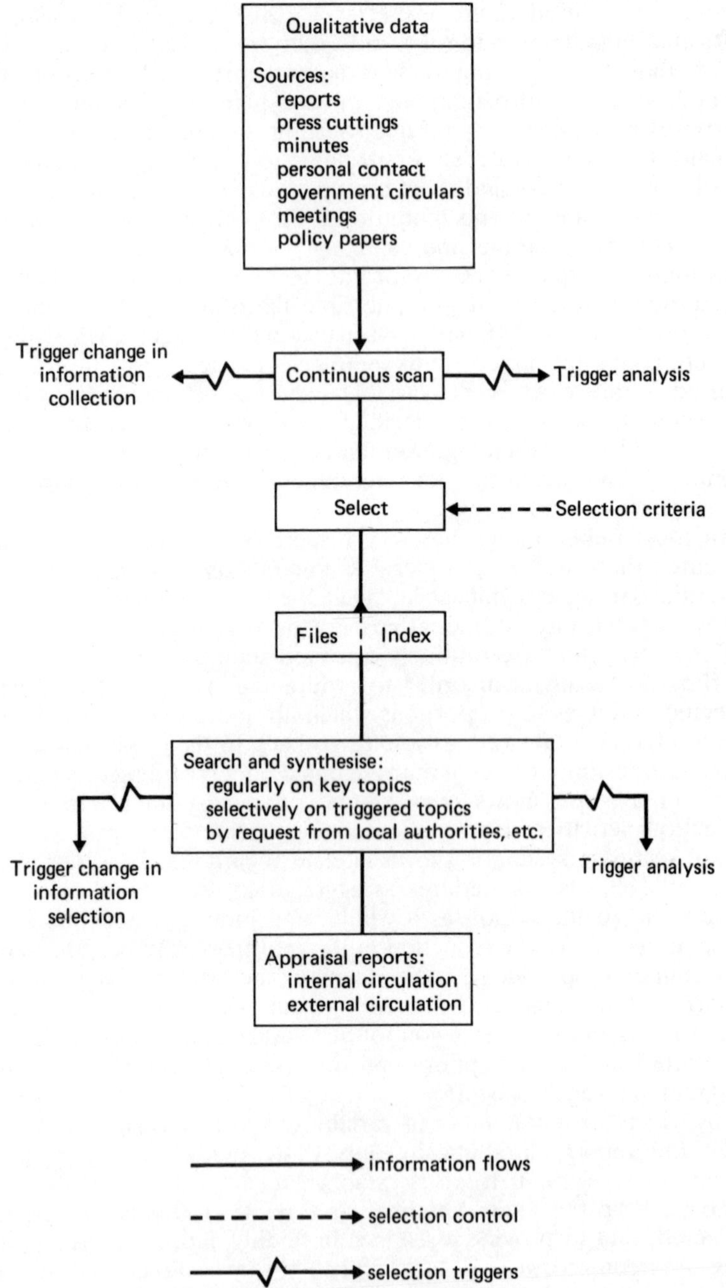

Figure 6.2 *Qualitative information: collection and processing system.*

geographical classifications are rarely possible and that series will need to be included where the appropriate aggregations or disaggregations can be done only approximately. It also has to be mentioned that such directories have not always proved a great success, perhaps because they too are designed in terms of past models and do not relate adequately to information required to examine problems in the future.

Qualitative Information

The monitoring function includes the collection of qualitative information, both 'hard' (for example, policies approved, commitments made, events that have occurred) and 'soft' (for example, information on implementing policies, proposals under consideration, assessments of a problem, attitudes towards certain issues).

Qualitative information is acquired during the normal course of work from a wide range of sources – published reports, internal papers, the press, personal contacts, committee minutes, and so on. This information should be seen as of direct relevance to the monitoring function and it should be a deliberate activity to extend the collection of qualitative information relevant to the region and to assess it. There has, however, to be a regular process of reviewing the information sources which are scanned and defining criteria of relevance. This process of selection of information to be stored is illustrated in Figure 6.2. This figure also represents the way items of information scanned may trigger off analysis in greater depth, or may trigger off a scan for other items of information.

By its very nature qualitative information is difficult to structure and to process. Files need to be kept and indexed in a manner which allows relevant items to be found according to a range of different concerns. Manual and computer techniques for indexing and cross-referencing unstructured material are available, and with the development of a context-based indexing system for computer storage and retrieval,[2] have recently become much more sophisticated.

The qualitative information index can be searched for information relating to certain topics (for example, the plan for a motorway), functional areas (for example, housing) or zones. By appropriate search a history of the matter of interest can be built up, and it can be examined from a number of points of view. This search and synthesis could be carried out as a result of some topic being triggered by a particular item of information, or possibly on a regular basis in relation to a limited number of key issues. These syntheses may in turn trigger off further analysis, or lead to topic appraisal reports.

Analysis

Analysis is at the heart of the monitoring function, as shown in Figure 6.3. Whenever other sources of information reveal issues of possible importance analysis, in varying depths, will be needed to understand the nature of the issue, to judge its significance, to predict its ramification in the region and to judge the consequences of possible

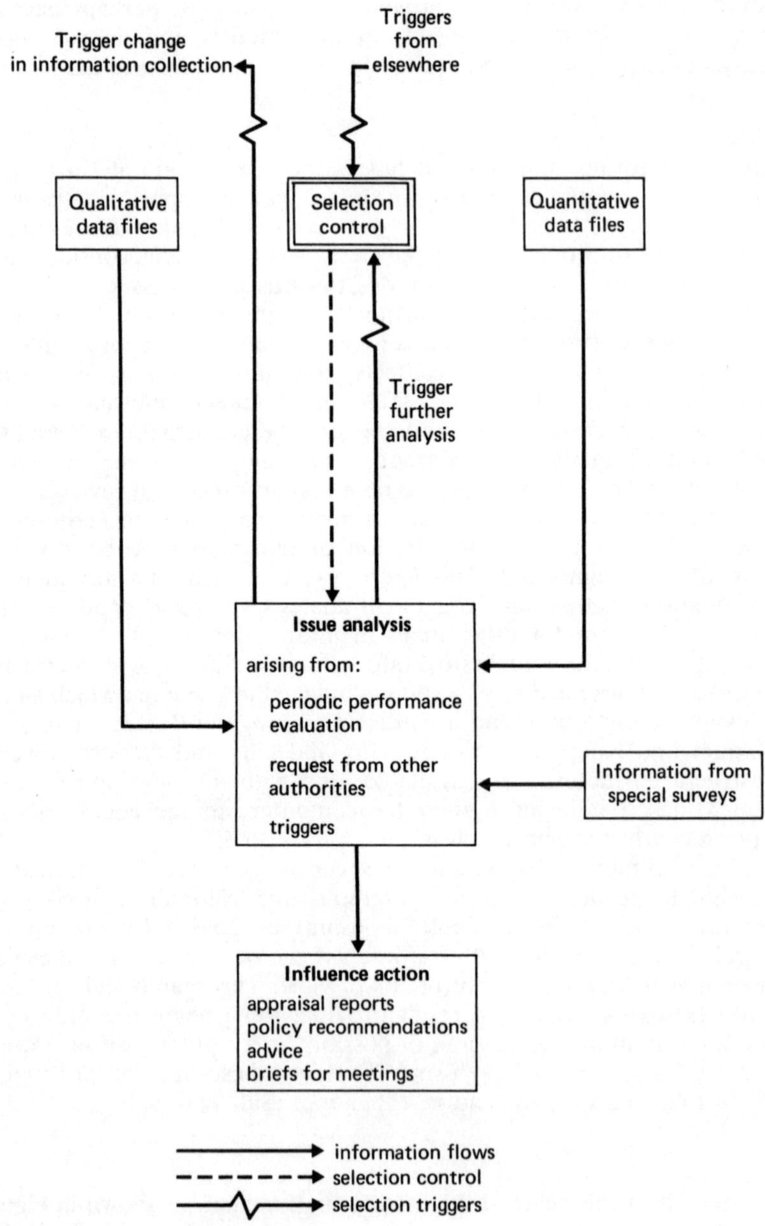

Figure 6.3 *Information analysis systems.*

responses. The general scanning activities give way here to an intensive collection and analysis of information.

An analysis may be carried out (*a*) at the request of a public authority in the region, where the issue is seen to have consequences beyond the boundary of the authority concerned; (*b*) routinely, after an appropriate period of time, to evaluate the effectiveness of regional policies in terms of current needs and aspirations; (*c*) triggered by an issue revealed from other data sources or by another analysis. Control will need to be operated over which issues will be responded to and analysed. This control function is indicated in Figure 6.3 and developed in Figure 6.4.

An analysis will not only draw on the sources of information within the monitoring system (see the information flow lines in Figure 6.3), but will almost certainly need to draw on information not currently stored. Use may be made of the directory of data series to find other sources. Where data sources do not already exist it will be necessary to carry out special surveys. The results of analysis may lead in turn to the need to analyse some interdependent topic, or it may lead to the recognition of some new category of information that needs to be collected in future. In this way each information-handling activity influences and is influenced by the others, breadth leading to depth which again affects the breadth.

THE CONTROL OF MIXED SCANNING

A number of references have been made earlier to the triggers that indicate the need for new information to be collected or a more intensive examination of certain issues. Here we will discuss this switching between different levels of scan – the articulation of mixed scanning. Given that there is such an abundance of information available, and that information-handling is expensive not only in terms of cost but in terms of the confusion caused by information overload, a control system has to be instituted which determines the information to be sought and the intensity of work to be carried out on each topic. The control system has to balance the degree of effort put into data collection as against data analysis and into the routine study of areas of known relevance as against investigating new sources of interest. The control system has to seek in a general sense to maximise the return on its information-handling activities.

The control system is illustrated schematically in Figure 6.4, though only the main links have been shown. The information that is to be sought has to be selected on the one hand so that information is available about topics known to be of interest, and on the other so that items that throw a new light on regional issues, or indicate new problems or opportunities, can be received. Topics of concern will be triggered as a result of analyses that have been carried out and also by the items of information themselves, picked up in the general scanning process. In addition to this triggering process a regular review needs to

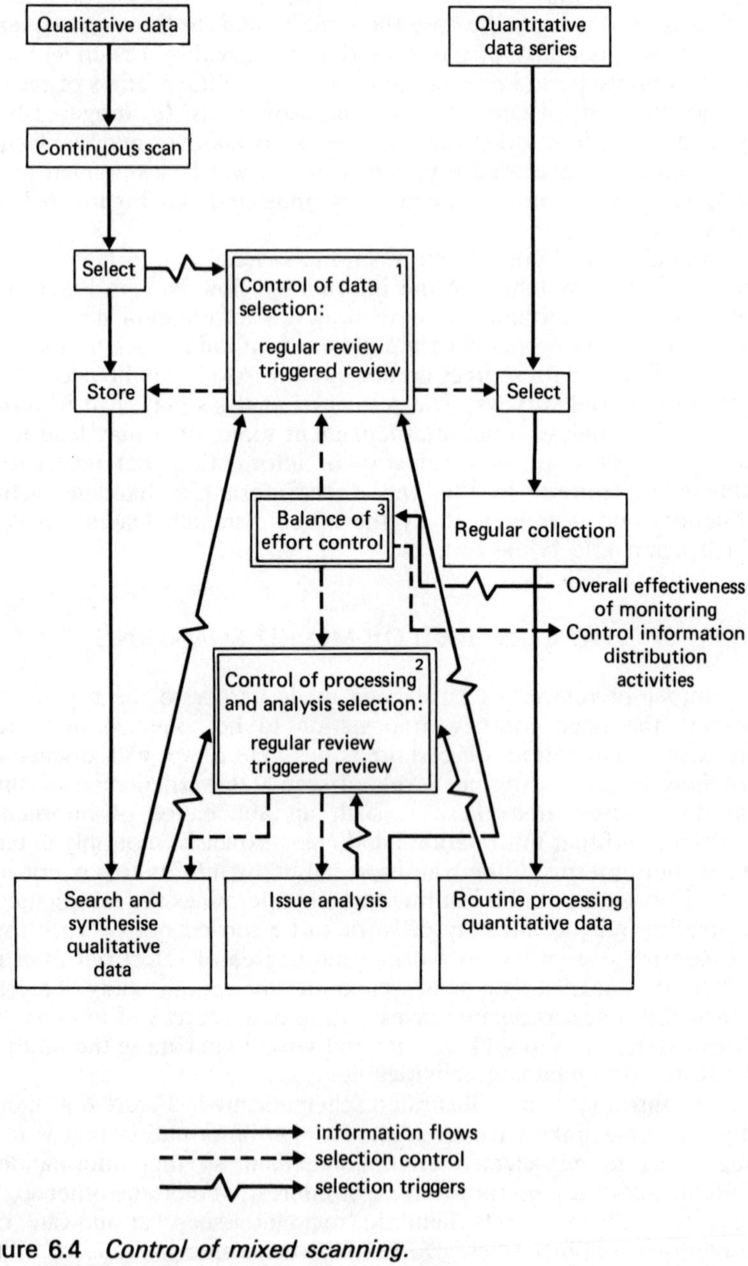

Qualitative data
Quantitative data series
Continuous scan
Select
Control of data selection: 1
regular review
triggered review
Store
Select
Balance of effort control 3
Regular collection
Overall effectiveness of monitoring
Control information distribution activities
Control of processing and analysis selection: 2
regular review
triggered review
Search and synthesise qualitative data
Issue analysis
Routine processing quantitative data
information flows
selection control
selection triggers

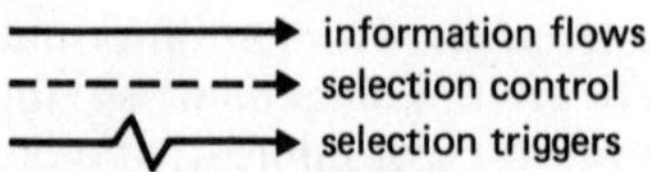

Figure 6.4 *Control of mixed scanning.*

be carried out of the data series to be collected and of the sources searched and the amount of detail to be recorded in the scan of qualitative sources. In Figure 6.4 box 1 represents this control over the information that is collected. This control is influenced by the triggers from various parts of the system.

Similarly box 2 indicates the selection control over the analyses that will be triggered by other analyses and by individual items of information. The control function includes regular review of the areas that should be routinely appraised from the qualitative information system and of the regional policies which should be evaluated. The control system is needed to carry out those regular reviews and to decide, on a general cost-effectiveness basis, to which triggers there should be a response.

Box 3 indicates the overall control of the mixed scanning system, in which control is exercised over the balance of effort that should go into the three activities of information collection, analysis and distribution. As a result of this process of internal control there should be a constantly evolving pattern of information dealt with and a changing pattern of work in response to changes within the region and as the monitoring function learns about the effectiveness of its own activities.

INFORMATION PRESENTATION AND DISTRIBUTION

Good information presentation and distribution is one of the important links in the planning and monitoring cycle (see Figure 6.5) and the impact of monitoring is dependent on it. Important considerations are the form in which the information should be presented, to whom it should be presented and when it should be presented. Although in general quick reporting is to be desired, detailed consideration of timing and of the people who are to receive the information have to be considered according to the issue. There is some generally applicable knowledge available, both practical and theoretical, relevant to the presentation of information. Particularly important is the need to reduce the sheer bulk of the information to proportions that can be absorbed and to appreciate that what can be absorbed varies between people according to the nature of their relationship to the issue dealt with. Therefore the amount of detail made available should initially be very restricted and the degree of resolution of parts of the issue only increased in stages according to the requests of the recipient. This approach has strong implications for the initial processing of the data.

Reports on particular issues should be made following examination of these issues, whether they be initial assessments or analyses in depth. One can envisage a steady flow of published reports following detailed analyses of regional problems and putting forward regional policies amounting over time to a revision of the original plan.

Regular routine reports should provide a wide-ranging assessment of events and trends within and external to the region. They would assess the impact of these on the region, both the current impact and the expected future impact. The aim should be to draw the attention of the

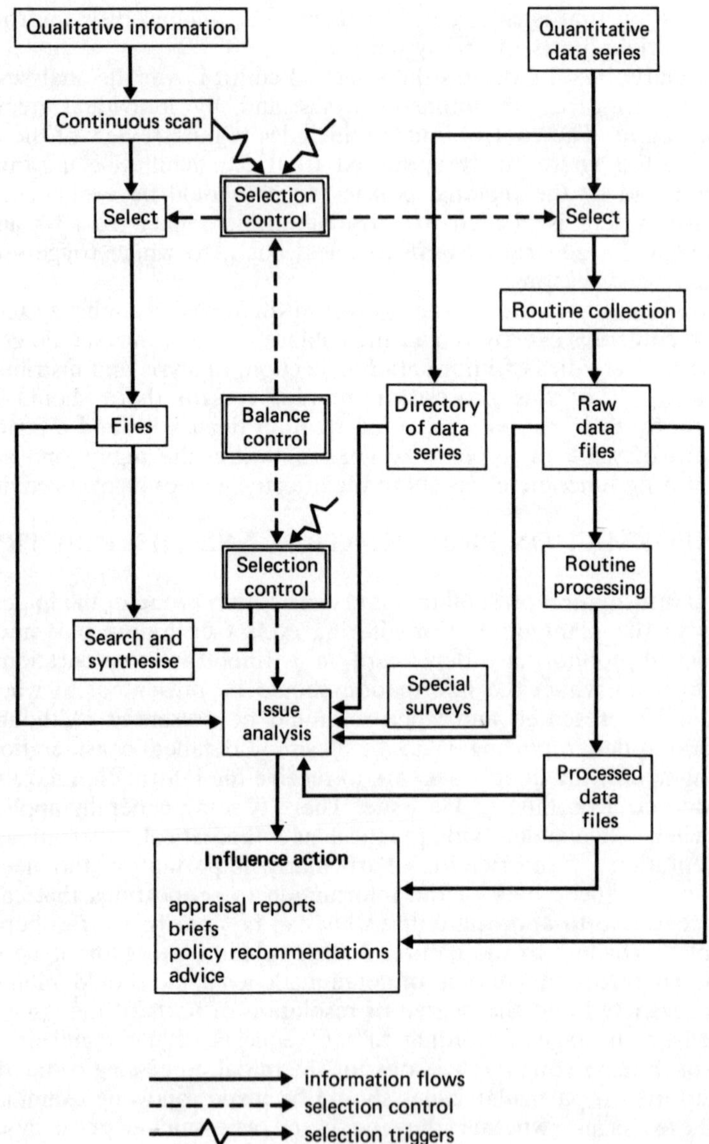

Figure 6.5 *A model of mixed scanning.*

decision-makers in the region to what are seen as the most significant developments in the region, and to encourage consideration of these developments. The description of a report as 'routine' does not imply the automatic rolling forward year by year of a set of standard figures. It should concentrate on change: change in factors affecting the regional environment, change in ways of looking at that environment, or change in social attitudes towards it.

Information will of course often be passed on informally and orally. Those involved in monitoring will have to keep in personal touch with key people in the region, not only to obtain 'soft' information, but also to pass it on. And in this context the information will not necessarily be neutral. It will often be in the form of advice or recommendations about actions to be taken in the regional interest. Influence can often be best wielded not by open reports but by individual meetings.

CONCLUSION

Although this examination of mixed scanning as an approach to monitoring in the regional context has been largely concerned with the technical process, many of the aspects discussed imply that monitoring is not a purely technical activity that can be left to a skilled statistical unit or even to an automatic computerised data-handling system. Though statistical expertise and efficient data-handling systems are important the social and intellectual characteristics of the people involved are critical. Information-gathering requires trust; information selection requires judgement; bringing information to bear on policy-making requires influence that stems from characteristics that go beyond a reputation for providing reliable information.

The case for strategic monitoring to be under the leadership of people with appropriate personal characteristics is particularly acute because there is inevitable resistance to the activity. Monitoring is inevitably more concerned with the failure of policies than with their success; with the gaps in policy rather than its adequacy; with what should be done better rather than what is being done well. For monitoring to survive there has to be considerable personal competence and considerable organisational commitment to good policy-making.

NOTES: CHAPTER 6

1 The 'hardness' of information is most usefully defined by the probability that the information accurately represents the real situation existing at the time to which the information relates. Thus prediction of unemployment levels in five years' time, or rumours that a minister is considering implementing a particular policy, are 'soft' information, in that although they may be valuable in allowing one to take account of certain possibilities the states described may not take place.

2 The GPO has developed a system called CAFS (content addressable filing system).

7

Planning Context and Planning Methodology in Regional Planning

CHRIS SKELCHER

INTRODUCTION

Public planning takes place in a complex and multifaceted *context*. The elements of planning's context are varied and include sentiments, values and ideology; organisations and social classes; the legislative framework; economic and demographic features; and physical resources and infrastructure. In the growing literature on public planning, however, scant attention is paid to the nature of the context and its relationship to the structure and organisation – or *methodology* – of the planning process. Yet this connection is of importance where the planning agency lacks powers of executive action or must work in collaboration with other organisations, in particular because an appreciation of context can aid the realisation of public intent. Regional strategic planning in England during the period 1968–79 provides an example, and will be used to explore and illustrate in greater depth the nexus between planning methodology and planning context.

This chapter reviews previous studies of the methodology–context relationship, showing why this issue is critical for public planning in general and regional planning in particular. The dominant methodology of English regional planning is outlined, and it is argued that certain components are inappropriate in terms of key contextual features. An alternative methodology is proposed, having a higher potential context-appropriateness. A study of the application of elements of this methodology in the West Midlands reveals a number of operational difficulties, and on this basis design considerations are highlighted.

CONTEXT AND METHODOLOGY

Environmental Responsiveness or Environmental Effectiveness?

Two basic interpretations of the relationship between planning context and planning methodology can be identified (Metcalfe, 1976). The first, termed *environmental responsiveness*, views planning methodology as highly responsive to features of the context, to the extent that context could be said to shape methodology, while the second approach, *environmental effectiveness*, is concerned with the manner in which the possibilities for change in the context can be enhanced.

Within the framework of environmental responsiveness, Friedmann (1965) and Faludi (1970) have both studied the connection between planning context and planning methodology. Their concern has been to explain or predict the type of planning methodology associated with a given context, and this task has been undertaken by developing theoretical schema which are then applied to the empirical cases respectively of Latin American economic development planning and urban planning in the United States and Britain. The planning approaches which have been adopted in a particular nation are then causally connected with, and explained in terms of, dominant features of that context.

This model of methodology–context relationships raises three main issues. In the first place, very abstract concepts are used to delimit the context. Faludi, for instance, talks in terms of 'level and pace of development' and 'cleavages in society', while Friedmann employs such notions as 'level of economic-technical development' and 'historical tradition'. The applicability of general concepts of this type is consequently limited to broad cross-national or cross-cultural studies. Secondly, the emphasis has been on descriptive/explanatory activity, with a linear relationship between context and methodology as independent and dependent variables respectively. Hence 'the concept of a planning environment [context] is a concomitant of a behavioural approach. Planning, instead of being an abstract, normative concept, becomes a dependent variable, dependent that is on the environment of decision-making' (Faludi, 1973a, p. 320). The underlying philosophy of environmental responsiveness thus bears a close relationship to the behaviourist approach to psychology and, more particularly, contingency theory in organisational sociology and the environmentalist school of political science (for example, Skinner, 1953; Lawrence and Lorsch, 1967; Salisbury, 1968). This leads to the third issue: that because the model views planning methodology as a dependent variable, it gives no guide for action on the part of the planner. Dror (1973), for example, notes that in practice there is an interactive relationship between planning and context:

> One of the more interesting characteristics of planning is its bidirectional relationship with its environment. On the one hand, the planning activity is shaped and conditioned by various environmental factors; on the other hand, planning is in many cases directed at that environment, trying to shape it to a greater or lesser extent. (p. 332)

The environmental responsiveness approach, therefore, is not oriented to the problems of decision-makers in trying to realise or implement public policy in the context, or to the particular issues they face in designing the organisational means of action.

It is in connection with this question that the second approach to context–methodology relationships, environmental effectiveness, comes into play through its concern with the conditions under which the impact on the context of organisational or planning action can be enhanced (see, for instance, Ackoff and Emery, 1972). In other words, it has a direct action focus. Etzioni (1968) has expressed the essence of this approach in his discussion of the debate between advocates of the rational model and supporters of disjointed incrementalism. He argues that it is of little value proposing one methodology as 'best' in the abstract since it is the context within which planning is to occur that provides the point of reference for judging appropriateness. Similarly, Bolan comments that 'the scope of today's problems impose special demands for awareness of the complex web in which the planner must function . . . *Understanding the nature of this* [*context*] *will help in determining appropriate strategies and techniques for intervention* (1973, p. 371, my italics).

There are two broad strategies for enhancing environmental effectiveness. One is to reorder the context itself so that it becomes more receptive to particular public policies or the desires of a focal agency. Thus the National Economic Development Council attempted to reshape its environment by bringing together industry, unions and government into working parties covering different sectors of the economy (Metcalfe, 1976), while the Tennessee Valley Authority co-opted interest groups in its context on to its management structure (Selznick, 1949). The second strategy is to design the methodology – the structure and organisation – of the planning agency itself so that it relates more closely to key features of the context, in other words to increase its degree of *context-appropriateness*. This is an approach in which interest has been developing, as in recent research commissioned by the Department of the Environment (DoE) which has been concerned with exploring such a strategy for environmental effectiveness. One study, for instance, had the following terms of reference:

> to suggest guidelines whereby regional strategy teams can most effectively shape their proposals, and their mode of working, so as to be in tune with the processes by which implementing agencies exercise their powers of discretion, whether at national, regional or local levels. (Carter, Friend and Norris, 1978, p. 1)

The problems of developing and applying context-appropriate methodology are the concern of this chapter.

The Importance of Context-Appropriate Methodology in Planning

The case that planning methodology should be context-appropriate rests on the belief that the potential impact of planned public intervention will be enhanced, *ceteris paribus*, by tailoring the method of policy formulation, implementation, monitoring and review to features of the context.

The history of the British development plan system illustrates this point. The first round of plans, prepared under the 1947 Act, largely adopted the 'blueprint' or master plan methodology developed in the work of Patrick Abercrombie and others. Built into this methodology were certain assumptions about the context of planning, primarily that it had a high degree of stability and predictability thus enabling planning (in theory) to exercise near perfect control (P. Hall, Gracey, Drewett and Thomas, 1973, p. 517). Experience in the operation of the development plan system in the 1950s and 1960s showed the inappropriateness of the master plan methodology to a period of rapid social and economic change. Not only was the machinery of planning cumbersome to operate but the actual form of the plan – literally a 'plan', a two dimensional map – was hardly conducive to effective guidance and control of change (Hart, 1976, pp. 27–42). As criticism of this planning methodology mounted, interest began to develop in moving from the 'blueprint' or 'unitary' approach towards 'process' or 'adaptive' methodologies which were considered more appropriate to a dynamic, systems view of the context (Foley, 1963; Faludi, 1973b), and this shift was given a quasi-official blessing in the report of the Planning Advisory Group (1965) which led to the 1968 Act.

Similar examples are documented by Ramirez (1974), who characterises the methodology of national development planning in Chile during the early 1970s as leading to 'planning in a social vacuum' with an 'extreme separation' between the planning exercise and policies on the one hand and the forces actually shaping national development on the other, and Galloway and Mahayni (1977) on US planning.

These cases illustrate how the potential of planned public action has been limited by employing a planning methodology having a low degree of 'fit' with the wider context. The response in Britain to the problems caused by using a master plan methodology to guide urban and regional change in a dynamic context has been to develop approaches towards the process end of the blueprint–process continuum. The important point, however, is that while the master plan approach is inappropriate at the scale of urban and regional planning, owing to a mismatch with contextual features, it is highly appropriate to local, site-specific, planning where there is a high degree of control over the context, for instance, in new towns under the quasi-autonomous New Town Development Corporations.

REGIONAL PLANNING: A CRITICAL CASE

The context-appropriateness of methodology assumes critical importance where the planning agency lacks executive power or control over resource allocation, and hence where any policies it develops are effectively only recommendations. This is because only by meshing with the context in the process of policy formulation can the planning agency hope to develop a common perspective and commitment to action by executive agencies along lines which it desires. Merely preparing a report in isolation from other agencies and then expecting action on it is to court disappointment. One area which illustrates this situation of attempts at non-executive intervention in a multi-organisational policy space is that of regional planning in England over the past decade.

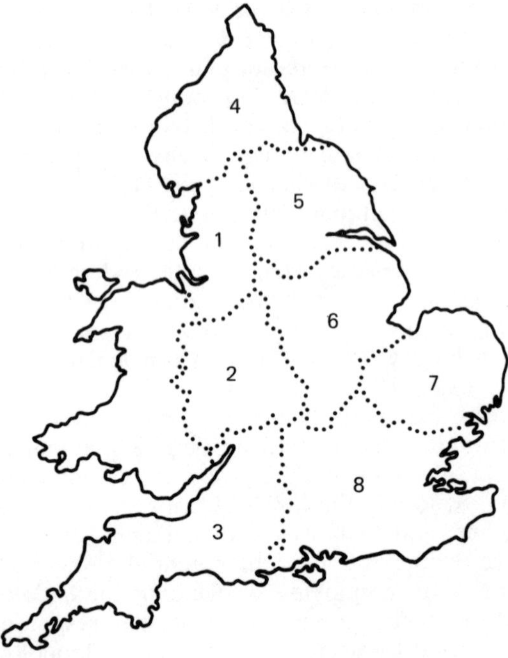

1 **North West**
Cheshire; Lancashire; Greater Manchester; Merseyside

2 **West Midlands**
Shropshire; West Midlands; Hereford & Worcester; Staffordshire; Warwickshire

3 **South West**
Cornwall; Devon; Dorset; Somerset; Gloucestershire; Wiltshire; Avon

4 **Northern**
Cumbria; Northumberland; Tyne & Wear; Cleveland; Durham

5 **Yorkshire & Humberside**
South Yorkshire; West Yorkshire; North Yorkshire; Humberside

6 **East Midlands**
Derbyshire; Nottinghamshire; Lincolnshire; Leicestershire

7 **East Anglia**
Cambridgeshire; Norfolk; Suffolk

8 **South East**
Kent; Hampshire; East Sussex; West Sussex; Surrey; Berkshire; Oxfordshire; GLC; Essex; Hertfordshire; Buckinghamshire; Bedfordshire; Northamptonshire; Isle of Wight

Figure 7.1 *England: planning regions.*

Regional Planning as a Field of Study

Perloff (1968, p. 153) provides a broad definition which underpins much regional planning practice in England.

> Regional planning is concerned with the 'ordering' of activities and facilities in space at a scale greater than a single community, and less than a nation . . . Such planning focuses on clarifying objectives and on designing means to influence behaviour (particularly locational decisions) so as to increase the probabilities of development in desired directions.

In England, eight regions are defined by DoE on the basis of aggregations of county councils (see Figure 7.1).

The definition employed by Perloff refers to the *intra*-regional allocation of resources and links closely with what Hall terms 'regional/local' planning. This can be distinguished from *inter*-regional or 'national/regional' planning, commonly referred to as regional policy and concerned with the distribution of economic activity between regions in pursuit of national objectives (P. Hall, 1970).

Gillingwater (1975) sees Perloff's definition as the 'good currency' view of regional planning. From this perspective the rationale for regional planning rests on two main points (Alden and Morgan, 1974). The first is that regional planning potentially has the ability to tackle certain problems affecting a number of agencies, as in the West Midlands where regional planning has been concerned with developing a coherent solution to the location of overspill from the conurbation to the shire authorities (P. Hall *et al.*, 1973; D. L. Saunders, 1977; B. M. D. Smith, 1972). The second point is that regional planning complements planning and decision-making at other spatial scales, a notion reflected in the twin aims contained in the terms of reference of recent regional strategies: to provide a framework for structure plans and a context for national resource allocation decisions (South East Joint Planning Team, 1970).

In recent years this 'top-down' good currency definition has begun to be challenged by an alternative perspective, based on the opportunity provided by the preparation of a regional strategy for local and regional interests to articulate their views and make advocacy statements to national government. Key examples include the *Strategic Plan for the Northern Region* (SPNR) (Northern Region Strategy Team, 1977), and the report on the regional economy produced as part of the updating and rolling forward of the regional strategy for the West Midlands (West Midlands Economic Planning Council/West Midlands Planning Authorities' Conference, 1979).

The Context of Regional Planning

The term 'context' has this far not explicitly been defined, in part because it has a residual connotation referring to that which remains after a planning agency has been delineated (Thompson, 1967). A starting point in developing a definition is to distinguish between that part of the context of which the planning agency must be cognisant because it is actually or potentially involved in transactions with it, and the more remote and less immediately significant context. This distinction draws on Dill's notion of the 'task environment', being that part of the context relevant or potentially relevant to goal-setting and goal-attainment (1958). There is thus part of the total context which may be delimited as having significance for regional planning activity. Hereinafter when the term 'context' is used it will refer to the significant context unless otherwise stated.

Elements of the context with which regional planning agencies will be involved most directly in transactions are other institutions, particularly government organisations. Large-scale institutions and the patterns of linkage between them have become basic features of industrialised societies at both national/international (C. Mills, 1958; Galbraith, 1967) and local/regional levels (see Friend, Power and Yewlett, 1974; Warren, Burgander, Newton and Rose, 1975). For regional planning agencies other institutions assume a particular importance. Lacking both a political power base and executive resource allocation functions, it is through such institutions that the regional planning agency must operate if its proposals and recommendations are to be realised. It must, then, enter into and attempt to influence the complex network of organisations bearing on its task.

The number and extent of institutions in the context of regional planning have increased substantially since the first of the (tripartite) regional strategies commenced in 1968, due largely to the changing and expanding issue agenda for regional planning. An analysis of the seven regional strategy documents prepared between 1968 and 1979,[1] based on an earlier study by Shaw (1975), reveals a shift from predominantly spatial, land use, growth allocation issues to questions regarding the regional economy, social welfare and the allocation of public finance, together with matters relating to the implementation of regional strategies (Table 7.1). This changing issue agenda is most marked in the case of the West Midlands. The original *Developing Strategy* of 1971 (West Midlands Regional Study, 1971) and subsequent approved strategy of 1974 (West Midlands Planning Authorities' Conference, 1974) were both principally addressed to the problems of formulating an agreed spatial pattern for the accommodation of metropolitan overspill, an issue which for two decades had been perceived as the key planning problem facing the region. By the time of the updating and rolling forward of the approved strategy in 1977, however, regional conditions had changed and questions about the West Midlands economy predominated.

The analysis shows that over time regional strategy exercises have gradually widened their scope to include matters far beyond the narrow, land use plan orientations of *Strategic Plan for the South East* (SPSE) (South East Joint Planning Team, 1970) and the *Developing Strategy*. SPNR has gone furthest in this direction, having a minor spatial dimension but substantial analytical and prescriptive work on

Table 7.1 *Issue Focus of English Regional Strategy Documents*

	SPSE	*West Midlands: Developing Strategy*	*SPNW*	*SCEA*	*RSPSE*	*SPNR*	*West Midlands: Updating*
Spatial	***	***	**	**	**	*	**
Economic	*	*	**	*	**	***	***
Public expenditure	*	*	***	**	**	***	*
Social welfare	*	*	**	**	**	**	**
Implementation	*	*	***	***	*	***	*

* minor focus
** medium focus
*** major focus

Table 7.2 *Institutional Focus of English Regional Strategy Documents*

	SPSE	*West Midlands: Developing Strategy*	*SPNW*	*SCEA*	*RSPSE*	*SPNR*	*West Midlands: Updating*	*Total agencies*
Local authority departments	2	2	4	5	3	4	2	5
Central government departments	1	1	6	6	3	6	3	9
Regional public agencies	—	—	1	3	—	2	4	5
Other	2	1	4	5	6	7	9	14
Total agencies	5	4	15	19	12	19	18	33

the functional areas of the economy, industry, housing, social welfare and public expenditure.

The expansion of the issue agenda has implications for the definition of its institutional context, since as regional planning moves beyond a basic land use remit it of necessity comes to relate to agencies other than local planning authorities, DoE and (pre-1979) the Economic Planning Councils (EPCs). The increasing significance of the regional economy on the issue agenda, for example, has led the Departments of

Industry (DI) and Employment (DE) to become important targets for strategy recommendations.

Four main sets of institutions can be identified as coming within the concerns of regional strategies – local authorities, central departments, regional agencies and other public and private bodies (Table 7.2). In terms of local authorities, strategies have moved beyond a focus on planning and housing departments to environmental health, education and social services. At central government level the original DoE and Department of Transport focus has been widened to include DI, DE, the Home Office, the Ministry of Agriculture, Fisheries and Food, the Treasury, the Department of Health and Social Security and the Civil Service Department; in fact all departments except those concerned with external affairs and defence. Prescriptive statements have been directed at the regional level of government and administration, including the regional health authorities, regional tourist boards and regional water authorities, the latter often being considered the *de facto* physical planning agencies (see, for example, A. J. Williams, 1977). Finally, there is a broad group of other institutions, including such national agencies as the Housing Corporation, the Development Commission, the National Enterprise Board and the Manpower Services Commission, the public utilities and nationalised industries and even in recent strategies the banks and building societies.[2]

The context of regional planning can best be characterised as a web or network of organisations having executive resource allocation functions in relation to substantive issues with which the regional planning exercise is concerned. The regional planning agency must, therefore, engage with such institutions if its recommendations are to be pursued positively. The ability to develop and maintain such engagement, however, will be influenced by the opportunities and constraints provided by the planning methodology – the way in which the process of planning is structured and shaped. Because regional planning in England has been perceived in terms of plan production rather than planning as an interactive process of goal selection *and* realisation, the dominant methodology has not been entirely appropriate to a strategy of engagement in the inter-organisational network.

THE DOMINANT METHODOLOGY OF REGIONAL PLANNING

During the past decade the dominant methodology of English regional planning has been based on three facets – the commissioning arrangements, the nature of the planning organisation and the form of the product.

Commissioning Arrangements

The dominant model for commissioning and steering regional planning activity has been 'tripartism', jointly involving central government, the appropriate local authorities (often represented through a standing conference) and the regional Economic Planning Council. This arrangement first emerged in the South East as central government's response to a situation in which it was faced by two competing strategies for the future of the region, respectively produced by the local authorities and the EPC (A. J. Powell, 1978). The solution adopted was to undertake a new study (subsequently published as SPSE) commissioned jointly by the three parties, and this approach was subsequently taken as a model for future regional strategies (HMSO, 1971).

While tripartism provided a solution to the particular difficulties facing central government in the South East, it in turn caused a new problem – the fragmentation of the political base of the planning activity. This arose because regional planning became the focus for joint decision-making by three sets of interests – central and local government and the EPC. But, additionally, neither central nor local government can be considered a monolithic entity pursuing one political line. Within each exists a series of semi-autonomous agencies and hence a variety of values, perspectives and 'assumptive worlds' (K. Young, 1977). At central government level, for instance, DI tends to have a view significantly at variance with that of DoE, and even within one department there are often differences of perception and strategy between headquarters and regional offices. Local authorities also have divergent values, particularly on matters of planning policy. In the West Midlands region, for example, the twenty-five years to the mid-1970s were a period in which there were sharp differences between the metropolitan authorities and surrounding shire counties (P. Hall *et al.*, 1973; D. L. Saunders, 1977). In effect, rather more than three interests are represented in the commissioning arrangements and the regional strategy process thus becomes an occasion for joint decision-making by a considerable number of organisations.

Nature of the Team

The preparation of tripartitely commissioned strategies has been undertaken by a joint team of officials seconded full-time or part-time from central government departments and the local planning authorities (in the case of the South East and the West Midlands from the technical unit of the appropriate planning authorities' conference). Teams are occasionally supplemented by consultants employed on contract, for instance, the housing policy specialists who worked on the Northern Region Strategy Team during 1974–7. The team thus faces the immediate problem of creating and establishing a corporate identity. Because team members come from a range of authorities there is the problem of overcoming differing loyalties and developing a shared assumptive world which, while permitting internal debates, at least sets an overall framework for viewing and interpreting the region.

During its period of operation the team builds up considerable knowledge about the region and establishes firm links into the network of institutions in its context. Because it is common for teams to be dismantled and their members dispersed once the regional strategy document is drafted, much of the value of this network-building for subsequent activity is lost. At a day-to-day level the team 'carries' the contents and policy themes of the strategy in its dealings with other agencies. In a situation where the ownership of the regional strategy and its formal standing are unclear (discussed below) the team members act as advocates, especially for those proposals which, like SPNR's recommendation for regionalising public expenditure planning, are novel and politically contentious. By abolishing the team after plan production, the possibility of using its links for realisation is negated.

The Form of the Product

Carter *et al.* make an important distinction between *visible* and *invisible* products of a planning activity. Visible products are those which 'once produced, are somehow placed on record – usually on paper – and in most cases imply some form of collective commitment to what they say', while invisible products 'remain in the consciousness of particular individuals, influencing their attitudes and perceptions as a result of personal "learning experiences" to which their participation in the process has exposed them' (Carter, Friend, Pollard and Yewlett, 1975, p. 20).

In the tripartite strategies the emphasis is on the visible product, on the preparation of a final report which contains a planning strategy for the future of the region. After a process of appraisal within DoE and consultation with other agencies and parties, the Secretary of State for the Environment publishes the response which comments on and in some cases amends the team's report. The response is typically prefaced by a statement to the effect that the response, read together where necessary with the strategic plan, sets out the approved regional strategy (Department of the Environment, 1975, para. 2). In fact the exact contents of the approved strategy remain unclear, responses having been

> brief and bland in the extreme, tending to assimilate the strategy to government thinking rather than to accept suggestions for changes in policy, dismissing matters which cannot be resolved without comparable information for all regions, and passing on other matters for further consideration at structure plan stage. (A. J. Powell, 1978, p. 10)[3]

The formal standing and ownership of these visible products is also a matter for debate. Government can easily deflect unacceptable recommendations, as in the decision not to respond to SPNR because of its wide-ranging economic and financial proposals, while local planning authorities are statutorily required only to have regard to the regional strategy and tend in structure plans to reflect only such policies and recommendations as coincide with county objectives.

The opportunity for developing invisible products is minimised largely because of the temporary nature of the regional strategy team, and yet in terms of developing joint decision-making and a commitment to action these invisible products need to be stressed. Personal commitment to a philosophy and set of priorities built up by individuals in agencies as part of a process of interaction on regional issues will undoubtedly be greater than that acquired by reading the final report of a regional strategy team.

This review of the dominant methodology for regional planning illustrates how the potential value and context-appropriateness of the tripartite commissioning arrangements, setting the regional strategy team at the focus of an extensive inter-organisational network of executive agencies, is limited by the short life of the team and emphasis on visible products. In the absence of a formal political and/or executive base English regional planning will remain an exercise in persuasion, yet features of the planning methodology act to limit the possibilities for exerting influence. Elements of the dominant methodology thus have a low degree of context-appropriateness.

AN ALTERNATIVE METHODOLOGY: DEVELOPING ORGANISATIONAL CONTINUITY

An alternative regional planning methodology can be developed, building on the opportunities provided by tripartite sponsorship, through the creation of a permanent team oriented towards the development of invisible products from a continuing process of regional exploration. Giving greater emphasis to invisible products, however, is dependent upon establishing the organisational continuity of the planning team by making it a permanent feature of the regional scene. As Powell argues, 'maintenance of some form of continuing regional planning unit is essential if the value of strategies is not to be dispersed' (op. cit., p. 10).

The case for creating continuity in the organisational base of regional planning has been made in a number of recent regional strategy team reports. In *Strategic Plan for the North West* (SPNW) the terms of reference included the requirements to make 'recommendations about the form of a continuous planning process for the region after completion of the Study' (North West Joint Planning Team, 1973, appendix 1), and in its final report the team argues for a small, permanent regional planning unit which should 'have the means of influencing decisions and policies' and to this end 'have access to information and to decision-making machinery on issues of regional significance' (op. cit., p. 261). *Strategic Choice for East Anglia* (SCEA) (East Anglia Regional Strategy Team, 1974) contains a proposal for 'bridging agencies' to co-ordinate the activities of the diverse range of executive bodies concerned with matters covered in the report, while SPNR follows the lead of these earlier strategies and proposes a strategic plan review committee serviced by a small full-time professional staff. None of these recommendations has been implemented.

Following the approval of the West Midlands regional strategy in 1974, however, monitoring arrangements were established jointly between the Economic Planning Board (EPB) comprising senior officials of central government departments concerned with the region, and the local authorities' West Midlands Planning Authorities' Conference (WMPAC). The Joint Monitoring Steering Group (JMSG), composed of EPB and WMPAC representatives, was supported by the technical working group, a small team of professional staff from the EPB and the West Midlands Regional Study (WMRS), an organisation funded by WMPAC. Staff worked on JMSG business for varying proportions of their time, and from their own offices. Monitoring reports were produced in 1975 and 1976 and between February 1977 and August 1979 JMSG, together with the Economic Planning Council, undertook an updating and rolling forward of the approved regional strategy. While joint central/local government monitoring has also been undertaken following SPSE and SCEA, an important feature of the West Midlands case is that annual reports were produced and published and that the updating and rolling forward was undertaken using existing staff and organisational arrangements. In the *Strategy for the South East: 1976 Review*, for instance, a number of extra staff were seconded full-time by the Department of the Environment to contribute to the work.

These examples illustrate an awareness of the need for an alternative regional planning methodology, having at its core the notion of organisational continuity. Such institution-building can be perceived as complementary to, and indeed aiding, the application of an operational strategy by the regional planning team emphasising less the technical plan production tasks and more the exercise of influence and persuasion in developing commitment around certain issues and policies. Organisational continuity, by enabling the team to become an established part of the regional scene and form relationships and linkages with institutions in its context, provides the opportunity to develop the role of invisible products beyond that which is possible with temporary teams. As Wedgwood-Oppenheim, Hart and Cobley (1976, p. 27) argue,

> it is essential for the success of the Unit that it be located . . . where it would be capable of exercising the greatest degree of influence and coordination over planning policy . . . [It] would not be in a position to *directly control* either the making of policy or its implementation. [It] could, however, be realistically expected to play a major part in *influencing and informing* the regional planning process on the basis of the quality of its information and the depth of its understanding . . . The Unit should therefore be placed in such a position that it is able to exert a significant degree of 'leverage' with regard to issues of regional significance.[4]

A key feature of the alternative regional planning methodology is change in the organisational basis of the activity, transforming the planning team from a temporary, quasi-independent unit into a permanent agency linked into institutions in its context. This organisational restructuring, a prerequisite to the development of invisible products around regional issues, rests on two concepts: the *network organisation*, reflecting the planning team's interactive role working with and between executive agencies; and the *multi-organisation*, descriptive of the team's composition of individuals drafted in from other organisations.

The Network Organisation

This concept is grounded in the notion of the network, a term which has assumed increasing importance and currency in public administration following in particular the work of Schon (1973) and Friend, Power and Yewlett (1974) (see also Friend and Spink, 1978; Healey, 1979). Based on the desire of social anthropologists to explore the interactions and interrelationships between all members of a social group (Barnes, 1954; Bott, 1957; Mitchell, 1969), the concept of the network was adopted as a descriptive and analytical tool in sociology following the realisation that clusters or networks of organisations linked by ties of interdependency could be identified (see, for example, Turk, 1970; Aldrich, 1974). For Benson (1975, p. 229):

> the interorganisational network is a fundamental unit of analysis in the study of advanced industrial societies [and] consists of a number of distinguishable organisations having a significant amount of interaction with each other.

Benson goes on to discuss the varying nature of inter-organisational networks:

> Such interaction may at one extreme include extensive, reciprocal exchanges of resources or intense hostility and conflict at the other. The organisations in a network may be linked directly or indirectly. Some networks . . . consist of a series of organisations linked by multiple direct ties to each other. Others may be characterised by a clustering or centring of linkages around one or a few mediating or controlling organisations. (Benson, 1975, p. 230)

It is possible, therefore, to identify inter-organisational networks focused on a particular region (for example, the West Midlands) or issue (for example, the regional economy).

Berry, Metcalfe and McQuillan (1974, pp. 1–20) argue that within the inter-organisational network a distinction can be drawn between *command organisations* and *network organisations*. The former are concerned with such substantive, technical tasks as house construction or vehicle assembly, while the latter focus on procedural, inter-organisational issues in the network, for instance, developing codes of building practice or working to resolve the component supply problems of motor manufacturers. Berry *et al.* and Metcalfe (1976) explore the operation of the National Economic Development Council (Neddy), and argue that this agency underwent an 'organisational metamorphosis' from a command organisation concerned with indicative planning and the provision of expert advice on economic and industrial policy to a network organisation reflecting a perceived need to focus attention on 'processes of negotiation and bargaining to coordinate the activities of the network of organisations which constitute the economic system' (Berry *et al.*, 1974, p. 7). Such a redefinition of task bears a strong comparison with the case of regional planning discussed in this chapter.

Following Berry *et al.* (1974) command and network organisations can be differentiated along four dimensions: terms of reference, environmental characteristics, management processes, and management characteristics. The terms of reference and goals of command organisations are set in relation to substantive tasks, as in the case of the South East Joint Planning Team (1970, p. 1) who were asked 'to report with recommendations on patterns of development for the South East' and on this basis defined objectives relating to the economy, transport, the countryside, and so on. The outcome of the exercise was seen in terms of a visible product – a documented planning strategy. By contrast the remit of a network organisation would be concerned with such procedural tasks as facilitating the creation of an integrated strategy on the part of executive agencies themselves by bringing together key actors or providing a regional intelligence function. The outcomes, therefore, will be invisible in nature.

Secondly, command and network organisations can be distinguished on the basis of their environment. Command organisations tend to exist in a well-defined sector of activity, in other words, to have a clear domain (Meyer, 1975). Thus in the dominant methodology regional planning was assumed to operate in a distinct segment of the hierarchy of plans between local physical and national economic planning. The domain of network organisations is less clear, in part since they are not concerned with substantive tasks but also because their environment consists only of other organisations. Thus the activities of a network organisation 'are only meaningful in the context of the limitations and potentialities of the command organisations with which it interacts'. It faces the problem of 'identifying a basis of interdependence with the command organisations operating in legitimated social fields' or domains (Berry *et al.*, 1974, pp. 4–5).

The third dimension is the management process. Berry *et al.* suggest that the management processes of command organisations have an internal orientation and are directed to defining intra-organisational objectives, assigning tasks, controlling work activities and evaluating performance. In the case of network organisations internal management processes are looser, as the primary orientation is a concern with managing aspects of the (external) inter-organisational network.

Management characteristics are the fourth dimension and those of command organisations tend to emphasise hard technical skills required for undertaking substantive tasks such as regional economic analysis, population projection and cost-benefit analysis. Network organisations, on the other hand, stress the softer political and interpersonal skills essential for brokerage and negotiation in the interorganisational network, for instance, when working to develop policy on an issue affecting two antagonistic planning authorities.

The Multi-Organisation

The second concept underpinning the alternative regional planning methodology is the multi-organisation which, Stringer suggests, has two main characteristics: first, that it consists of parts of several other agencies, and secondly that each component part consequently has its own primary allegiance to its parent organisation, 'its own affiliations, its own goals and its own values'. In other words, the multi-organisation is 'a union of parts of several organisations, each part being a subset of the interests of its [parent] organisation' (Stringer, 1967, pp. 106–7). For Gillis *et al.* (1974, p. 13) the multi-organisation is 'a grouping of representatives of independent bodies in order to take joint decisions', while Pfeffer and Salancik (1978) prefer the term 'joint venture', referring to a new organisational entity jointly owned and controlled by two or more parent organisations. Both Warren (1967) and Harris and Scott (1974) have begun to explore and categorise different forms of multi-organisation, primarily on the basis of the nature of relations between agencies facing common issues.

Hood (1976) sees multi-organisations arising in response to perceived interdependent problems facing a number of agencies, and this view is supported by events in English regional planning. Examples include the creation of the South East Joint Planning Team and steering machinery as government's response to competing strategies, and the formation of WMPAC and the WMRS in response to a concern by local authorities that they might lose to central government the initiative in resolving the West Midlands intractable overspill problems (Painter, 1972).

In theory there is a strong complementarity between the concepts of network organisation and multi-organisation, given an operational strategy for regional planning which stresses the development of invisible products. Where the planning team operates as a network organisation the fact that its structure internalises the interorganisational network will potentially aid the transfer of commitment to joint courses of action back to executive bodies. Thus regional strategic planning will be the product of institutions themselves rather than an outside independent team, and this may be expected to aid the development of linkages and 'appreciative systems' (Vickers, 1965) between the executive agencies. Because of the complementary relationship between the operational strategy embodied in the concept of the network organisation and the structural features of the multi-organisation, the alternative regional planning methodology may be said to rest on the notion of the *network multi-organisation*.

THE NETWORK MULTI-ORGANISATION AND PATTERNS OF INTER-ORGANISATIONAL RELATIONS

While a case has been made in theory to show the higher degree of context-appropriateness of the alternative regional planning methodology when compared with the traditional dominant approach, it is important to appreciate that the network multi-organisation will be operating within a complex field. As Hanf (1978, p. 12) notes, 'the application of coordination strategies occur within a set of [interorganisational] relationships, and once new mechanisms are formed the interorganisational network will impinge upon their operation'. Since the planning team will exist only by virtue of and in relation to its organisation set,[5] it is important to ask questions about the pattern and nature of inter-organisational relations as this will have important implications for the role of the team, its ability to influence external events and the detail of its operational strategy.

The Exchange Model of Inter-Organisational Relations

There has been a tendency by writers on inter-organisational relations to perceive a predisposition to co-operative behaviour, a view grounded in the concept of exchange which, as R. H. Hall *et al.* (1977) have pointed out, provides the dominant theoretical perspective on inter-organisational behaviour. This emphasis is due to the focus of much research on the development of strategies to aid co-ordination between agencies in the delivery of local public services (Zeitz, 1975).

Levine and White (1961, pp. 583–661) originally formulated the exchange approach to inter-organisational relations, predicated on the assumption that interaction between agencies was voluntary behaviour motivated by the mutual benefits derived by participating organisations. The philosophical basis of this approach rests on the work of such writers as Homans (1958) and Blau (1964), who see behaviour leading to exchange when ends are only achievable through interaction with others. Propensity to exchange, they suggest, will increase as benefits tend to maximise. Exchange is thus voluntaristic and goal-directed.

This explanatory model of the inter-organisational behaviour has filtered through to inform studies of public planning agencies at regional and subregional level, often because they focus on situations in which there are potential or clear benefits to organisations from joint planning and decision-making, and hence where there is a strong predisposition to co-operative exchange-type behaviour. Friend, Power and Yewlett's (1974) study of the decision to proceed with town expansion at Droitwich can be located within this perspective, since each of the three parties involved gained from the joint decision. Droitwich itself acquired funds through the Town Development Act to finance an urgently needed sewerage treatment works, Birmingham City Council found a site for some of its overspill population, and for Worcestershire County Council (in whose area Droitwich is located) growth at this location relieved pressure on the Green Belt and hence helped to contain peripheral expansion by Birmingham at the expense of Worcestershire countryside (Friend *et al.*, 1974). At a strategic level an exchange relationship developed, town expansion at Droitwich meeting the respective goals of participating agencies. While at the tactical level there were conflicts and disputes about the details of the scheme, these must be seen in the wider context of mutual benefits. In such a situation the operation of a network multi-organisation would be relatively straightforward, facilitating an awareness by the parties of their compatible goals and hence providing the basis for an exchange relationship and mediating on detailed issues subsequently arising.

It is on a similar basis that Rondinelli (1975, p. 197) develops a set of prescriptions for urban and regional planning activity, arguing that the 'formulation and implementation of policy occurs through processes of reciprocal exchange'. His proposal for a strategy of 'adjunctive planning' recognises that

> coordination among semi-autonomous decision-making units can be promoted effectively only along lines of shared interest . . . Coordination cannot be imposed through hierarchical integration, centralised control, or structural consolidation. The basis of coordination is exchange. Mutually beneficial rewards must accrue to parties. (1971, pp. 35–6)

The theme of Rondinelli's work is that policy integration in a complex inter-organisational context can be achieved through adjunctive planning – in effect networking between executive agencies as a means of exposing the possibilities for exchange and hence realising the co-ordination and coherence of policies and programmes. Yet there will also be situations in which exchange is not possible because a gain to one participant means a loss to another, and where organisations employ strategies to preserve their self-interest (see, for example, White, Levine and Vlasak, 1975). It is therefore important to explore inter-organisational networks where there is a propensity to conflict rather than co-operation, in order to draw out the implications for the operation of a network multi-organisation.

Divergence on Issues and Outcomes

The form of conflict between organisations can be expressed in a number of ways. For Pondy (1969) conflict can be *strategic*, concerned with the allocation of resources, functional responsibilities and legitimacy between organisations, or *frictional*, resulting from poor operational co-ordination or ambiguous jurisdictional boundaries, as in the case of county–district relations in physical planning (Leach and Moore, 1979). Self (1972) makes a distinction between *agency competition* and *agency conflict*, according to whether organisations operating separate programmes make indirect competing demands on limited resources or engage in direct conflict over an issue of common concern. The distinction to be used in this study, however, is based on Warren's (1972) observation that in situations of concerted inter-organisational decision-making each party will have an interest in the *issues* to be covered and the *outcomes* of the process, and hence that there may be convergence or divergence between participants at either or both of these levels.

The inter-organisational context for the network multi-organisation can thus be characterised as one in which constituent agencies have a stake in both the issue agenda and outcomes or products of the process of regional exploration, and where their interests concerning these may be convergent (and hence potentially co-operative) or divergent (and hence potentially competitive or conflictual). In the former situation, as in the case of exchange relations, the operational strategy of the planning team is relatively straightforward, but where issue and/or outcome divergence between participants occurs a challenge is presented to the alternative methodology of regional planning. This is because the multi-organisational structure means that the planning agency itself is composed of individuals from organisations who are in dispute, and hence it may become a focus for conflict and attempts at dominance by participating interests which in turn constrain the operational strategy of the planning team.

PATTERNS OF INTER-ORGANISATIONAL RELATIONS: THE WEST MIDLANDS

The updating and rolling forward of the West Midlands regional strategy provides an example of the likely impact on a network multi-organisation of conflict and divergence between agencies in its context. In particular, it reveals the way in which the multi-organisation's direct and concrete linkages into the institutions and politics of the context can confound or severely limit its operation, particularly through attempts by agencies to shape the issue agenda and outcomes of the planning activity.

The team undertaking the updating (described earlier) can be defined as a multi-organisation, a variety of different interests and agencies being represented on the Joint Monitoring Steering Group and the technical working group (collectively these will be termed the joint team). While the tasks of the joint team were defined principally in substantive, technical terms, to some extent its activities involved procedural, organisational questions. Consequently, the joint team can be seen as a 'partial' rather than 'full' network multi-organisation, but despite this it is believed that the issues faced can be generalised to the latter.

The Team–Context Relationship

In order to understand the impact of the context on the joint team it is necessary to develop an appreciation of its role in the inter-organisational network, and in particular the manner in which the substantive task of updating and rolling forward the regional strategy related to the interests and activities of other institutions. The work of Benson provides a useful starting point. Extending the view of the 'system-resource' theorists, who hypothesise that organisational decision-makers are typically oriented to the acquisition and defence of a supply of resources adequate to meet agency goals, Benson argues that competitive or co-operative interactions between agencies are ultimately dependent upon and shaped by resource contingencies. In other words, inter-organisational relations are fundamentally affected by considerations of access to and control over resources, which Benson (1975, p. 232) sees as being authority – 'the legitimation of activities, the right and responsibility to carry out programmes of a certain kind, dealing with a broad problem area or focus' – and money.

From this analysis Benson has identified four 'action orientations' pursued by agencies in their dealings with other organisations in the network.

(1) *The fulfilment of programme requirements*. 'The organisation's claim to a supply of resources will typically be based upon the adequacy and effectiveness of its established programmes. Thus agency officials are reluctant to undertake tasks or to tolerate practices of other agencies which interfere with the fulfilment of present programmes . . . They will exert pressure upon other agencies to cease practices disruptive of programme requirements.'

(2) *The maintenance of a clear domain*. 'Such a domain is characterised by one or more of the following attributes: (i) exclusiveness – a claim untrammelled, unchallenged by other organisations; (ii) autonomy – a claim permitting the performance of activities independently, without supervision direction or shared authority; (iii) dominance – a claim permitting authoritative direction of other agencies operating in a specified sphere.'

(3) *The maintenance of orderly, reliable patterns of resource flow*. 'Organisations are oriented to see that the support network operates in a predictable, dependable way that permits the agency to anticipate an adequate and certain flow of resources.'

(4) *The extended application and defence of the agency's paradigm*. 'The organisation participants are committed to their agency's way of doing things – to its own definitions of problems and tasks and its own techniques of intervention . . . Organisations which use or espouse other approaches are seen as irresponsible and immoral. Efforts are made to see that the 'proper' definitions and techniques are adopted.' (op. cit., pp. 232–3)

The activities of the joint team in updating and rolling forward the approved regional strategy presented a challenge to participating institutions in terms of each of these action orientations, for three main reasons. First, the planning exercise involved undertaking a fresh analysis and interpretation of regional conditions and trends, and by implication assessed the continuing validity of the substantive assumptions underlying agency policies and programmes. For example, work by the joint team on changing demographic trends and household formation rates led to the suggestion that there was 'overprovision' in the structure plans of the shire counties. Secondly, the updating included an explicit assessment of agency programmes in terms of their compatibility with existing and future regional conditions. The plans of executive agencies were evaluated for continuing appropriateness. Analysis of the regional economy and related policies, for instance, raised questions about the adequacy of DI, DE and Manpower Services Commission programmes. Thirdly, the visible product of the planning exercise was a set of policy recommendations and guidelines which, potentially, could alter the resource base and resource access of institutions in the region. For example, an updated strategy oriented to urban regeneration could have disbenefits for population and employment levels in the shire counties.

While a regional strategy will not necessarily bear directly on the distribution of the resources of money and authority in the network, it can have a substantial indirect effect through its influence on secondary resources such as population distribution, employment location, economic development and infrastructure provision. In the West Midlands, which is currently experiencing a low rate of population growth, out-migration from the metropolitan core to villages in and beyond the Green Belt and poor economic performance, the recommendations of the updating can have an important influence on the distribution of the primary resources of money and authority: money, because changes in population, households and employment can have consequences for local authority finances through the rate yield, criteria for allocating central grant, and for the local economy because of income multiplier effects; and authority, because adverse recommendations can affect the political standing of local councillors and officials (who may have seen the exercise as a means of 'delivering the goods' in terms of jobs for their area) and central departments (whose role and ability may be criticised).

However, while the updating presented a challenge to the existing distribution of resources in the inter-organisational network, agencies were clearly aware that it might hold out benefits as well as costs by providing an opportunity to alter the balance of resources in an individual participant's favour. Agencies in the region thus faced the problem of engaging in the updating and rolling forward to ensure at least that their resource position was not worsened, but that if possible outcomes would be to their advantage. The joint team was thus confronted with differing and competing demands from the constituencies or parent organisations commissioning the exercise, and because of the relatively open multi-organisational structure of the team participating agencies acted to shape the issues covered and outcomes developed.

Issue Divergence

An example of issue divergence concerns the case of the regional economy. Changes in the economic structure of the region, identified in the 1976 annual monitoring report, led to the decision to update the approved regional strategy, and the issue of the economy subsequently dominated the exercise. Although DI was involved as one of the parties to the updating, it was concerned at the interpretation of economic analysis. Early on in the process, while the local authority side argued that the regional economy was undergoing structural change, DI posited the view that it was in fact at the bottom of a cyclical process. But DI also questioned that the regional economy should be the main issue in what it perceived as essentially a DoE-local authority physical planning exercise, and was aware that the updating could lead to policy recommendations as challenging to its role and position as those contained in SPNR. This question was eventually resolved at national level when DoE accepted the DI view that economic issues should only be included in the updating to the extent that they had physical planning or land use implications, and hence that non-spatial economic matters should be excluded from the issue agenda at least as far as central government was concerned. WMPAC and the West Midlands EPC did not accept this position, however, and consequently two final reports appeared in September 1979. One, endorsed by all three parties on JMSG, was essentially a physical planning strategy for the region (Joint Monitoring Steering Group, 1979), while the other was a report by WMPAC and WMEPC on the regional economy which argued that the JMSG strategy paid insufficient attention to underlying and fundamental economic issues (West Midlands Economic Planning Council/West Midlands Planning Authorities' Conference, 1979).

Outcome Divergence

Outcome divergence is illustrated by considering the spatial strategy. Early on in the process the local authority side were concerned that the Middle Ring, one of five subregions employed by the joint team (Figure 7.2), was not defined flexibly enough to take account of commuting patterns, and so on, and that acceptance of this subregion for analytical purposes would, because it had a buoyant economic structure and high rate of population growth, lead to prescriptions for peripheral growth just over the border from the conurbation. Long-standing concerns about development encroaching into the Green Belt and possible future boundary extensions by the metropolitan authorities, which in 1974 had led to the loss by Staffordshire of its Aldridge/Brownhills growth point, were raised. Not until October 1978, eighteen months after the start of the exercise, was the problem resolved with a distinction being drawn between definitions of the Middle Ring for 'statistical' and 'policy' purposes, the latter based on recognition of 'the emergence of the Metropolitan County and the Middle Ring as inter-dependent parts of a wider city-region' (Figure 7.3) (Joint Monitoring Steering Group, 1979, p. 187). The policy definition was designed to achieve two objectives: first, to emphasise the free-standing towns in the statistical Middle Ring by excluding more rural areas such as parts of North Warwickshire, Rugby, Stratford-on-Avon and Wyre Forest; and secondly, to include free-standing growth centres from the statistical Outer Ring – for example,

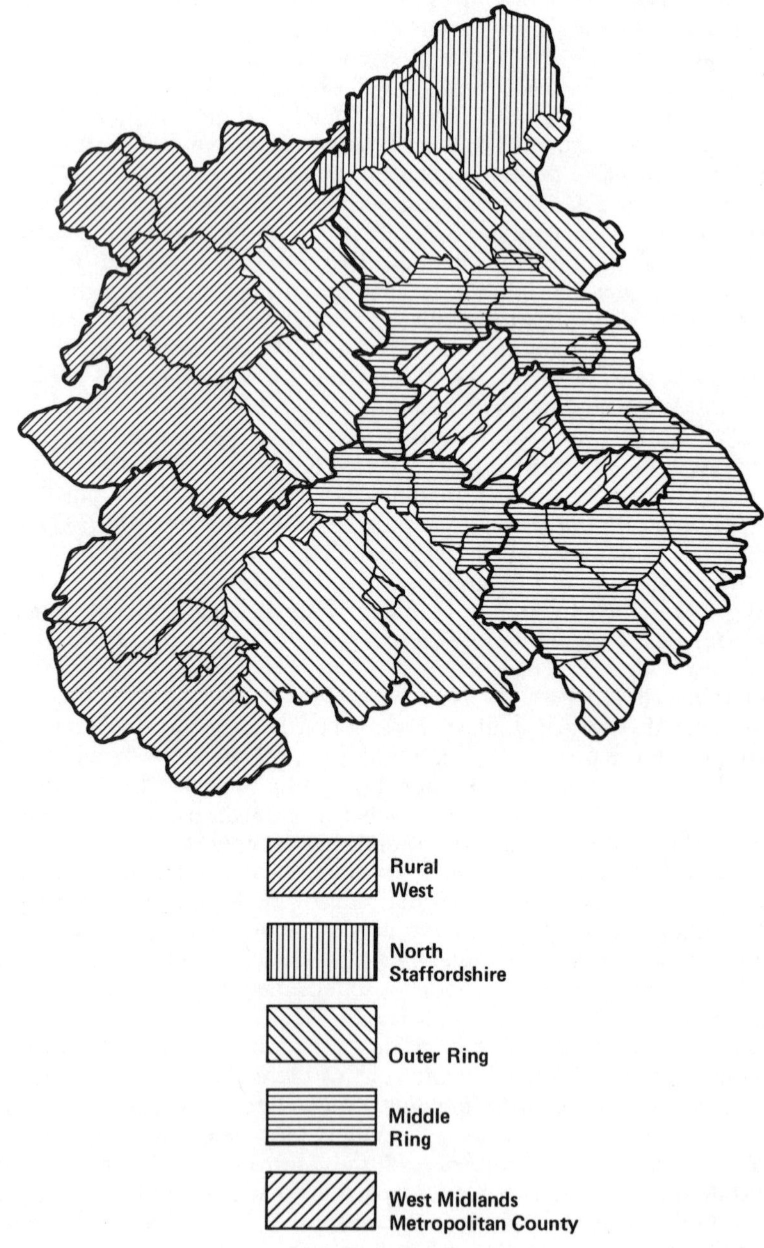

Figure 7.2 *West Midlands: statistical subregions.*

Figure 7.3 *West Midlands: policy Middle Ring.*

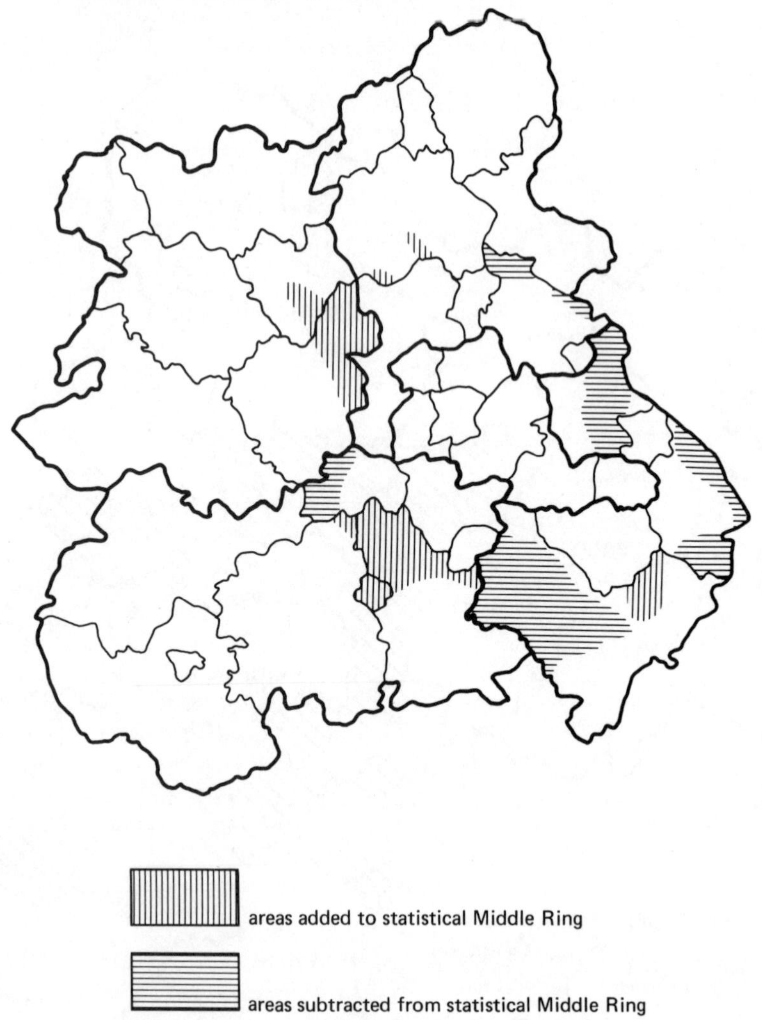

Figure 7.4 *West Midlands: statistical and policy Middle Rings: analysis of difference.*

Telford, Worcester and Stafford – by developing spurs or 'fingers of growth' out from the regional core (Figure 7.4).

Although the distinction between policy and statistical definitions of the Middle Ring enabled participants' divergent views on outcome to be resolved, it did so at the expense of clarity. Thus in the updating reports it is unclear where the boundary of the policy Middle Ring lies, nor is it apparent from the text when one definition rather than another is being employed. By minimising the potential constraints in the recommendations of the updating and rolling forward, authorities are pursuing a basic political strategy of holding options open where possible.

OPERATIONAL CONSIDERATIONS FOR NETWORK MULTI-ORGANISATIONS

The phenomena described above are not peculiar to West Midlands regional planning, but are regularly to be found in inter-organisational decision-making. As Walton points out:

> I have been struck by the amount of behaviour that is not directed towards either problem-solving or bargaining over [agencies'] respective preferences regarding the substantive issues which divide them, but rather is devoted to defeating the interagency process and *to making the outcome as ambiguous or innocuous as possible.* (Walton, 1972, p. 108, my italics)

In terms of Benson's perspective this strategy of avoidance represents a rational response to a situation where divergent outcomes have differential resource consequences for participants. As Walton observes, 'interdependent ventures seldom have symmetrical gains for participating agencies' (op. cit., p. 109). Since tactically it would be disadvantageous for one party to withdraw from the updating, in the sense that the remaining participants could combine to make decisions unfavourable to that party, the solution is to dilute the substantive outcome of the exercise. The relatively open form of the joint team as a multi-organisation permitted commissioning parties to undertake this task and neutralise certain issues or outcomes threatening their resource position.

This conclusion presents something of a challenge to the alternative regional planning methodology developed earlier, while recognising that the joint team in the West Midlands was operating to some extent as a command rather than network organisation. In particular it illustrates that close linkages by the planning team into institutions in the context can act to constrain rather than enhance the development of invisible products, because executive agencies will operate to manage the disturbance the team causes to the resource environment. This is done by reducing the impact of the network multi-organisation in seeking commitment to common lines of action. Consequently the lessons of the West Midlands study have implications for the design and operational strategy of a network multi-organisation.

The role of the network organisation is described by Metcalfe (1978, p. 79) in the following way.

> Network organisations provide a mechanism for exploring the interconnections among problems as perceived by different interests and a context for thinking through ways of arriving at mutually acceptable solutions. Network organisations facilitate the emergence of a shared frame of reference and the means of dealing with areas of conflict, but do not presuppose an identity of views or complete consensus.

It was argued earlier that in certain circumstances there would be at least the potential for 'an identity of views', if not actual consensus. Such exchange-type situations raised few difficulties for a network multi-organisation; its task was to expose the compatibility of organisational objectives or strategies. Where there was divergence on issues or outcomes, however, such as the West Midlands example, the position of the planning team appears more problematic. One solution to this issue would be to insulate the network multi-organisation to some extent from agencies in its context, for instance, by reverting to the quasi-independent team structure of the dominant planning methodology. A different approach, somewhat closer to the spirit of the alternative methodology, would require the planning team itself consciously to establish a power base or position of legitimacy in the inter-organisational network.

Within a network the basis of differential power, and by implication the ascription of legitimacy or 'usefulness', relate either to an organisation's position in the internal network structure or to its external linkages. Some organisations gain power, for example, because they are a focal point in the network, providing services or managing resources which affect other agencies. Others have links with institutions who are outside the network but nevertheless control or possess strategic contingencies (information, extra resources, and so on) affecting network organisations (Benson, 1975). The achievement of one of these positions within the inter-organisational network will provide a more effective basis for the network multi-organisation to manage attempts by agencies to dominate and shape its activities to individual advantage.

THE DEVELOPMENT OF CONTEXT-APPROPRIATENESS

The message of this chapter is that in the design of planning structures and processes an awareness of the context is essential. While public planning is about a process of design – of goals, proposals and programmes – questions of the design of the process itself are often given low priority. In this meta-design activity a crucial issue is the relationship of the planning methodology to its context: what contextual features are significant? How can the planning process be shaped to take account of these elements?

The example of English regional planning 1968–79 was used to explore the notion of context-appropriate methodology and it was argued that the dominant methodology was not completely appropriate to key features of its context. While regional planning was chosen as an example because it represents a critical case for context-appropriate methodology, because of the absence of any executive, resource allocation or political base for the activity, and hence a relationship to the organisations in its context is essential, the notion of context-appropriateness has wider applicability.

Within the public sector ties and mutual dependencies between agencies have become more significant during the last decade. Both the reorganisation of national and subnational government and the rise of new issues on the political agenda have resulted in the creation of an increasing number and variety of institutions (regional water authority, regional and area health authorities, Manpower Services Commission, and so on) and planning systems (transport policies and programmes, housing investment programmes, public expenditure survey committee process, and so on).

In Chapters 9 and 10, for example, the theme of context-appropriateness can be identified as a key development in practice in certain fields and in relation to some agencies, but it has seldom explicitly been discussed. In practice context-appropriate methodology has often appeared following the unsatisfactory introduction of an 'ideal type' model. In local authority corporate planning, for instance, the rejection of Bains's organisational structures and the high-technology, PPBS-based, processes resulted in local authorities developing planning methodologies which were appropriate to their particular circumstances (Haynes, 1978; Honey, 1979; see also Chapter 3 of this book).

In a period of major structural change in the economy and a significant shift in dominant political philosophy, however, it is important that public agencies – who are facing increasingly severe societal problems with a reducing resource base – should be able to short-cut 'learning through experience' in their development of planning methodology. Learning through experience in the case of corporate planning took about a decade, from the articulation of the original ideas and proposals in the mid-1960s, their application in the late 1960s/early 1970s, the retreat in the mid-1970s and the emergence of more appropriate systems in the latter half of the 1970s. The argument of this chapter is that the explicit consideration of contextual features in the design of planning methodology may reduce the time-lag in the planned response of public agencies to perceived priorities.

NOTES: CHAPTER 7

This chapter is based in part on the author's participation in a research study of regional planning methodology undertaken with D. A. Hart, of the University of Reading, M. E. Norris and Allen Hickling, Centre for Operational and Organisational Research, Tavistock Institute, to whom thanks for advice and criticism are due. The research study was commissioned by the Department of the Environment. The views expressed here are the author's own, and in no way commit the Department or fellow researchers. Certain elements of this paper will be found in earlier form in Mawson and Skelcher, 1980, and Skelcher, 1980a.

1 The South East Joint Planning Team, 1970; West Midlands Regional Study, 1971; West Midlands Planning Authorities' Conference, 1974; North West Joint Planning Team, 1973; East Anglia Regional Strategy Team, 1974; South East Joint Planning Team, 1976; Northern Region Strategy Team, 1977; Joint Monitoring Steering Group, 1979; and West Midlands Economic Planning Council/West Midlands Planning Authorities' Conference, 1979. While the *Developing Strategy* report of 1971 was not commissioned on a tripartite basis, central government staff were closely involved at a number of stages and subsequent regional planning in the West

Midlands has been tripartite. Other documents termed 'regional studies' or 'regional strategies', and commissioned solely by the appropriate regional Economic Planning Council, are not considered here.

2 This analysis is, in some cases, based on an interpretation of the intended target agency as not all regional strategies clearly identify the specific agency towards which a recommendation is directed.

3 While the most recent government response has been produced in a different format, many of the above comments still apply. See Department of the Environment, 1978.

4 See also Chapter 6 of this volume.

5 On the concept of the 'organisation set' see Evan, 1972.

8

County–District Relations in Town Planning

STEVE LEACH

INTRODUCTION

Less and less can the problems of developing and implementing public policies at the subnational level be seen as the responsibility of one particular type of organisation. One of the major effects of the 1974 reorganisation of local government was to fragment the institutional basis for policy-making in local government in cities. Before 1974 there existed a system of unitary authorities (county boroughs) and county councils, although counterbalanced by a wide range of different lower-tier authorities within their boundaries (municipal boroughs, urban districts, rural districts) were usually in a dominant position *vis-à-vis* such authorities (see, for example, Lee *et al.*, 1974, ch. 4; Marshall, 1977, ch. 16). Since 1974 that dominance has lessened as the new shire counties have been faced with fewer, larger, and arguably stronger, districts. The county boroughs have disappeared, many of them in the major conurbations forming the nuclei of the new metropolitan districts, which have had to learn to live with a new type of strategic authority, the metropolitan county. In 1974 Friend, Power and Yewlett (1974, p. xxi) argued (with reference to a town development scheme implemented under the pre-1974 local government system) that 'corporate planning was no longer enough' to cope with the problems faced – an *intercorporate* dimension was also needed. That prescription is even more relevant in the post-1974 local government world than it was when it was written.

This growth in the significance of the inter-organisational context of subnational policy-making has perhaps nowhere been more evident than in the field of land use planning. Prior to 1974 there were inter-organisational disputes over planning policy, notably between the large cities and the surrounding counties over the location of overspill development (Lee *et al.*, 1974, ch. 2). However, in the 1972 Local Government Act (p. 182), land use planning became one of the few explicitly 'shared' functions. Counties had the responsibility for the preparation of structure plans; development control was shared between counties and districts, with the county dealing with applications 'of county significance', and the districts with all the rest; local plans could be produced by county, district, or county and districts jointly (it was anticipated that it would normally be a district activity). In the case of district-produced local plans, certification was required from the county that the plan was in accord with the county structure plan. Distribution of planning applications was normally governed by a document known as a Development Control Agreement. The preparation of local plans was covered by a Development Plan Scheme. The latter had a formal legal standing which the former had not. Counties and districts were exhorted and expected to work together co-operatively to implement the new planning machinery.

Since the research on which this chapter is based was carried out this machinery has changed. The new Local Government Planning and Land Act 1980 (section 86) contains clauses which in effect recognise that the required co-operation has not necessarily materialised. Apart from one or two very limited categories, development control will become the clear responsibility of the districts and certain other provisions arguably lessen the county's influence over the content of local plans. An institutional separation between policy-making and implementation has been introduced whereby counties 'make' land use planning policy and districts 'implement' it. An arbitrary institutional separation of this kind between policy-making and policy implementation is likely to create as many problems as it solves. But the proposed changes do not alter the necessity to study land use planning policy from an inter-organisational perspective.

Land use planning has always been an anomaly within the range of a local authority's functions. Both at structure plan and local plan level, the relationship between land use planning and the broader processes of local authority policy planning (in its various forms) has never been clear. In some authorities the two processes intermesh at particular points; in others, and this is perhaps the more common situation, they proceed more or less independently. Stewart and Eddison (1971, pp. 367–9) have argued that structure planning can in no sense be seen as a substitute for the more corporate processes of local authority policy planning. Faludi (1972) has argued that land use planning would make more sense within the range of a local authority's policy activities if it were seen as a 'land-budgeting exercise' constraining and expressing a set of authority-wide policies which are not in themselves developed on a spatial basis.

This chapter first demonstrates the importance of understanding the inter-organisational context in which the formulation and implementation of land use planning policy takes place; secondly, it illustrates the kind of constraints which this network imposes and, finally, draws some conclusions about appropriate approaches to policy-making. Some of the concepts and conclusions may well be applicable, in principle, to other substantive areas of 'local' policy-making (for example, joint care planning). The proposed changes in the legislation may alter the balance of the county–district relationship and some of the policy outcomes. They do not decrease the need for the analysis of the inter-organisational context and the prescriptive application of this analysis.

THE STRUCTURE AND PROCESS OF CHANGE IN COUNTY–DISTRICT RELATIONSHIPS

In the research on which this chapter is based (Leach and Moore, 1978; Leach, 1978) considerable variation in the quality of county–district relationships was found. Three broad factors are useful in understanding these differences; the structure of the interrelationship; the 'assumptive worlds' of the key actors (councillors and officers); and the nature of the legal and quasi-legal agreements (for example, Development Plan Schemes, and so on) which were used during the course of the relationship.

The Structure of the Interrelationship

Before two parties can develop a relationship there must be some reason for their coming together. The implication of this truism is that the quality of the interrelationship between any county–district pairing will be based on the range of different ways in which the *functions* of the two bodies are related. The type of conflict that is of real significance for an organisation is that which stems from the *structural interdependencies* between itself and the other organisation. This statement is not to imply that personality clashes are not significant but rather that they are only significant when the 'personalities' concerned occupy functionally related positions in the two authorities.

There are a variety of different ways in which counties and districts are structurally interrelated. The following classification attempts to categorise these structural interrelationships.[1]

(*a*) *Dependence on common resources*. There are a number of ways in which counties and districts in effect compete for the same resources, for example, rates income and the locally determined sector of loan sanction.

(*b*) *Hierarchical dependency*. There are also a number of ways in which districts act as agents for the county. The most significant example are highways agency arrangements. However, delegated powers (for example, in development control matters) also fall into this category.

(*c*) *Functional interdependency*. This type of relationship implies some kind of shared function, where both county and district have powers, and where what one of the parties does inevitably affects the other. The interdependency involved may be *sequential* (for example, waste treatment, in which districts collect and counties dispose); *pooled* (for example, industrial development, certain recreational provisions); or *reciprocal* (for example, structure/local planning; joint use recreation).

Town and country planning provides an important example of functional interdependency with, sometimes, some elements of hierarchical dependency.[2] However, the quality of the inter-organisational relationship in town planning is often affected by experiences in county–district points of contact which embody other kinds of interdependency (for example, dependence on common resources).

While interaction develops in particular functionally related areas, the *quality* of this interaction is considerably affected by the values, attitudes and interests of the actual participants concerned: their 'assumptive worlds' (Young, 1977, p. 3). A variety of different actors may be involved at the county–district interface – councillors, chief executives, heads of department and professional and non-professional staff. These actors may well share certain authority-wide values and attitudes and there are likely to be common attitudes also at the departmental level. However, individual attitudes can also play a part. For example, many of the key personnel in a district may share a common predisposition towards the county which reflects their reaction to the results of reorganisation. In a department particular professional attitudes towards 'doing a good job' are often widespread. Finally, the personal antagonism of a chief officer to his counterpart in the county may have a considerable effect. To summarise, the structural independencies outlined earlier present *opportunities* for conflict or co-operation between authorities. The different values and attitudes of the key actors involved, and the balance of power between them, largely determines the way in which these opportunities are realised.

In particular it seemed from our research that there were certain key values which councillors, chief executives and departmental heads constantly referred to in singling out particular sensitive areas at the county-district interface for their attention. Councillors were often particularly concerned about local autonomy, financial restraint and individual freedom. Chief officers were more concerned with professional standards or departmental growth. Such values, which may usefully be termed *reference values*, may operate both as *filters* through which more specific policy matters or organisational routines are interpreted by these different groups and selected for action, or *scanning devices* by which policy matters and organisational routines are actively sought out and utilised to promote the values. The reference values operating in an organisation may or may not reflect self-interest, and may change over time in response to changes in the organisation (for example, change of party in power) or its environment (for example, threat of further local government reorganisation).

In the development of a county–district relationship the role of *legal and quasi-legal documents and agreements* (for example, Structure Plan, Development Plan Scheme, Development Control Agreement) has been crucial. In all but the most benign and consensual of relationships these documents tend to be used as, at the very least, bargaining counters, and sometimes almost as weapons if overt conflict develops. Thus the approval of a Development Control Agreement, or by the DoE of a Structure Plan, can be critical events in the development of county–district relationships. This type of document can be used as a power resource in the development and deployment of *strategies* for coping with the interdependency with the other authority.

For example, a county holding an approved Structure Plan, and a Development Control Agreement allowing a minimum of latitude to its districts, is clearly in a very different power position from a county which has not yet submitted its Structure Plan and operates a very lenient and district-oriented Development Control Agreement.[3]

The pattern of a county–district relationship, once established, can change over time in a number of ways. A change in the *political party in power* in either county or district can be crucial. In this case what often happens is that in effect a new range of reference values is injected into the policy-making arena. Alternatively, a particular issue (for example, a Green Belt dispute) can suddenly release the opportunity for conflict that has previously lain dormant between two authorities. Sometimes the process of stereotyping occurs whereby one or both authorities develop an *idée fixe* about the other which hardens over each new incident, and a vicious circle of misunderstanding and mistrust may develop with predispositions dominating every response.

KEY FACTORS INFLUENCING THE QUALITY OF COUNTY–DISTRICT RELATIONSHIPS

Three more specific aspects of the three broad variables outlined above were found to be particularly important in understanding the pattern of county–district relationships; the attitude of the two authorities concerned to reorganisations; the politician/officer power balance; and the strategies used at the interface for coping with the interdependency.

(1) *Attitude of the Authority to Reorganisation*

Crucial to an understanding of the pattern of county–district relations in any county is the attitude of the county and the districts concerned to the 1974 reorganisation. Some pre-1974 authorities were bitterly disappointed with the results of reorganisation and this disappointment was carried through to the new authorities by the often high proportion of councillors and officers who made the transition. First, resentment was caused over *loss of powers*. In particular the change experienced by an authority that had been a county borough prior to 1974 and then became a shire district with considerably reduced functions often led to an anti-county predisposition, which one or two incidents involving disagreement could easily develop into overt antagonism.[4] Such predispositions and potential for conflict were particularly significant in the large cities, for example, Bristol, Nottingham. Secondly, districts which following reorganisation found themselves in counties other than the one they themselves would have preferred tended to develop a similar predisposition and a similar potential for conflict. This tendency applied both in cases where the parent county still existed after reorganisation, (for example, Lincolnshire), and in cases where it disappeared completely in 1974 (for example, Herefordshire), and was accentuated where the new county was much less ready to delegate functions than the old.

On the other hand some districts were relatively happy with the results of reorganisation, particularly where they escaped transfer to a different, less preferred, county. This response was especially true of districts on the fringe of a conurbation area which managed to avoid being incorporated into a metropolitan district, where they would have completely lost their identity. Districts which had to struggle to exist at all were equally prone to be well disposed towards the county. Either a pro-county or anti-county disposition may become modified over time as new issues arise, or new parties gain power. But the resilience of attitudes formed at reorganisation can be quite remarkable. There is a sense in which the new 1974 two-tier system has not operated as a 'new start', or a 'break from the past'.

Clearly the initial anti-county predisposition is more likely to have been sustained if there still exist considerable numbers of councillors who served in local boroughs and districts prior to reorganisation. In 1977 there was sometimes as many as 60 per cent of sitting councillors who had served prior to 1974, and figures of 40 per cent were commonplace. Every year, of course, this will tend to reduce somewhat. In authorities where the degree of member continuity is relatively low it is less likely that the initial reaction against the results of reorganisation will have been sustained over time. The degree of officer continuity may also be important.

A number of other influences can be identified which either mitigated or intensified these potentialities for conflict. Where there is a relatively large number of districts in a county (seven or more) then the ability of any one district to win disputes with the county is reduced, because of the relative smallness of the district lobby at county headquarters, the relative improbability of common pressures from, or organisation of, a united front of districts, and the corresponding ease with which the county can operate a divide-and-rule strategy. Alternatively, if a county has a relatively small number of districts (five or less), the conflict potential is correspondingly increased, for all the converse reasons. In such a situation, particularly if faced with one large and influential district among its limited complement, the county may well make conflict-preempting concessions.

County-district pairings varied considerably with regard to the number of dual members involved. In some part of the county dual membership was encouraged by local party associations, while in other parts it was discouraged, or even prevented (see Richards, 1975, p. 76). Where it exists, dual membership by and large appears to increase the likelihood of co-operation between two authorities. In any crisis of divided loyalties, however, the dual member tends to favour his district.

Finally, the likelihood of the potential for county-district conflict actually becoming realised is reduced if there exists within the environment of the district some other organisation with whom it is in conflict. In other words, if much of the district's energy is directed towards battles with a new town authority, a water board or area health authority, or a central government department, then it is less likely to take on the county, whatever conflict preconditions or predispositions exist.

(2) *The Political/Technical Power Balance*
Attitudes to reorganisation tend to be particularly strongly held by members, although there are certainly officers whose status or influence has been reduced as a result of reorganisation who do have similarly strong feelings about it. However, by and large the behaviour of officers is motivated by other values, attitudes and interests. This means, of course, that the differential influence of councillors and officers on both policy-making and policy implementation becomes important. It is widely accepted that there is considerable variation between different authorities in the degree to which the political level actually initiates policy. In some authorities it is undoubtedly true that a political party comes to power with a wide range of policies and programmes which it more or less succeeds in introducing. In others, however, it is clear that much of the initiatory momentum for policy comes from officers, whose advice the various committees invariably accept. In any event, as Bulpitt (1967, pp. 118–23) points out, the number of 'live issues' with which councillors are concerned at any one time tends to be limited, and in addition departments have the ability to modify or generate political issues through the information that they receive, collect and feed to elected members and through their powers of implementation. Thus of the areas of a local authority's work which involve interdependency of some kind with the other tier, some will be of concern to members and will be significantly affected by their attitudes (for example, with regard to reorganisation), while others will be of less importance to members and will be largely influenced by officer attitudes. The values and attitudes of key officers will also, therefore, be to a greater or less extent an influence on the course of county–district relations.

In situations where the attitudes and assumptions of officers are important a number of significant variables may be identified. Perhaps the most important is the extent to which key officers *have knowledge and experience of the other authority*. Though local government reorganisation involved a considerable upheaval of staff, many of the movements involved were local ones. Thus in town planning in particular it is quite common to find situations where considerable numbers of county staff have moved to the districts within the new county.[5] In addition some chief executive positions in districts have been filled by ex-county men. Where these kinds of move have taken place it should be apparent that there exists a potential *personal* network for coping with problems that might arise. A new district planning officer who previously worked in the county in which the district is situated will invariably find himself confronted with many of his former colleagues still in the county. Normally this kind of situation makes co-operation more likely, although not inevitably so. The new district planning officer may not have fitted in at the county, or he may feel that his talents had been overlooked by the county planning officer. He may also be under some pressure from his new authority to demonstrate that he is now a 'district man'. However, it is far more common for the network of personal links to be used in a positive way, to sort out conflicts before they become serious, or to prevent them occurring. Other members of his staff may be involved in similar networks. The same generalisation (with the same qualifications) also applies to district chief executives, who were formerly based in the county. Similarly district officers who have developed experience of and personal links with county officials on the basis of the pre-1974 two-tier system often also find they have a personal network which they can use to secure co-operation and limit conflict. Many of the district highways and administrative staff have this kind of experience. In those counties which in the pre-organisation era had operated a *decentralised system of development control*, with district offices scattered around the county dealing directly with district politicians and officers, the transition to the new two-tier planning system was often smooth – perhaps because an embryo two-tier system was already a familiar experience to both parties.

However, inherited from pre-reorganisation days there may exist within counties a concern over the ability of district staff to perform an adequate professional role. This concern is particularly likely in highways agency agreements, where the financial and administrative terms of the agreement often reflect a desire by the county to keep a firm control over the actions of district staff, who tend to be more confident about their ability to carry out their professional duties adequately. Similar problems may apply over the shared function of town and country planning. It is often felt at county level that, whatever the competence of the professional staff, parochial and irrational political interests are much more likely to influence what happens in districts than in counties – hence the need for firm control. These beliefs and attitudes often cause concern on the part of district staff, a concern that may be aggravated by the hierarchical and autocratic management styles of (particularly) county surveyors' departments.

The politician/officer power balance may be abruptly changed by a switch in party control of a county or district following a local election. There is little evidence that a difference in party control between county and district is in itself a conflict-generating factor. As many examples were found of poor relations between a county and a district which were run by the *same* political parties as instances of poor relations between authorities of different political complexions; and the same was true for good relationships. A party political difference may intensify conflict, but the forces generating the conflict usually lie elsewhere. However, a *change* in political power can have a significant impact, especially if the incoming party is particularly concerned with issues such as local autonomy or financial restraint, which may be expected to impinge on the county-district interface. The possibility also exists that change in political power might improve the relationship.

(3) *Strategies for Coping with Interdependency*

Legal and quasi-legal documents such as County Structure Plans and Development Control Agreements can be both *sources* of conflict, and bargaining counters or weapons in the playing-out of the conflict that results. Such documents do not inevitably create conflict; there exist many situations where counties and districts have little disagreement about the context of a Structure Plan, and where a Development Control Agreement works very smoothly. However, such documents operate as potential sources of conflict and as resources which may be utilised if the circumstances are felt to be appropriate.

There was a considerable amount of awareness among local authorities that Structure Plans and Development Control Agreements were by no means neutral documents in the county/district power balance. County planning departments which were experiencing difficulty (in their terms) in securing from districts decisions and policies which were in the county interest looked forward to the day when they possessed a formally approved Structure Plan as a legal back-up to their efforts. Districts often felt a corresponding unease about an impending Structure Plan, and several examinations in public have involved objections from districts (sometimes operating together), particularly over the level of detail in the plan. It is of course also much easier for a county to influence the content of local plans when it possesses an approved Structure Plan, and to assess an application as a 'county matter'.

A similar potential resource is provided by Development Control Agreements. Many such agreements were drawn up on the assumption that co-operative harmonious relations would prevail between county and districts, and hence the Agreement left much leeway to the district in terms of application classification and acceptance of local commitments. In relationships where expectations of co-operation have not been fully realised there has often developed a desire at county level for a more county-oriented Agreement which gives more scope for control. Alternatively those districts which operate within a very restrictive (from their point of view) county-oriented Agreement have often come to resent the limited scope for manoeuvre which results.

Thus a county-oriented or district-oriented Development Control Agreement, and the existence of a County Structure Plan or the lack of one, can all significantly influence the quality of county–district relations in planning and can all be used (by one party or the other) as a power resource in the playing-out of a conflict. The same argument applies to Highways Agency Agreements, which may similarly be 'restrictive' or 'permissive', Waste Processing Agreements and other documents which govern collaboration between the two authorities.

Significant increases in a county *rates precept* were often a conflict-intensifying factor for districts which were attempting to hold their rates steady (given that even if they were successful in doing so a large increase in the county precept would mask this achievement, for the ratepayer). Similarly any attempts by a county to transfer the cost burden of joint ventures (for example, joint use recreation projects, information centres, sheltered housing) were often resented by the districts.

There was also some indication that difference in character between county and district was a conflict-intensifying factor (for example, the position of an urban industrial district in a predominantly rural county). Also the proximity of a district to county headquarters sometimes aggravated developing conflicts.

SHIRE/METROPOLITAN DIFFERENCES

In understanding the different patterns of county–district relations in shire and metropolitan counties one factor is of paramount importance. In shire counties the balance of power is tilted very much towards the county, while in metropolitan counties it is tilted very much towards the district.

In shire counties there is far more that the county can do at the county-district interface to harm the district than the district can do to harm the county. One shire district's chief executive writes: 'The County Council, not because it is perverse, or heavy handed, is in a much stronger position than each of the District Councils individually. It is also (at present) stronger than the Districts collectively.' This strength stems from a number of factors. Because of rate-precepting, counties in general are not as accountable to the electorate as the districts, nor are they as accessible. Financially shire counties are in a stronger position, with a revenue budget typically many times greater than that of a district[6] (reflecting that both education and social services are county functions). Given, in addition, the much wider range of functions which a county performs, it is not surprising to find that a district has to cope with county actions (for example, a withdrawal of funds, or a change in policy) much more often than a county has to cope with district actions.[7] While a shire county is invariably the most important organisation in the environment of a district, the same is not true of any one district from the point of view of its county.

In metropolitan counties the balance of power is quite different. Metropolitan districts are altogether more powerful entities than shire districts in functions and budgets. Some large metropolitan districts have revenue budgets of the same size as those of the counties in which they are situated; in all metropolitan districts the budgets would be at least roughly the same size as their counties'. Thus the financial impact on the district of a county action will be much easier to incorporate than for a shire district. In addition much of the annual expenditure of a metropolitan county is on police and fire services – neither particularly controversial subjects for county–district relations. Metropolitan districts have responsibility for education and social services, leaving highways the only major spending department at county level with powers that directly impinge on the districts, and strategic planning as the only other department which can significantly affect the activity of the districts. Thus the metropolitan county was seen by districts as at best a resource to be exploited and at worst an irrelevance (though sometimes an irrelevant nuisance). In the metropolitan counties there was often an awareness of the county's limited power *vis-à-vis* the districts and in several cases a painful search for a distinctive identity seemed to have begun – particularly in planning – together with a related attempt to carve out for itself a piece of territory at the county-district interface. However, the strategies that could be adopted in pursuit of these aims have to be carefully assessed. An attempt to 'impose' a regard for county interests on the districts would be likely to meet with determined opposition from them (and indeed, has done, in those few instances where this approach has been attempted). Strategies have to be far more subtle and oriented towards persuasion, bargaining, or opportunism.

Some interesting differences emerge in the three main groups of factors influencing metropolitan county–district relationships.

(1) *Attitude of the Authority to Reorganisation*

Attitudes towards reorganisation have played a much smaller part in influencing the course of county–district relations in metropolitan counties *vis-à-vis* shire counties. The metropolitan counties are completely new authorities, and thus have no previous history on the basis of which they can act or, initially, be evaluated. The metropolitan districts are in most cases amalgamations of ex-county boroughs, municipal boroughs and urban districts. In the common situation where the new metropolitan district is dominated (in terms of influence) by a former county borough, then the politicians and officers of that county borough, who were present both before and after reorganisation, are in a position where, although they have lost a limited range of powers to the new county (for example, police, fire, highways, strategic planning), they have gained significantly in territory and population. These gains tended to damp down any potential antagonism to the results of reorganisation.

The main exceptions to this general pattern were those large and powerful ex-county boroughs at the centres of conurbations which had not gained boundary extensions or new population to compensate for loss of powers at reorganisation and whose civic pride did not in any event predispose them to welcome the imposition of any kind of two-tier system. Such authorities apart, the widespread lack of initial antagonism may, however, quickly change if the county attempts a heavy-handed or dictatorial stance in its dealings with its districts.

Neither the number of districts in the county nor the existence of dual membership seems to make much difference to the quality of the relationships which develop in metropolitan counties. The former varies only within a narrow range;[8] and the latter rarely seems to be widespread enough to have much impact. Metropolitan districts have dealings with a much wider range of bodies than do shire districts (for example, central government departments, area health authorities) and only rarely is the metropolitan county seen as the major organisation in a district's environment.

(2) *Strategies for Coping with Interdependency*

Metropolitan districts tend to be much more politically active bodies than either shire districts or shire counties. There is more likely to be a governing party with a reasonably wide-ranging and coherent programme and an equally well-organised and policy-oriented opposition. This political emphasis means that changes in the identity of the party in power can be particularly traumatic, with sudden switches in policy as the new party seeks to demonstrate its differences from the party replaced and from the party in power in the county (if the county is of a different political persuasion). However, partly because of the much wider range of functions in a metropolitan district, and the more limited range of overlap with the metropolitan county (of shire districts and counties), this greater degree of political organisation does not necessarily have much impact on the county-district interface. Apart from odd isolated issues,[9] the main areas of inter-authority concern are highways and town planning. The former is normally relatively uncontentious politically (although of widespread irritation to district officers) while in the latter area metropolitan counties have in general adopted such a low profile that most districts have not felt their autonomy to be threatened.

This relative lack of political controversy in town planning has meant that relationships between officers at both head of department and middle management levels have been very important. In metropolitan counties there has often been, at reorganisation, a movement of planning staff in *reverse* direction from that described for shire counties. No equivalent body to the metropolitan county existed before 1974. Its planning staff predominantly came from the planning departments of the larger county boroughs within the conurbation, with a much more limited movement of staff from the county areas which were involved prior to 1974. In addition many of the staff from the larger county boroughs either stayed where they were or moved to the new expanded planning departments of the districts which had previously not contained a county borough or had one with only a small planning staff. Thus, as in shire counties, a close-knit network of staff often exists, spanning county and districts, which normally seems to act as a force for co-operation unless personality incompatibilities or career disappointments are involved. Most of the new metropolitan county planning staff will have had experience in authorities which are now part of the new metropolitan districts and will often know both key officers and councillors alike. Their approach to the management of county–district relations is thus likely to be, at the very least, 'realistic'.

In some cases this network of common experience and professional expertise is used to avoid the possibility of what is seen professionally to be a bad political decision (for example, through the classification of an application) and in some cases also these interprofessional links have come to be regarded with some disquiet by other district officers (for example, chief executives) as not being in the district's best interests.

Given the size and experience of the planning and surveying staff of the new metropolitan districts, it would be surprising if concern developed at county level over the professional competence of the two district departments concerned. Indeed the hierarchical and autocratic nature of some county surveyors' departments is a particular source of irritation to the well-experienced and qualified staff in the districts.

(3) *Nature of Agreements and Issues at the Interface*
There are some interesting differences between shire and metropolitan counties under this heading. At the time of the research it was less likely, in metropolitan counties, that a County Structure Plan had been formally approved and in operation,[10] and, given that such counties did not exist prior to 1974, there were no pre-reorganisation county policies to be carried over which might act as constraints on district activities. The most that the majority of metropolitan counties had were a limited number of interim policies on subjects such as offices, shopping, or Green Belts. Similarly there is little input a county can make, without a Structure Plan, to local planning (although there are corresponding difficulties for a district in getting a local plan formally approved, prior to the approval of the Structure Plan). In addition most Development Control Agreements in metropolitan counties acknowledge the expertise that exists in district planning departments, and the power of districts *vis-à-vis* the county, in the way they effectively delegate the vast majority of development control decisions to the districts,[11] and in their acceptance of policy commitments made in districts prior to reorganisation. Thus even if a county planning department were predisposed towards adopting a hard line with its districts it would have very few bargaining counters or weapons at its disposal. One common device is for counties to develop their specialist services divisions (for example, conservation, derelict land reclamation), which are put at the disposal of districts, partly in an attempt to develop with them good relations and working arrangements.

In general, therefore, in town planning, relations between counties and districts in the metropolitan counties have been relatively uncontroversial; partly, it can be argued, because county planning staff are aware of the relative weakness of their position and do not push controversial issues or disputes with districts. The test will come when more metropolitan counties possess approved structure plans as legal backing in inter-authority planning disputes which arise. The problems then would be that once they have established low-profile consensual strategies towards the districts, it may prove difficult for counties suddenly to change their approach. It is unlikely that there would be much corporate, authority-wide support; and to develop a new strategy or a more conflictual nature would be likely to generate *political* resentment at district level over what would be seen as interference in, or a challenge to, district autonomy. The most likely way in which a county planning department can come to be positively valued by its districts is if it acts as an advocate for resources for the whole area generally, rather than attempts to allocate already existing resources amongst the different districts.

COUNTY–DISTRICT RELATIONSHIPS AND PLANNING POLICY

The development of a land use planning system is as much a matter of institutional design and interaction as it is of finding an appropriate version of rationality to apply to the problems faced. Land use planning is one of the new policy arenas where a commitment to the concepts and assumptions of purposive rationality is widespread. The use of the language of rational policy-making (issues, objectives, alternatives, evaluation, monitoring, and so on), is now widespread,[12] following their 'discovery' and development in planning education from the mid-1960s onwards.[13] The use of a common model does not guarantee agreement about appropriate substantive policies but it helps structure the debate. In addition there exists in land use planning – almost by definition – an acceptance of the importance of taking a longer-term[14] view of policies. Incrementalists, disjointed or otherwise, tend to be outnumbered in the planning world.[15] Thus many of the problems that face corporate planners in authorities which are not easily persuaded of the need to take a longer-term view, or of the benefits of even modest versions of the rational model, are not issues for land use planners.

The problem of the land use planning systems since 1974 is much more a problem of institutional arrangements. This chapter shows that there often exists amongst professional planners in particular county-district groupings a series of common assumptions about appropriate land use strategies and about an appropriate division of responsibilities. This loose alliance is always liable to be overriden by political drives towards autonomy and minimal co-operation, fuelled by resentment over the redivision of powers in the 1972 Local Government Act. How then can this potential at officer level best be utilised in the light of the new provisions of the 1980 Local Government Planning and Land Act?

The first point to raise is whether or not there is a significant set of planning problems which exist at the county level. Some districts have argued that a strategic land use planning tier is hardly needed when population is stable, new economic activity is limited, new house-building is at the lowest level since the war, and the finance for new large-scale public capital projects is drying up year by year. The contextual issues faced by strategic planning have certainly changed since the days when they were dominated by overspill problems and the allocation of economic growth. However, it is very hard to argue that a set of related planning problems at a level higher than that of a district does *not* still exist. This argument is particularly true of the conurbations, where the metropolitan counties coincide roughly[16] with large journey-to-work catchment areas. Where one has a structuring of work and residential activities and opportunities which cover a set of adjacent districts, and one or more service centres which serve in a number of ways the same broad area, it is hard to argue that planning at the level of the district alone is sufficient. This case is harder to make for shire counties, which only in a few instances correspond with journey-to-work catchment areas.[17] But even where they do not, all counties contain such catchment areas which involve two or more districts, and indeed there are other rural issues (Green Belts, major recreation areas, rural settlement and transportation policy) which arguably imply some kind of supra-district dimension. The existence of these issues does not necessarily imply that such a dimension could not be provided by institutional means other than those that exist at present (for example, some kind of standing conference of constituent districts). Nor does it imply that the counties as they are presently drawn are the most appropriate size for strategic planning (cf. Derek Senior's 'regions', Royal Commission on Local Government in England, 1969, Vol. 2, or indeed the existing, officially defined regional units).

However, the present two-tier arrangements are likely to be with us for some time, and the problem is how they can be made to work in a way which ensures that structure planning is more than the sum of what constituent districts lobby for (or are prepared to accept) and is something which is a major influence on implementation patterns. How can counties increase their influence on strategic issues (that is, those involving more than one district) in a way which is acceptable to districts? On the face of it the prospects are not promising. Even where the county possessed a series of substantial weapons (the County Structure Plan, the Development Control Agreement, the power of direction, the power of certification), the power balance has come to rest, in most cases, very much with the districts. The present Act removes the power of direction, renders the Development Control Agreement irrelevant, gives districts increased powers over local plans (see Local Government Planning and Land Act 1980, section 88), and raises a series of major questions about how structure plans are going to be implemented. It seems not unlikely that structure plans may follow the path of regional plans – invoked occasionally at public inquiries, but otherwise manipulated or ignored according to what suits the interest of constituent authorities.

There are two signs that even given these new circumstances Structure Plans may become influential documents. In the event they will have to become very different kinds of document. One sign is the increasing, though fragile, unity of purpose within the local government world in face of the perceived threats to local government autonomy generally posed by the new Bill. The other is the tendency in some recent regional plans, and indeed Structure Plans, to develop a challenge outwards towards central government rather than, or as well as, an attempt to look inwards and allocate scarce resources between local authorities. The two issues are not of course unrelated, in that the latter could be seen as both supporting the former and providing a channel for it.

The differences between counties and districts which were accentuated, for perfectly understandable reasons, in the years after reorganisation were one reflection of a divided local government world. 'Organic change' and the vitriolic debate which developed around it was a striking manifestation of that division. The fundamentally opposed positions of the two associations (the ADC and ACC) were a major feature of the debate. But since then the world of local government has changed. For the first time since 1974 the three local government associations have demonstrated unity over a major issue. For the present, and in the foreseeable future, given a government apparently concerned to reduce local government discretion, differences between county and district may well be played down, in a world where differences between central government and local government have become paramount. A similar phenomenon was noted by a number of writers prior to 1972 (see, for example, Lee *et al.*, 1974, pp. 70–4), when many counties and their constituent smaller districts forgot their differences in united stances to oppose proposals for change within their particular areas. At a recent Inlogov seminar on the planning aspects of the Bill it was noticeable that the main issue for most of the (local government) participants was not the division of powers between county and district, but the effect of the proposed changes on the central/local power balance. There is surprisingly little evidence of a widespread victory celebration by the districts. The context of the problem has changed and is seen to have changed. That changing context is likely to affect what happens to the land use planning system over the next few years.

How might this changing context be reflected? There already exist professional networks of planners within counties and their constituent districts committed as much to 'the principles of good planning' as to the political assumptions in the areal units to which they are attached. As already argued, those political assumptions are themselves already changing in a direction that is likely to minimise the problem of county–district relations. In many counties there already exists potential machinery for working on common problems between counties and districts – that is, the various versions of the County Joint Committees and District Joint Committees advocated by Bains, together with officer committees of chief executives, particular chief officers. This machinery has tended to become dormant or be dismantled over the past few years. It may well become increasingly activated in the new situation. There then exists a potentially rich set of cross-cutting networks – political and professional – which could become forums for, among other things, the development of a new, more constructive, county-district approach to planning.

The idea of 'networking' and the associated concepts of 'reticulism', 'facilitating', 'enabling' and the 'multi-organisation', have been developed and applied over the past decade, mainly through the work of John Friend and his associates at the Institute of Operational Research (IOR) (see Friend, Power and Yewlett, 1974; Friend, 1980). This group of ideas is concerned with the conscious building-up and manipulation of the kind of network discussed above, as a way of tackling inter-organisational problems. The normative connotations of these concepts have been criticised by Healey (among others) who argues that they are inappropriate in inter-organisational issues where the participants have different interests (1979, pp. 64–6). Brazier and Harris (1975, p. 256), writing from a similar operations research perspective to that used by the IOR, incorporate Healey's point to some extent by arguing that inter-organisational conflict can be usefully categorised into three types – *technical*, *procedural*, and substantive or *political*. Whereas skilled reticulism cannot hope to resolve substantive political issues – although it can clarify their existence and nature – it can reasonably hope to resolve technical and procedural conflicts.

Town and country planning is moving into an era where the scope for technical and procedural conflict is arguably decreasing (that is, problems of who does what, and classification of applications, will be largely removed by the provisions of the 1980 Act). It may also be moving into a period where county/district conflicts are, if not replaced, at least toned down by increasing central-local conflicts. In this kind of climate one would expect a much greater political readiness to co-operate and develop a common stance on the part of counties and their constituent districts. It has already been argued that this readiness would be backed up by a professional network already predisposed to co-operate. The role of the County Structure Plan could in these circumstances become very different. The potential role of the County Structure Plan as an advocacy document for the county as a whole already has precedents in the form of certain regional plans[18] and metropolitan structure plans.[19] Whatever the impact of County Structure Plans on the policy discretion of local authorities, they do, as statutory documents, have an important *symbolic* significance. Under a perceived threat from the centre, the County Structure Plan could become a vehicle for the expression of a new-found common ground for county and district. Indeed, given these signs of an increased predisposition to co-operate there may develop an inter-organisational climate where it actually proves possible to discuss, develop and agree policy on some of the real issues of, for example, housing and shopping policy, on which it has so far proved difficult to develop a county perspective that has any real hope of being implemented. The changing context of county–district relations could, therefore, begin to produce a very different pattern of interaction from that which prevailed in the research discussed here.

NOTES: CHAPTER 8

This chapter is a modified and extended version of an article written by myself and Nicholas Moore which appeared in *Policy and Politics*, vol. 7, no. 2, 1979, under the title 'County/district relations in shire and metropolitan counties in the field of town and country planning: a comparison'. I am grateful for the permission of *Policy and Politics* to reproduce the material here.

1 The classification used is an amalgam of J. D. Thompson's classification of types of inter-organisational interdependence and L. R. Pondy's classification of forms of inter-organisational conflict. See Thompson, 1967, pp. 54–7, and Pondy, 1969, pp. 296–320.

2 It contains elements of hierarchical dependence in situations where the district has acted as development control agent for the county, over a specified range of county matters.

3 It was of course the case that both counties and districts had powers to determine planning applications under the 1972 Act. However, the way in which county matters were classified, the extent of delegation of certain types of county matters to districts and the ability of the county to comment on certain classes of district-determined applications varied considerably.

4 This argument also applies to a lesser extent to large ex-municipal boroughs, particularly where these were accustomed to a considerable degree of delegated power from the county.

5 In Cheshire, for example, six out of eight district planning officers had had previous experience with the county planning department.

6 County revenue expenditure in Cheshire was in 1976/7 running at £165m per annum, compared with £3m for the average district.

7 The major exception to this generalisation was in the field of town and country planning where it was apparent that the districts enjoyed the balance of power.

8 The number of districts in metropolitan counties varies from four to seven, with the exception of Greater Manchester which contains ten.

9 For example, Greater Manchester Council's attempts to provide free school milk throughout its authority's area in 1976.

10 The West Midlands Structure Plan, which has existed since reorganisation, is somewhat untypical in that it was to a large extent an amalgam of district structure plans existing before 1974.

11 For example, through the way in which county matters were defined (see note 3, above).

12 As a quick skim through any structure or local plan documents will demonstrate.

13 Due largely to the influence of McLoughlin, 1969, and Chadwick, 1971.

14 Most definitions of planning incorporate an element reflecting the desirability of a long-term view. See Faludi, 1973b, chapter 2.

15 See Lindblom, 1959, for a concise statement of the theory of incrementalism.

16 Although given the tightness of the way the boundaries of metropolitan counties were drawn in 1974 it could be argued that the metropolitan counties fall within such catchment areas.

17 Notably in Avon, Cleveland and Humberside, the new 1974 counties.

18 See, for example, the *Strategic Plan for the Northern Region* (Northern Region Strategy Team, 1977).

19 For example, the Merseyside Structure Plan – see Struthers and Williamson, 1979, p. 168.

9

Area Management and Responsive Policy-Making

BARBARA A. WEBSTER

It is often the case that management innovations which appear simple and logical in concept prove difficult to put into practice. Those who propose new approaches to policy-making or planning in local government often pay scant attention to the way the ideas can be translated into practice and underestimate the difficulties and resistance that may be encountered. Those in local authorities who have responsibility for policy-making activities often themselves fail to trace through the implications of the ideas and give insufficient thought to how they can be applied in the context of a particular authority. The development of area management is no different from previous innovations in this respect.

The concern of this chapter is to evaluate recent efforts to develop an area perspective in local authority policy-making through the introduction of area management.[1] Policy-making is here interpreted widely, so as to include the making of decisions concerning the authority's objectives and how they will be achieved, decisions about the allocation of resources, and the establishment of guidelines governing how services are to be provided and to whom. Of specific interest is the way these decisions affect the future level and nature of services, and the future actions of the authority, in particular geographical areas or neighbourhoods. The chapter will examine both the philosophy underlying the area management approach and the way that philosophy has been put into practice. Different authorities have adopted quite different schemes which attempt to alter or adapt the existing policy planning system in a variety of ways, and the effectiveness of these alternatives in achieving the aims embodied in the original philosophy is assessed. How successful have they been in bringing about changes in the decision-making processes, and what difference have they made to the substantive nature of the decisions themselves?

THE PHILOSOPHY OF THE AREA MANAGEMENT APPROACH

It is difficult to attribute the development of the area management approach to local authority policy-making to the influence of a single coherent philosophy. Rather it can be seen as a response to a set of related ideas, articulated in different forms by a number of commentators on the operations of local government. The views espoused often exhibit different emphases, which derive from their different theoretical and/or ideological perspectives on the role of local authorities and their functioning in practice. Central to most of them, however, is a concern with the notion of 'responsiveness' and a criticism that current policy-making in local government somehow fails to respond to the needs and problems of the community or environment it serves. More specifically, local authorities are seen as insensitive to the needs and priorities of particular areas within their boundaries and ineffective in designing and providing services to meet them. This perceived failure has been seen in the United States as providing an important 'administrative' argument for some form of decentralisation in local government (Schmandt, 1969; Yates, 1974). In Britain it led to an interest in the development of area management, which was seen by central government as 'a means of adapting local government organisation so that it can respond more sensitively and effectively to the particular needs of areas' (Department of the Environment, 1974).

This concept of responsiveness is, however, a rather generalised notion, and it is necessary to examine three somewhat distinct strands of thought within it to begin to appreciate its implications for the way in which local authority policy decisions are made. These arguments are concerned with the diverse socioeconomic character of different areas and the resulting diversity of needs, the need for co-ordinated approach to local problems and the need for policy decisions to reflect more closely local preferences and priorities.

Meeting the Diversity of Needs

Geographical areas or neighbourhoods within the jurisdiction of a particular local authority, it is argued, differ in their social and economic characteristics. They exhibit different population structures, different industrial and employment structures, different physical features and different ethnic compositions. These differences create varying needs for local authority services and different local problems. Proponents of area management argue that local authorities should recognise these differences and adjust their policies and provide services so as to take account of them. And it is not simply that the amount and quality of service required may vary but that the type of service which is appropriate may also differ.

The prevailing tendency, it is suggested, is for local authorities to adopt policies which apply to the whole authority and to provide uniform levels of service. A uniform standard of service may be adopted because of a principle that all areas should be treated alike or in order to avoid any charges of discrimination or favourable treatment (V. Ostrom, 1975). It can arise from the application of professional standards of service provision which take little or no account of the circumstances which can result in varying needs for those services

(Stewart, 1980). Open space standards, for example, take no account of variations in the proportion of children in the population, the availability of garden space, or the mobility of residents in different areas; yet these factors could be argued to result in different levels of need for open space. Uniformity may also be encouraged because it is seen as good administrative practice to treat all cases or areas in a like manner (Stewart, 1977). Whatever the reason for it, formal uniformity in provision can lead to unfairness or inequity (Stewart, 1975).

This tendency towards uniformity has been seen by some only to be reinforced by recent developments in policy-making, specifically the development of corporate planning. Together with the emergence of larger governmental units, policy-making approaches which focus on the need for local authorities to plan their activities as a whole in order to secure the most effective use of resources have encouraged administrators 'to perceive the environment as uniform in its needs and homogeneous in its objectives' (Benington and Skelton, 1972). The same writers went on to suggest that data collection and analysis to support policy decisions related to an aggregated, often city-wide, level and did not reveal important differentials in the distribution of needs in the population.

Thus an area approach to policy-making is believed to allow these difficulties to be overcome by emphasising the fine grain, and enabling policies and resource decisions to be tailored to the specific needs and problems of particular localities. This implies, for example, that an authority might vary the amount and accessibility of open space, provide different types of recreation facilities and adopt different policies, for instance, towards charging for those facilities, in different areas.

A Co-Ordinated Response to Local Problems

An improved response to diverse area needs and problems could simply be seen as requiring a greater recognition of such variations and for them to be reflected in the policies and priorities of individual services, such as housing or education. For many of its advocates, however, an area approach to the policy-making would imply more than this. It would be concerned to develop a more co-ordinated or comprehensive approach to the needs and problems of particular areas. The argument is that some of those problems are not amenable to the functional approach, founded on professional specialisms, typical of the organisation and planning systems of many authorities (Greenwood *et al.*, 1976). Urban problems are often complex, highly interrelated, and locality-specific. Thus in planning future provision in a particular area, the authority must encompass these relationships if duplication and non-complementary policies and actions are to be avoided and appropriate solutions developed.

Important antecedents of this view can be found in many of the initiatives undertaken in the late 1960s and early 1970s which were concerned with urban problems. The Shelter Neighbourhood Action Project forcefully made the point that the problems experienced in Granby were of a highly interdependent nature, and their report catalogued the difficulties caused by the inability of the local authority to respond corporately to particular problems such as multi-occupation. Central to the solution of urban problems was seen to be the establishment of a governmental apparatus which could co-ordinate 'new policies down through every level' (Shelter, 1973). The experiences of this project, and its recommendations on local authority planning and management, had, it has been suggested, an important influence on the urban strategy subsequently developed by government (McConaghy, 1978). Both the Urban Guideline Studies and the Inner Area Studies, initiated by the Department of the Environment in 1972, expressed the need for a comprehensive or 'total' approach to the problems of particular areas. The Sunderland Study, in proposing a community review process as the basis for local authority planning, argued that grouping problems on an area basis would enable the local authority 'to identify problems that might be overlooked by using only a functional division' (Department of the Environment, 1973a). The relationships between different problems at the local level would also need to be carefully examined if the solutions or actions identified were not to prove ineffective because they were based on inadequate analysis of the essential nature of the problems. The Inner Area Studies have further documented difficulties caused by the lack of co-ordination between different services or departments of the authority (Department of the Environment, 1977a).

There is another case to be made for a co-ordinated approach, based not on the complex and interrelated nature of local problems, but on the different pattern of needs likely to be found in different localities. If the need for individual services can vary spatially, then overall patterns of needs can vary, giving rise to different priorities for service provision. Where the functional perspective predominates, local authority policy-making systems will tend to be based on priorities determined between different services, or between different aspects within a particular service, with area priorities generally being considered once this overall framework has been set. Yet local priorities between services may not be the same as those at an authority-wide level. Thus if the most effective use is to be made of the resources available, the allocation of those resources needs to be considered in relation to the overall needs and problems of particular areas.

Essentially this is the argument for corporate planning applied at the local level. The failure of corporate planning systems built at the centre of the authority to meet the special needs of deprived neighbourhoods has been identified in several studies (Department of the Environment, 1973a; Shelter, 1973). The Sunderland Study pointed out that corporate planning systems continued to emphasise the functional, with the focus being on 'functional needs such as housing and leisure' (op. cit.). It is difficult to sustain this criticism since in a number of authorities corporate planning has also focused on cross-functional issues, particularly in relation to client groups such as the elderly or under-5s. None the less it remains true that policy planning systems have not generally encouraged local authorities to focus on wide-ranging issues such as deprivation, or on problems experienced at the local level (Stewart, Spencer and Webster, 1976; Stewart, 1980).

Recognition of these deficiencies led Stewart (1975) to suggest that what is required is a local authority organisation which can recognise and respond to problems at different scales, in particular to those at the authority-wide city level and those at the more local neighbourhood level. An area approach to policy-making was perceived as a necessary and natural extension of corporate planning:

> The organization based merely upon the city, often built on a powerful central organization, neglects immediate and often pressing needs, but the organization based merely upon the locality neglects the capacity for fundamental change. What is required . . . is for a multi-levelled management and political process . . . The local authority which recognises diversity would add to the corporate dimension at the centre of an area dimension at the periphery. (pp. 14 and 18)

Thus a whole new dimension, the area dimension, is to be introduced into the policy process. This view was certainly reflected in thinking about the development of area management. The Liverpool Inner Area Study, in establishing an experimental area management scheme, saw the fostering of a corporate approach to the area's needs and problems and to the allocation of resources as one of its major functions. This concern to bring the corporate approach down to the local level was later echoed in the consultation paper on area management sent to urban authorities by the Department of the Environment (1974). It was seen by the Department as 'a means of identifying priorities and objectives at area level, seeing their relevance locally and putting them in their district-wide context' which would help the authority to 'analyse problems, formulate policies, and monitor their effects in a corporate way at an area level'.

Reflecting Community-Defined Problems and Priorities

For some the argument for the area approach to policy-making is not so much a question of recognising another scale of dimension in the policy process as a concern with the balance of influence between the local authority and the community in that process. This view goes beyond a recognition that the views and opinions of those living or working in a particular area may be helpful in identifying and understanding needs and problems. It argues that 'responsiveness' implies reacting to local perceptions or definitions of needs and local priorities for service provision. Different preferences may arise from variations in the socio-economic character of the population, or from the unique geographical characteristics of a particular area, and it is suggested that:

> Provision of identical services in two neighbourhoods can hardly be considered equitable if the residents of one area deeply desire the service while those of the other feel no need for it and would prefer

to see an allocation of funds to other services. (Rich, 1977)

Local authority policy processes have been criticised for failing to provide opportunities for such local preferences and priorities to be expressed. Where efforts to enable public participation have occurred, these have been limited in scope and structured by the authority so as to afford little real public influence (Damer and Hague, 1971; Batley, 1972). In particular, participation has tended to occur at the stage when the authority is moving towards formal approval of policies and decisions about resources, thus excluding the community from the critical earlier stages of defining problems and issues and formulating possible policies (Benington and Skelton, 1972).

The Coventry Community Development Project argued that, if anything, the early development of corporate planning reduced rather than enhanced the potential for the expression of local community views. The tendency to concentrate on authority-wide issues, discussed earlier, was seen to be associated with a concentration on more general and abstract goals which obscured rather than illuminated the different priorities, and conflicting interests, of different sections of the population, such as geographical areas of client groups. Corporate planning was having a centralising and de-politicising effect on policy-making. Not only did the techniques and modes of analysis employed mystify the process and make it more difficult for elected members to control and determine policy decisions, but those who represented the interests of specific neighbourhoods within the formal political system, the backbench members, were increasingly remote from those decisions (op. cit.). These themes have been reinforced by later studies (Davis, McIntosh and Williams, 1977; Cockburn, 1977). While the nature of corporate planning systems is more varied than these writers imply (see Chapter 3 of this book), and the centralisation of political power may be due to increased politicisation or external circumstances rather than corporate planning itself (Hinings *et al.*, 1980), few policy-making systems have been structured to facilitate the expression of local views and priorities.

The case for an area approach to policy-making is, then, that it would make the process more democratic by allowing greater influence for community demands and priorities in the decisions made. Opinions vary on how far this could be achieved by enhancing the role of the backbench member, through, for example, area committees, and how far it implies the direct involvement of the general public and residents' groups, or even some form of community control (Stewart, 1974; Yates, 1974; Davis *et al.*, 1977). The concept is, however, as put by Benington and Skelton, of an 'inductive policy process' which would begin with concrete particulars and the definition of local problems. It would comprise an open debate involving ward councillors, residents' groups and fieldworkers at all the key stages of the policy process, including the identification of problems and issues, the formulation of policy, and monitoring and review. Policy-making would become a 'bottom-up' rather than a 'top-down' process (Benington and Skelton, 1972).

DEVELOPMENTS IN PRACTICE

Although it is possible to identify the general philosophy which has underpinned the development of an area management approach, the extent to which, and the way in which, the different strands of thought have been embodied in the objectives of the area management schemes varies from authority to authority. As a result they have adopted different types of approach in attempting to develop an area perspective in policy-making and resource allocation within the authority. An appreciation of how the philosophy has been applied in practice thus depends on an understanding of these different approaches and the role they play in the authority's policy planning system.

The schemes vary in their objectives, their organisational features and their activities.[2] The most important aspects of variation in the present context can, however, be conveniently summarised in three characteristics: the power or decision-making responsibility afforded to area management in the policy process; whether the approach seeks to change the nature of the policy process itself in a systematic way; and the extent to which the approach emphasises a community input to policy and resource allocation decisions. Thus different approaches can be broadly typified according to the following three dichotomies, although it should be noted that the categories are inevitably simplified and do not reflect fully the differences in emphasis which exist.

Executive/advisory. This dichotomy identifies the extent to which the scheme, whatever organisational form it takes, has an executive responsibility for the ongoing policy processes of the authority. Approaches in the executive category would involve the delegation of some degree of power, for at least part of the policy process, to an area committee or other area-based elected member/officer group. In the other type of approach such a body would be ascribed a purely advisory function. It would be intended only to provide information and proffer advice on the needs and priorities of a particular neighbourhood to those bodies which do have executive responsibility for policy and resource allocation decisions.

Systematic/ad hoc. This categorisation enables approaches which are concerned to change or alter systematically the policy processes of the authority, so that they take account of the needs of particular areas, to be differentiated from those which adopt a more *ad hoc* style in attempting to influence specific decisions of importance to the area. The former is purposive in its attempt to identify and analyse policy issues and feed them into decision-making, and often aims to be comprehensive in its coverage. By contrast the *ad hoc* approach tends to be much more reactive in style, responding to specific, substantive, policy issues as and when they arise. Such issues may be raised by area management itself, by other bodies within the authority, or externally to the local authority.

Authority-oriented/community-oriented. This dichotomy is intended to distinguish broadly between those approaches which are concerned with improving the authority's response to neighbourhood needs and problems as defined by the authority, and those concerned with responding to needs and problems defined by the community. Thus it focuses on who is involved in developing the area approach to policy-making. The term 'community' is not intended to imply some cohesive section of the public which has common interests, but is used here to refer to all those who have a responsibility or special interest in a particular area, whether it be the local councillors who represent it, the field officers who work in the area, residents' groups, or the general public. Approaches vary in the extent to which they involve these groups and most have some form of 'community' input. However, it is generally possible to distinguish schemes which are primarily oriented towards those at the periphery, whether or not they are formally part of the local authority organisation, and approaches which are predominantly oriented towards the centre of the authority.

Executive Approaches

Approaches which involve some executive responsibility for policy-making being afforded to an area body imply a significant change in the existing structure of decision-making in the authority. In theory, at least, some decisions on the nature of services, priorities for service provision and resource allocation could be delegated to local committees (Stewart, 1974; Davis *et al.*, 1977). In the United States such responsibilities have been delegated to bodies controlled by local residents or community groups, although such delegation occurs most often in relation to single services or functions, such as health and education, rather than in relation to the whole range of local authority services (Yates, 1976a). Although some of the area management schemes in Britain have delegated power to spend specially allocated budgets, these are usually very small and are not intended to be spent on normal services and activities.[3] Generally speaking, the schemes have little executive responsibility for policy-making and in no case does it relate to the formal approval of policy and resource decisions.

The only authority where a substantial executive function could be regarded to exist is in Middlesbrough, where a number of Area Policy Subcommittees have a key and integral role in the annual policy process of the authority (see Figure 9.1). Having regard for the prior recommendations of three other Policy Subcommittees, concerned with Recreation, Housing and Industrial Development, the committees have responsibility for preparing a policy plan for their area embracing all the services and activities of the council. These plans contain a statement of objectives over fifteen years, a statement of issues and evaluation of alternatives, recommendations for proposed courses of action and a work programme for the following five years, with resource implications. Thus the committees have some executive responsibility for the stages of the policy process concerned with the identification of problems and issues and the formulation of policies, being able to establish officer working parties to undertake analyses of specific policy issues. Formal adoption of the plans, in terms of their incorporation in the annual Middlesbrough Policy Plan, however,

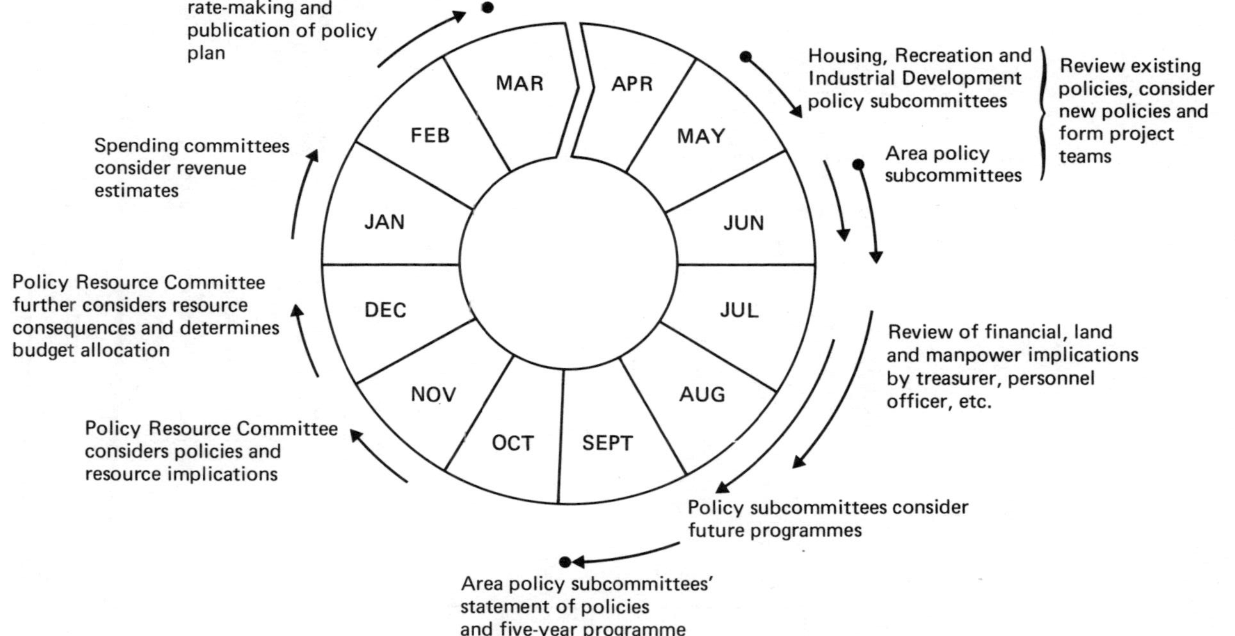

Note: The outer cycle refers to the activities of the area policy subcommittees and the inner cycle refers to the activities of other committees.

Figure 9.1 *Middlesbrough policy process.*

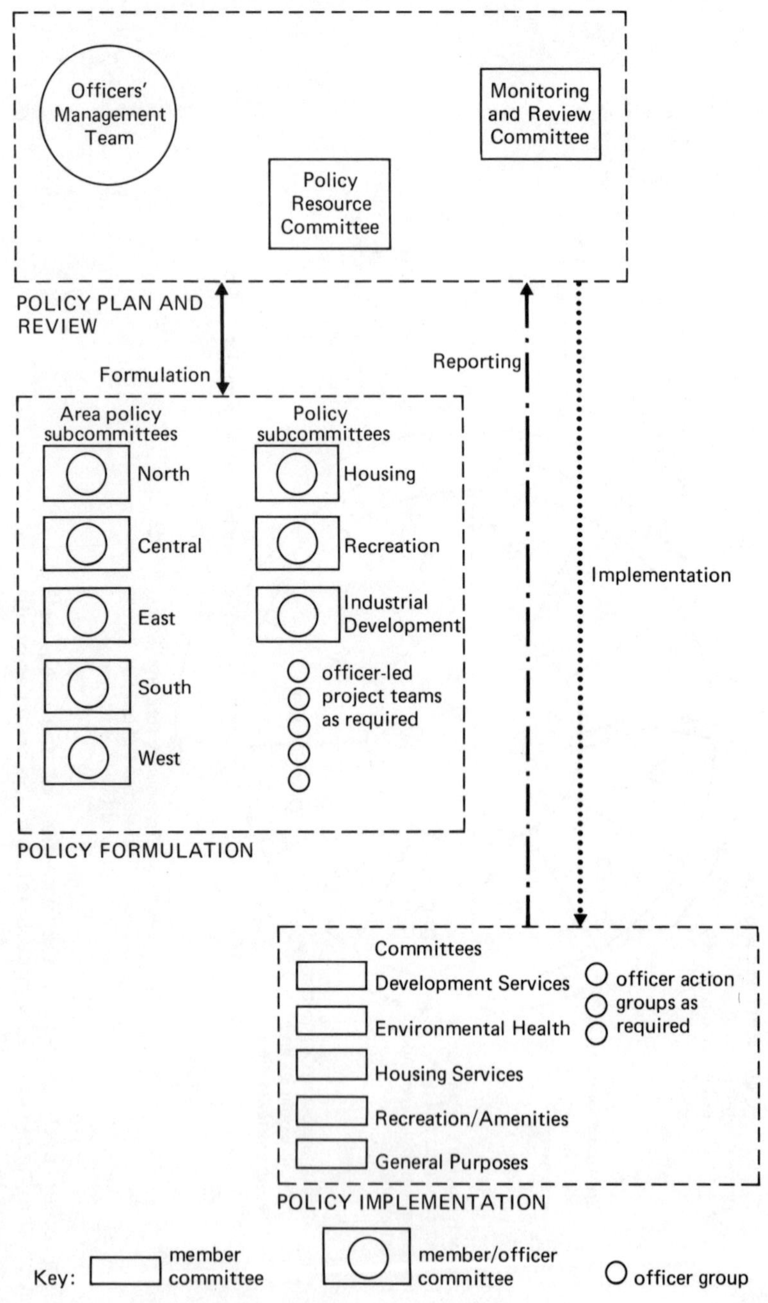

Figure 9.2 *Policy-making in Middlesbrough.*

remains the prerogative of the central Policy Resource Committee of the council, and policy implementation is explicitly separated from policy formulation, being the responsibility of a number of service or functional committees (see Figure 9.2). Although monitoring and review is also a central responsibility, involving the Policy Resource Committee and a special Monitoring and Review Committee, the Area Policy Subcommittees consider the impact of existing policies when developing their plans for subsequent years.

The approach in Middlesbrough is systematic, operating through a regular policy cycle and designed to achieve a comprehensive approach which will 'unite council policy, across a range of services and areas, into an integrated statement set out in a single policy document' (Harrop *et al.*, 1978). The policy processes of the authority have been changed so as to incorporate the area perspective as an essential part of them. It is, however, authority-oriented rather than community-oriented. Although in establishing the Area Policy Subcommittees the authority was aware of a need for increased and meaningful consultation with local groups, public participation in the activities of the committees has been limited. The committees involve ward members, but there is an overall balance between 'local' and 'non-local' members with six of the leading members and committee chairmen of the council being represented on each of them. The tendency, then, is for the approach to be centralised, operating at a high level and involving senior officers, often chief officers, rather than fieldworkers with an area responsibility. The seniority of the officers and involvement of key politicians may none the less be essential to the effectiveness of the committees, given their concern with major policy matters.

Advisory Approaches

The advisory approach relies on feeding information about the area, analyses of local issues, and views and recommendations concerning neighbourhood needs and priorities for resource allocation, into the existing policy processes of the authority. Individual authorities vary in the combination of these inputs which is utilised, but all the advisory approaches essentially adopt the role of advocate of neighbourhood concerns and interests. The area committees or groups do not have the power to act independently at any stage of the policy process. They rely on influencing and bringing pressure to bear on other bodies. This type of approach to policy-making is much more prevalent amongst the monitored authorities, indeed the development of area management in general can be characterised as advisory rather than executive. However, because individual schemes differ with respect to their location on the other two characteristics, systematic/*ad hoc* and authority-oriented/community-oriented, a number of quite distinctive variants have emerged. They are most usefully considered by examining systematic and *ad hoc* approaches separately.

A Systematic Area Perspective

Both Stockport and Liverpool sought to introduce a systematic area

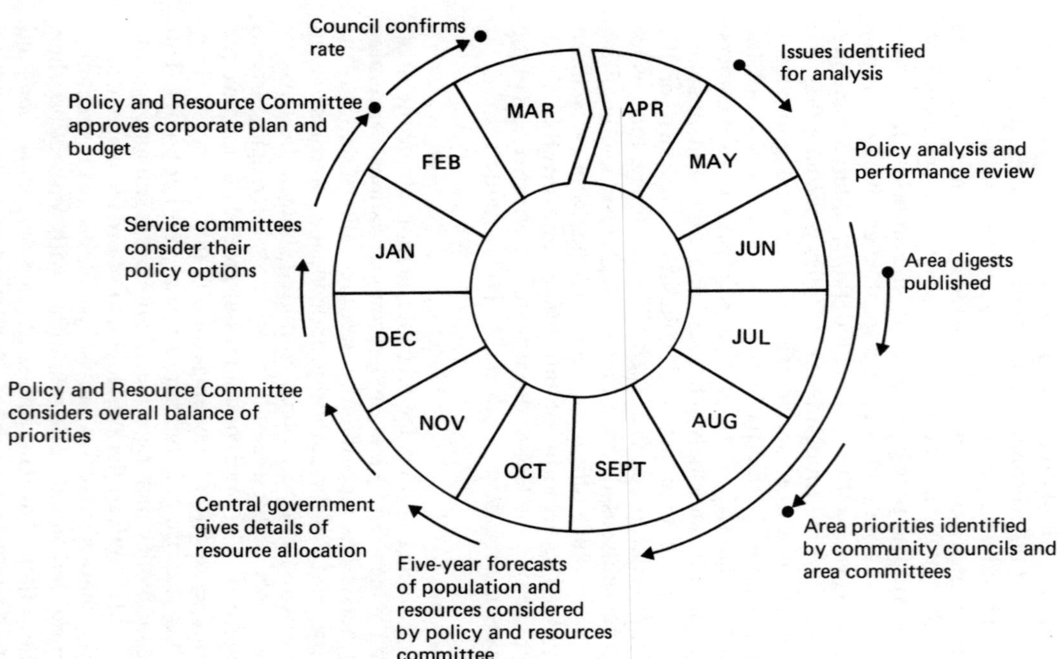

Note: The outer cycle refers to the activities of the area committees and the inner cycle refers to the activities of the main council committees.

Figure 9.3 *Stockport annual planning budgetary cycle, 1974/5 (after Hambleton, 1978).*

perspective in policy-making, in the first case by developing existing policy processes and in the second by introducing new policy processes. They also differed in that the Stockport scheme emphasised a community orientation, whereas the one in Liverpool was authority-oriented. These differences in style will become clearer from a description of the two approaches.

The proposals for the area organisation established in Stockport embodied both a concern to facilitate a corporate approach to planning and policy-making at the local level and the desire to make the local authority more accessible and responsive to the needs and aspirations of residents in different parts of the borough. Prior to reorganisation the council had encouraged the development of community councils and created a special relationship with those recognised by the authority.[4] The new council, building on the earlier foundations, established eight generalist area committees, comprised of the appropriate ward members, supported by three area co-ordinators and a system of information and advice centres (Harrop *et al.*, 1978; Hambleton, 1978).

The expression of these concerns in the new organisation, combined with the fact that corporate planning was already well established within the authority, led to a consideration of how opportunities could be provided for local needs and problems to be identified and fed into the corporate process. In the first financial year of the authority, 1974/5, an attempt was made to introduce an area dimension into the annual planning budgetary cycle of the authority through the Priority Problems Exercise. The process is described in detail by Hambleton (1975) but the main stages are shown in Figure 9.3. Initially the authority prepared area digests which provided a fairly simple statement of local services and some census information on socio-economic conditions in each area committee area. These were circulated to the community councils who were asked to list priorities for action in their locality. The area committees then considered these and prepared statements of local problems, together with their recommended actions, what those actions were intended to achieve, and the order of priority of the various recommendations. These recommendations, together with their priority rating, were forwarded to the service committees for consideration when developing their policy options reports, which fed into the annual corporate plan and budget statement. Thus the exercise was intended to advise service committees on the identification of needs and problems and the formulation of policy.

This effort to establish a systematic and comprehensive consideration of area needs in the policy-making of the council, providing the area dimension, was not sustained subsequently. The potential for the area organisation to be involved in corporate planning was greatly affected by changes to a more centralised and inward-looking corporate process, instituted in 1975–7 as a response to the cutbacks in public expenditure (Harrop *et al.*, 1978; Hambleton, 1978). There was a concern that the Exercise would raise expectations for expenditure which could not be fulfilled, and certainly criticism has been made of the Exercise that it focused too much on the identification of extensive lists of needs and problems, paying insufficient attention to opportunities and ways of saving resources (Hambleton, 1978). In any event it was questionable how far the approach had in fact been concerned with policy, many of the issues raised by the community being matters relating to the day-to-day provision and operation of services, rather than priorities for future services or policy suggestions.

Although the area committees' formal role in the annual planning/budgetary cycle ceased, there was continued support in some areas for the development of a community input and in subsequent years it took the form of enabling and assisting community councils in exploring particular local issues and bringing them to the attention of the authority. This community issues approach was quite different from the earlier Priority Problems Exercise in several important respects. First, although the approach as originally conceived had a strong community orientation, the role of residents' groups was restricted by the standard format for the presentation of local priorities through area committees. Moreover it was felt that insufficient time and information had been provided to community councils for them to formulate useful comments. In identifying community issues the initiative lay very much more with the community councils and the approach, being divorced from the annual cycle, became much more *ad hoc* in nature. Specific issues were selected as important, following consultation with local councillors, and then a more extensive analysis of the problems undertaken and proposals generated, with the support of the area co-ordinator. Reviews were undertaken of, for example, shopping centre provision, the local transport system and entertainment provision, and presented to the authority. Thus the focus became a more detailed and sophisticated input to policy formulation, but on a very restricted set of issues.

Underlying the system established in Liverpool lay a similar concern to foster a corporate approach to the needs and problems of areas, in this instance one particular part of the city called District 'D'. The proposals of the Inner Area Consultants for area management made it clear that they envisaged the establishment of a corporate planning process for the area, which would be comprehensive in its coverage.

> The first main field for area management would be the identification and definition of corporate planning objectives for the area based on an analysis of its needs from the perspective of individuals and communities in the area. The work would involve an evaluation and reconciliation of the short and long term policies being developed for each local authority service by each department, and an assessment of how they meet local needs and circumstances. The aim would be to recommend programmes for action by each department that would, in combination with each other, represent a co-ordinated and socially effective programme. Initially, implementation of this function would take the form of participation in the

> annual budget cycle, by preparing evidence on the allocation and use of resources for the area as a whole, covering all District Council expenditure directly affecting the area, both revenue and capital. To this end, the budget proposals of each programme department should be scrutinised and reported on by area management before decisions are finally made on next year's budget. (Liverpool Inner Area Study, 1974)

The consultants also envisaged a community orientation for the approach, seeing the concept of area management as implying the delegation of some of the authority's responsibilities to subordinate committees and officers and efforts to bring government closer to the community it is designed to serve. Those involved in implementing the scheme, however, were primarily concerned to influence central decision-making in the authority as it affected District 'D', and chose to concentrate on corporate planning activities rather than community development. This revised orientation was reflected in the fact that the Area Management Unit, which provided officer support to the District 'D' Committee, was located in an office in the town centre rather than in the area itself.

Although the Liverpool scheme had similar objectives to Stockport in wanting to create a systematic approach to policy-making for an area, the nature of the approach differed because of the different contexts of policy-making in the two authorities. While corporate planning was well established centrally in Stockport, there was no similar tradition in Liverpool which was organised along strong functional/professional lines. The climate afforded little support for an approach based on generating a comprehensive view of needs and problems, as 'the city's corporate management system instituted under the McKinsey reorganisation fell into disfavour and effectively disappeared on local government reorganisation' (Duerden, 1979). Hence area management was seen as an alternative means of developing corporate working within the authority as a whole (Harrop *et al.*, 1978). It had to establish a new corporate policy process rather than develop and extend an existing one.

The Area Management Unit began by drawing up a programme structure for the area and identifying a number of key issues, in an attempt to implement the comprehensive corporate approach intended by the consultants. But this type of approach proved unrealistic, given the staff resources available and the lack of appropriate information. The idea of a regular annual input to budget plans based on analysis of existing expenditure could not be achieved, because the area resource analysis undertaken by the Inner Area Consultants (Liverpool Inner Area Study, 1976) was not repeated in subsequent years as they had anticipated. Thus in the absence of the analytical capacity to build up a rigorous system of area-based corporate planning, the Area Management Unit decided to adopt a more selective approach to policy analysis on a limited number of issues. Studies were undertaken, for example, of the availability of land and buildings for industrial development, the problems of vacant land and derelict housing and current provision and council policy for services for the under-5s. The reports produced were intended primarily for officer-level discussions, and were aimed at influencing the policy and resource allocation decisions made by various bodies in the authority on these specific matters.

Ad Hoc *Inputs to Policy-Making*

In both Stockport and Liverpool the failure to sustain a systematic area approach to policy-making led the schemes to become much more pragmatic in attempting to influence decisions on specific substantive issues. None the less their initial efforts can be clearly distinguished from the more consciously *ad hoc* methods adopted elsewhere. The approach in Newcastle, Haringey and Dudley has generally been one of taking up specific policy or resource matters as they arise, or are identified as important, and pressing for decisions in accordance with area interests. There was no explicit effort, at least in the earlier phases of the schemes, to alter or adapt the existing policy processes of the authority as a whole.[5] Since two authorities which favoured a systematic area perspective found the *ad hoc* approach the only viable one in practice, understanding the role of the latter in policy-making is all the more important. This role is considered in relation to four different types of change that the approach has sought to achieve: to change existing policies or plans of the council; to change local authority priorities in resource allocation; to develop new policy initiatives or new forms of service provision by the authority; to influence the policies, plans and programmes of other agencies. The following examples illustrate for each of these themes the way area management has been involved.

(1) *Changing existing policies and plans*. The Area Management Advisory Committee in Haringey has responsibility for public participation on matters relating to the area, and early in the life of the project two major and controversial planning issues were referred to the committee for advice and comment. One involved proposals for the redevelopment of part of the area and the other an application to allow the redevelopment of an individual site for a hypermarket. In both instances local opinion was against the Planning Committee's proposals. The Area Management Advisory Committee mounted an extensive programme of public participation, and the willingness of the local councillors to fight the plans combined with the capacity of area management to channel public opinion led to both redevelopments being rejected by the council.

Plans for the development of a large new private residential estate which had already been accepted by the council in Dudley were re-examined through area management. The officer team was particularly concerned that insufficient attention had been given to the provision of community facilities. After extensive consideration had been given to the matter, area management proposed that the plans for the new school to be built be adapted to make it suitable for community use.

They persuaded the private developers concerned to accept responsibility for 50 per cent of the cost of adapting the building.

In both these instances area management was largely responding to initiatives within the authority. In Newcastle the close liaison between officers, councillors and the public has often encouraged the identification of issues by local people themselves. This led one of the priority area teams to take up the idea of the development of a community school as a focus for the area. This was strongly supported by parents but was contrary to the Education Department's established policy of socially mixed catchments. The team explored how the community school concept had been developed elsewhere and pressed for one to be established. As a result of these efforts some of the funds available through the Inner City Partnership are to be used for this purpose. Although it is questionable whether this would have occurred in the absence of special resources, the scheme did bring established council policy into question and has helped to lessen opposition within the authority towards the community school concept.

(2) *Changing priorities in resource allocation*. The issues of resource allocation encompass the use of manpower, land, buildings and equipment, as well as the use of financial resources. Area management has sought to change the priority of one area *vis-à-vis* other parts of the authority, the emphasis attached to different aspects of a particular service, and the priority given to different types of service as they affect a particular area. An example of the first is the attempt in Liverpool to change the priority of District 'D' in the authority's pre-school provision programme. The Area Management Unit undertook an analysis of the need for pre-school classes in different parts of the authority and compared them with existing services and the established priorities of the education service. Although they felt the report demonstrated a clear case for increased priority for District 'D', the scheme was unable to persuade those responsible to alter existing priority rankings. However, a pre-school experiment was subsequently established by area management itself using special funds.

The availability of a local budget was crucial in enabling the area management elected-member working party in Dudley to tidy up a number of small eyesore sites in the area, thus changing priorities within a particular service. The smaller sites were not being dealt with by the authority, for the working group on derelict land was concentrating its attention on the larger sites which would attract government grants. As a result of area management's efforts most of the small sites have been cleared, those remaining not being in council ownership.

The more substantial budgets provided for the priority areas in Newcastle have been used to supplement departmental spending on services, for example, hiring extra road-sweepers, social workers and advice staff and providing additional books for local libraries. The original intention of the scheme was that such expenditure should be carried by the appropriate normal service budget after the first year, but this additional financial burden was not welcomed by service committees and departments and the idea has not been adhered to. Given the size of team budgets and the inability to transfer responsibility in this way, the scheme has only been able to influence overall patterns of inter-area service provision in a very marginal way. A large proportion of the teams' budgets have, however, been spent on leisure and recreation facilities, including play provision and the laying-out of allotments. This service was most affected by recent expenditure cuts in the authority, and the activities of the Priority Area Teams have not only resulted in a higher level of recreation provision in those areas than would otherwise have been the case, but have helped to change attitudes in the council so as to increase the overall status and priority accorded to recreation provision.

(3) *Developing new policies and services*. The focus on the needs and problems experienced in particular areas has in some cases led area management to identify needs which had hitherto gone unrecognised by the authority, often because they did not fit neatly into the responsibilities of a particular service. As a result of the involvement of the Haringey scheme with the problems experienced by ethnic minorities in the area, the need for translation and interpreting services was identified. Following discussions with council departments and voluntary organisations the Area Management Unit proposed the introduction of a borough-wide translation service to be used for all major pieces of information about council facilities and services. This proposal was accepted by the council. In Newcastle some of the teams became interested in the problems experienced by elderly people living in high-rise flats. Although initially they helped to solve some relatively minor day-to-day management problems, this developed into a wider concern with the housebound elderly and led to a survey of their needs. By bringing this issue and information about the problems to the attention of the authority the teams have heightened awareness of needs not currently catered for, and as a result a new working party has been established to consider future provision for the elderly.

(4) *Influencing other agencies*. Some of the area management schemes have identified issues of local importance which have resulted in attempts to influence the policies, plans and programmes of agencies other than the local authority itself. The residents in one of the Priority Areas in Newcastle were especially concerned about the Area Health Authority's plan to close the local hospital. The team took up the issue, persuaded representatives from the Area Health Authority to attend meetings with the residents, and pressed the health authority to maintain the building for local health care provision, or at least some form of community use. In the event they were unsuccessful because of opposition from a group within the local authority who wanted to use the site for an alternative purpose, as well as from the health authority itself. There was also concern about the lack of cancer screening within the priority wards, and in this case the special Priority Area funds were used to provide the service, which proved very successful in terms of

take-up. This demonstration of the need for, and effectiveness of, cancer screening will be used to bring pressure to bear on the Area Health Authority to give higher priority to community health services in the inner city areas. A further example is provided by the community councils in Stockport who undertook a study of the local transport system which identified a number of changes which would improve services in the area. The Area Committee persuaded the appropriate agencies to reschedule some existing bus and rail services and introduce new ones to meet the needs identified.

Thus the *ad hoc* approach has in many instances led to issues of local concern being taken up within the authority. Many have been initiated by residents and community groups, some have stemmed from the proposals of the local authority and other agencies, and others have been identified by area management itself, based on knowledge of local problems and conditions and awareness of gaps in, or inadequacy of, existing policies. Area management's role has often been one of identifying problems, bringing them to the attention of other groups or bodies in the authority and making recommendations on what decisions should or should not be made. On occasions, however, the schemes have been involved in formulating appropriate policies, based on a more extensive survey and analysis of specific problems, rather than simply advocating a particular course of action.

THE IMPACT OF AREA MANAGEMENT APPROACHES TO POLICY-MAKING

Assessment of the impact of area management approaches to policy-making can be considered at two different levels. At the first level we can examine to what extent they have influenced the local authority's policy-making and resource allocation: have they altered the nature of policy planning processes within the authority; and how far have they resulted in changes in policy decisions or the initiation of new policies and services? Essentially this is concerned with their impact on the internal operations of the authority. The second type of impact is the extent to which they have achieved an improved response to local needs and problems: how far have they enabled different policies to be applied and different levels and types of service to be provided in response to the diversity of local needs; have they achieved a more co-ordinated response to local problems and priorities; and have they resulted in the views, aspirations and priorities of the community being more closely reflected in the provision of services? While it may be regarded as inappropriate to evaluate how far a particular scheme has achieved aims which were not part of the authority's intentions, it is legitimate and useful to consider how far such approaches have, in general, achieved the various aims embodied in the philosophy discussed earlier.

Impact on Policy-Making and Resource Allocation

Not all of the schemes were intended to change the overall nature of policy-making within the authority. However, only in one of those authorities where area management was specifically designed for that purpose, Middlesbrough, could it be argued that policy and resource allocation processes were substantially different as a result of its introduction. The feature which distinguishes the Middlesbrough scheme from the others is the clear executive responsibility which the Area Policy Subcommittees have for certain aspects of the policy process. It is significant that these committees were established as an integral part of a new policy-making and management system for the authority as a whole, unlike other schemes where the introduction of area management was intended to augment or adapt an existing, well-established, policy system. In the latter authorities the ideal of a systematic approach, integrating the area dimension with the functional or programme dimension, proved unattainable. The attempts to change the nature of policy-making through a purely advisory approach were frustrated by a number of difficulties which arose in linking area management to the ongoing decision-making system.

The Liverpool scheme encountered considerable problems in feeding policy reports and recommendations into the local authority. Not only was there no clearly agreed way of dealing with reports of a corporate nature, there being no strong central policy-making machinery, but it proved difficult to get service departments to consider and respond to their recommendations (Harrop *et al.*, 1978). This experience might suggest that the potential for area management to develop a systematic approach would be greater where there was more acceptance of the need for a unified and 'rational' approach to policy-making and an established central policy cycle. The experiences in Stockport and Dudley, however, indicate that it can be just as difficult to establish such an approach where there is a corporate policy system as where there is a departmental or highly functional system. In Stockport the Priority Problems Exercise proceeded in parallel with the central policy process, the problems identified by the Area Committees not being considered until the relatively late policy options stage, when issue identification and policy formulation by the service committees was largely complete. Moreover it proved hard to relate the specific area proposals to the highly generalised nature of the policy option statements (Harrop *et al.*, 1978). In Dudley area management encountered problems in creating links with the key elements of the corporate management system, particularly the Programme Area Teams, and thus remained isolated from the main policy-making machinery in the authority for much of the project's life.

The lack of success of several schemes in their attempt to create an area dimension in the authority's ongoing policy processes has to be seen in the context of the changes that were taking place within local government at the time. Many local authorities were having to alter their policy and budgetary processes in order to cope with the need to make cuts in expenditure. These changes generally led to the streamlining and centralisation of decision-making (Hinings *et al.*, 1980). Thus the climate was not conducive to an innovation which implied greater complexity and, possibly, the delegation of decision-making responsibility. None the less it seems likely that such difficulties would have been encountered even in the absence of these new centralising tendencies. The fundamental problem is that whatever the specific form of the authority's policy planning system, functional and departmentalised or corporate, area management's role in those processes lacks legitimacy.

This problem has affected the ability of all advisory approaches, systematic and *ad hoc* alike, to influence policy and resource allocation decisions. Those bodies responsible for taking such decisions, departments, service committees and even programme area teams, see area management's activities as an unnecessary and irritating intrusion into issues which are regarded as their proper concern. The open-ended nature of area management's interest means that it is not perceived as having a new or distinctive role to play. The tightening financial situation encouraged decision-making bodies to become more entrenched and protective of their own, often professional service, interests, thus making an innovation which appeared to threaten their control over decisions even less acceptable.

Such attitudes can create particular difficulties for the *ad hoc* approach which often relies on issues being referred to the area committee or group from other parts of the council. In several authorities there has been a reluctance to involve area management in policy decisions, and many key issues have not been referred at all, or too late for a meaningful area input to the decision. For example, the Area Management Advisory Committee in Haringey was not involved in the development of the Borough Housing Strategy, and in Dudley a highly controversial debate concerning primary school provision in the area was confined to the central committees of the council.

Given the likely resistance to area management initiatives, advisory approaches which attempt to influence the nature of the policy-making machinery in a systematic way probably have less potential for change than those which seek to influence specific decisions. Being more focused, the latter approach is in a better position to make a concerted effort to change attitudes on particular issues, monitor the response of the decision-making body concerned and sustain pressure if it proves unfavourable. This type of approach is likely to be particularly appropriate in an authority which has a diffuse and departmentalised system of policy planning. The experiences of the advisory schemes demonstrate that the issue-specific approach can be effective. Many of the more *ad hoc* initiatives have, as has been shown, achieved some significant changes in policy or new policy initiatives. Several of the analyses undertaken in Liverpool did, in conjunction with other pressures, have an influential role in shaping council policy on, for example, land for industrial use, school site extensions and wider land use policies. Similarly the Haringey scheme played an important role in relation to redevelopment policies; the teams in Newcastle affected thinking on education and provision for the elderly; and in Stockport the area committees, in conjunction with local people, influenced transport planning and recreation provision. Generally, however, the influence of area approaches is more evident on issues related to planning, recreation and the environment than on issues related to housing, social services and education.

Lacking formal decision-making power, the potential of advisory approaches depends on the resources they can utilise in bringing pressure to bear on those bodies with executive responsibility. Community-oriented approaches may have an advantage over authority-oriented approaches in this respect, since they appeal to certain interests within the organisation of the authority which have been underrepresented in the policy process, namely, backbench members and lower-tier field officers (Harrop *et al.*, 1978, p. 202). The support of local councillors, particularly when coupled with a mobilisation of public opinion, can provide an effective political force for securing decisions in the interests of a particular area: this is well demonstrated by Haringey's Area Management Advisory Committee in relation to planning policies. No such political resource was available in Liverpool, where the District 'D' Committee had a low public profile and where its work was continually interrupted by party political disputes and personality clashes (op. cit., p. 150).

Another resource possessed by some schemes is information. As was shown in both Liverpool and Stockport, the existence of extensive data, especially new data, and a comprehensive analysis of a particular policy issue can provide substantial support for the recommendations of an area body. In the face of such 'hard' evidence it is much more difficult for other bodies to dismiss area demands as special pleading. Authority-oriented schemes are perhaps more likely to possess the staff necessary to create a policy analysis capacity, but the Stockport scheme shows that it is also possible to draw on the resources available within the local community itself.

A substantial local budget can also be used in attempting to influence policies and resource allocation. The examples discussed illustrate how the Newcastle priority area teams used their special finance to alter priorities and provide new services. But such budgets can also be used in persuading other bodies to institute changes. First, area management can threaten to provide the service if a particular department or committee is unco-operative; this option is often unacceptable because it implies a loss of professional control. In the second place, the budget can be used to demonstrate the feasibility and effectiveness of new and different services, thus weakening one source of opposition to their provision by the authority or another agency.

Whichever of these various resources are available, the prospects of success in influencing local authority policies and resource allocations are likely to be greatest where the aims of area management coincide with the interests of other political or professional groups within the authority. Thus area management can extend its sphere of influence by identifying and gaining the active support of those interests and by enabling others to use area management in creating effective lobbies for change.

An Improved Response to Local Needs and Priorities?

The first test of a new approach to policy-making must inevitably be whether it changes the policy process itself and the way decisions on service provision and resource allocation are made. But in monitoring or evaluating such innovations it is easy for attention to become focused solely on issues relating to the internal organisation and operation of the local authority and for questions concerning the impact of those operations on the local environment to be neglected. The ultimate test of the area management approach must be whether it actually achieves an improved response to local needs and priorities. This responsiveness can be assessed by examining how far the various approaches adopted in practice have succeeded in meeting the three main aims contained in the philosophy set out at the beginning of this chapter.

(1) *Meeting the diversity of needs.* Some of the changes in local authority decisions which have been achieved by area approaches undoubtedly represent an improved response to the needs or problems of particular areas. The allocation of additional land for industrial development in Liverpool; the defeat of redevelopment proposals and the introduction of a translation service in Haringey; the provision of a community school, a cancer screening service, extra street sweeping and recreation facilities in Newcastle; and the prevention of the closure of a suburban railway station and the allocation of more land for allotments in Stockport are all examples of such a response. However, the schemes have not always been successful in securing the changes desired. In addition these responses do not represent significant alterations in existing patterns of service provision, and are only rarely radical in the sense of providing a new or different type of service or representing a change in council policy for a particular area. In some schemes the response to certain local needs has depended on the existence of special budgets, rather than being the outcome of efforts to influence decisions on resource allocation and service provision in the authority as a whole. Whether such direct provision represents the most appropriate response to local problems and can provide a sustained solution to them remains an open question.

Obviously it will not always be possible for the authority to respond to the specific needs and demands of particular areas. Some services, such as provision for the homeless or juveniles in care, are likely to be unpopular in all areas. More important, in a situation of limited resources it is impossible to satisfy all needs and demands. Thus a concern to relate service provision and resource allocation to the relative needs of different areas necessitates certain areas being given priority over others and some demands not being met at all. This leads on to the question of whether area approaches have enabled local authorities to achieve a better overall matching between provision and resource allocation and the spatial pattern of needs in the community.

Some of the schemes considered here, namely, Haringey, Liverpool and Dudley, cannot be used to assess this, for they were established in one area of the authority only, often on an experimental basis. It is therefore questionable whether changes similar to those achieved for that particular area could have been achieved simultaneously in all parts of the authority. It is in any event exceptionally difficult to undertake such an evaluation because of the general lack of information on inter-area variations in needs and provision.[6] Although the question of the match between needs and provision cannot be answered directly, it is possible to consider how far area management has enabled different policies to be applied and different levels or types of service to be provided in accordance with local needs. This issue is most appropriately examined in the Middlesbrough context, since it is the only scheme to sustain a systematic area approach covering the whole authority. There new initiatives have been developed in response to particular local problems, for example, community projects in particular council estates, and the involvement of the area policy subcommittees in preparing the authority's policy plan does enable the level of services to be varied according to local needs and objectives. However, it is questionable how far it really achieves the kind of differential policy and service response referred to. It will be recalled that the recommendations of the area policy subcommittees are drawn up within the overall framework of council policies and the strategies for housing and recreation and industry established by the other policy subcommittees. Moreover, although in theory policy formulation is separated from implementation, in practice the area policy subcommittees deal with 'major' policy issues whereas 'minor' policy changes are the responsibility of the service committees. This distinction is inevitably a fine one and means that the area policy subcommittees do not control policy formulation on certain aspects of council policy, for example, housing allocation. These factors, together with the common central representation on the various area policy subcommittees, could be argued to lead to a tendency towards standardisation of approach, or uniformity, thus limiting the capacity for a response to the diversity of local needs.

(2) *A co-ordinated response to local problems*. A co-ordinated response to particular localities was argued to have two different aspects, one concerned with the complex and interrelated nature of local problems and the other concerned with meeting local priorities for services. Some of the problems with which area management has been concerned have been related to particular services or functions, such as planning, education, or community health, and have not been seen to require a corporate response. Other issues have been of a more wide-ranging nature and involved a number of different services. For example, both the problem of service provision on a new private estate

in Dudley and the translation service in Haringey were felt to require a corporate response. Attempts to consider local priorities for services as a whole and to relate those to the allocation of resources within the authority were pursued in Stockport, Middlesbrough and Liverpool.

Only in Middlesbrough, however, could a comprehensive corporate approach on the part of the local authority to planning for the needs of particular areas be argued to have been achieved. The area policy subcommittee provides a forum in which the problems of a particular part of the borough are considered as a whole, and a response made in terms of an annual corporate policy plan, with resource recommendations, for each area. The plans are normally accepted for inclusion in the Middlesbrough Policy Plan without substantial changes being made by the Policy Resource Committee of the Council. It has already been noted, however, that certain aspects of policy may not be determined by the area committees. In addition it is important to point out that Middlesbrough, being a non-metropolitan authority, does not have responsibility for education or social services functions, services which it will be recalled have featured little amongst the changes achieved by area management. Although county council representatives are invited to attend the area policy subcommittees the plans do not incorporate these important services and thus do not represent the fully integrated approach to local problems envisaged by many commentators.

Other schemes have experienced difficulty in achieving a co-ordinated response to local needs. Although the Area Management Unit in Liverpool itself adopted a corporate approach to its work and undertook policy analyses which cut across particular service responsibilities, it found difficulty in obtaining a corporate response to its recommendations. The main interdepartmental body, the Area Management group of officers, was disbanded when it became clear that it could not operate as a corporate management function for the area, and, given the highly functional structure of the authority, there was no other body with a clearly defined corporate responsibility to which area management could relate. In Stockport the Priority Problems Exercise endeavoured to look at the overall priorities for services within particular areas, but despite the existence of the corporate planning system these priorities were never responded to corporately by the authority. The recommendations of each area committee were split up and sent to the appropriate service committee. The latter committees were each aware of the priority ranking attached to proposals specific to their responsibilities, but nowhere were the various proposals of an area considered as a whole and a report fed back to the area committee on the action taken (Hambleton, 1978).

(3) *Reflecting community-defined problems and priorities*. One important characteristic of an area approach has been defined as the extent to which it is community-oriented, that is, the role which those who represent local interests, particularly councillors and the public, play in the policy process. Clearly the community-oriented schemes, such as Haringey, Newcastle and Stockport, are the ones which are

most likely to encourage local definitions of problems and priorities to be reflected in the policies and services of the council. However, there has been some questioning of the extent to which these schemes really represent local interests.

The first aspect of this issue is the power afforded to the public or community groups, as opposed to elected representatives. The area committees in Stockport are conducted in a formal manner, community councils making a contribution to the debate when invited, and in the Priority Problems Exercise it was the area committees which made the final decisions on priorities, amending or adding to the recommendations of the community councils as they saw fit (Harrop *et al.*, 1978, p. 7). Similarly, some of the priority area teams in Newcastle have operated in the accepted style of council committees. In contrast, other priority area teams and the Area Management Advisory Committee in Haringey have managed to break free from the traditional type of committee meeting, and have operated in a much more open style with members of the public contributing freely to the debate and decisions normally being reached by consensus. However some of those involved in articulating the philosophy of the 'bottom-up' approach to policy-making might not regard even these schemes as representing a significant step in this direction (Benington and Skelton, 1972). Ultimate responsibility for decisions remains with councillors, and local residents do not possess an effective bargaining or equal partnership position, as in Dayton (Hambleton, 1978), let alone having some form of community control (Arnstein, 1969; Yates, 1974). In the second place there has been some questioning of the representativeness of the members of the public who attend, and concern has been particularly expressed in Haringey about the lack of involvement of some of the minority ethnic communities.

Despite these reservations concerning their role, residents and community groups in these schemes have had considerable opportunities to define needs and raise issues as they perceive them. This is an important development, given past criticisms of public participation in local government. Further, the schemes have had some, if not widespread, success in securing policies and services in tune with community opinion. However, the influence of local views is inevitably limited by the primarily advisory nature of many schemes. It is also debatable whether the interest of community groups and the public can sustain the systematic type of approach. Although in both Haringey and Stockport it proved possible to mobilise public opinion around one or two controversial policy issues currently affecting the area, the experience of the Priority Problems Exercise suggests that it may be more difficult to obtain community views on matters of policy and priority for service provision, particularly on a regular basis.

CONCLUSIONS

In one way or another the area management schemes have all enabled the identification of local needs and policy issues and the expression of community interests. That their efforts have resulted in the authorities being more aware of the problems and priorities of particular areas is widely accepted (Spencer *et al.*, forthcoming). This achievement is not insignificant since such an identification of needs and problems, involving both objective and subjective information, is essential to any attempt to develop a policy-making system which is more responsive to those needs. However, the schemes have been much less successful in affecting other stages of the policy process. They have resulted in certain changes in policies and service provision but it is evident that their overall impact on policy-making and resource allocation in the authorities has been limited. The actual achievements of area management seem to fall well short of the aims espoused in the underlying philosophy. Why should this be the case? The answer lies partly in the way the ideas have been put into practice, and partly in the unrealistic expectations and inherent contradictions contained within the philosophy itself.

The difficulties encountered in developing area management and the various factors which account for the general impacts of the schemes have been discussed in detail elsewhere (Harrop *et al.*, 1978, ch. 10). There is no doubt, however, that the type of area management which has been implemented in British local government is much weaker, in terms of the powers afforded to the area body in the policy process, than many of its proponents envisaged. These writers generally anticipated the delegation of certain powers to area committees, and some have advocated giving the area committee 'substantial autonomy to adjust local services within an overall budget' (Davis *et al.*, 1977). Only one of the schemes discussed here has executive responsibility for some part of the policy process, the majority being afforded only an advisory function.

The limited nature of the schemes which have been established reflects both the nature of the initiative taken by central government and the attitudes of the local authorities involved to the role of an area approach. The Department of the Environment's aim was to encourage local authorities to experiment with area management, by offering financial assistance as an incentive. Unlike certain experiments in the United States, such as the Model Cities Programme and the Community Action Programme, it was a limited initiative, and no requirements concerning the powers and functions of the scheme or the form of community involvement were imposed. In fact it was argued by the Department of the Environment that many different forms of organisation were possible to achieve the perceived objectives of area management. The only conditions which central government sought to impose were that it should not be simply an administrative exercise but should contain 'some kind of political representation in the committee structure of the Council', and that it should involve the 'co-ordination of the Council's activities at area level by a full-time manager' (Department of the Environment, 1974). In subsequent negotiations with individual authorities the latter condition was not in fact closely adhered to.

In the absence of any requirements to do otherwise, the majority of the authorities which developed area management chose to implement schemes which were advisory and did not fundamentally change the existing bases of decision-making in the authority (Horn *et al.*, 1977). Executive responsibility for policy-making has rarely been delegated to area bodies, and it is interesting to note that in the one authority where this has occurred, Middlesbrough, the area policy subcommittees were established at the time of reorganisation and not as a response to the offer of financial assistance from the Department of the Environment. Moreover even where opportunities for community involvement in policy-making have been provided, these have not always been extensive or afforded a very influential role for local groups and the public.

It could be argued, therefore, that the limited impact of area approaches to policy-making is attributable to the limited nature of the schemes themselves, and that those which have been implemented so far do not reflect the 'stronger' or more powerful forms of area approach which could potentially be established. However, it is important to consider the reasons why the authorities concerned chose schemes which were primarily advisory, and hence what the prospects are for the development of more radical approaches. The limited powers afforded to area bodies can be explained by the fact that the underlying philosophy contains a number of fundamental challenges to the principles on which the existing local government system is based. The call for differentiation in the policies and activities of the local authority to meet diverse local needs challenges the principle of uniformity: it threatens the power of leading politicians to determine overall council policy and priorities in resource allocation, exposes conflicts of interest between the needs of various localities and the authority as a whole, and questions national and professional service standards adopted by the administrative system. The aim of achieving a comprehensive or co-ordinated approach to particular localities runs counter to the often predominant functional basis on which the local authority is organised: it threatens the service interests of committee chairmen and professional autonomy, and by establishing new patterns of responsibility additional to the normal hierarchical administrative structure of departments it challenges the authority of chief officers. Finally, by advocating a greater role for the 'community' in the decision-making of the council it is contrary to the interests of those individuals and groups currently in positions of power in the authority: the argument for direct involvement by the public and community groups can be seen as particularly threatening because it challenges the traditional system of representative democracy, facilitating influences on decision-making which are external to the authority and its systems of control (Harrop *et al.*, 1978, ch. 10).

Given the extent of these challenges which area management, by its very nature, represents to the existing organisation and ongoing decision-making processes, it was perhaps predictable that its powers would be limited. In particular, it is not surprising that community-oriented schemes have generally had only a limited, and often *ad hoc*, role in policy-making, and that the scheme with the greatest degree of executive responsibility for policy-making, Middlesbrough's, is authority-oriented and demonstrates a tendency towards centralisation. This analysis also raises the question of whether the underlying philosophy established realistic expectations of what might be achieved within the existing structure of local government. Three particular aspects of that philosophy will be considered here.

First, the idea of developing an 'area dimension' in the policy process, which would enable local authority decisions to match the diversity of local needs, was perhaps an unattainable objective. The concept was of a systematic consideration of area needs and priorities and the provision of services to take account of inter-area variations, the area dimension being additional to the authority-wide corporate dimension and the existing functional framework of the authority. It seems to be underpinned by an assumption of rationality in the policy-making processes of the authority, an assumption which in some instances proved unrealistic. Even for those authorities which had progressed quite far in the development of a policy process based on rational principles the 'area dimension' implied a level of complexity and sophistication which it is difficult to envisage being sustained. Many local authorities have experienced difficulties in creating an effective corporate planning system integrated with the existing functional machinery, given increased organisational staff resource and information demands, and have moved away from the comprehensive ideal to a more selective approach (see Chapter 3 of this volume). Certainly the information on area needs and provision necessary to support a systematic area approach is not readily available in most authorities, and would require the establishment of new systems for information collection and analysis. Indeed the lack of such information makes it difficult to validate a critical underlying assumption of the philosophy, namely, that needs and priorities for services differ significantly between geographical areas.

This point relates closely to the second aspect of the philosophy which needs to be questioned, the emphasis on a co-ordinated approach at area level. It is assumed not only that needs and priorities vary between areas, but also that the problems which occur in particular localities are highly interrelated. Undoubtedly there are local problems which can only be solved by a cross-functional approach, and various studies which have demonstrated the importance of these have already been referred to. However, there may be needs which do not exhibit such interdependencies, and it could be argued that obtaining an improved response to localised needs *within* existing functional divisions may be as important, if not more important, than enabling area problems and priorities to be considered as a whole. Moreover an area approach is likely to be easier to develop in a service-specific context since although it may challenge the centralised power of senior officers and committee chairmen it operates within the functionally differentiated structure of most local authorities (Mason *et al.*, 1977). Certainly the prospects for the delegation of executive functions to area committees are much greater where such committees are confined to a single service, such as housing or social services, than where they have a general responsibility for an area.

Perhaps the most fundamental criticism which can be made of the philosophy is that it contains a number of internal tensions or contradictions. First, there exists a tension between responding to the aggregate pattern of area needs and responding to the specific needs of particular areas. The first emphasises the local authority's role as arbiter between the competing needs of different areas, with policy-making being seen as having a distributive function. This requires general criteria by which the overall allocation of resources and services to different areas is to be judged, and is often associated with arguments for 'social' or 'territorial' justice (Harvey, 1973; B. Davies, 1968). This function may not be compatible with a response to the individual needs of all areas, particularly since many policy and service provision decisions relating to one area may have wider implications or effects on other parts of the authority. Such incompatibility relates closely to a second contradiction, between the need for centralised decision-making and the call for greater autonomy over decisions to be delegated to the area level. For a local authority to respond more sensitively to variations in need between areas and to allocate resources in accordance with those needs implies strong control from the centre, yet the specific nature of the needs and problems occurring in particular localities is often argued to require those with knowledge and/or interests in the area having greater decision-making responsibility.

A further tension, which may be aligned with the previous two, is that between the responsibilities and interests of the 'authority' on the one hand and the 'community' on the other. The responsibility of the local authority for its area as a whole and its role as a distributor of resources implies that the response to different neighbourhoods should be based on some 'objective' analysis of their needs, whereas the philosophy also emphasises the importance of local preference and the subjective definition of needs and priorities by those with an interest in a particular area. This tension is expressed in the role strains often experienced by area co-ordinators, who are employed by the local authority yet who may interpret their role as one of facilitator and advocate for the local community.

Area approaches, then, have been advocated as a response to a group of different, yet interrelated, problems concerning local authority policy-making, rather than as the outcome of a single, clearly articulated and coherent philosophy. This lack of clarity and coherence is often reflected in the objectives of those authorities who have adopted some form of area management (Horn *et al.*, 1977). In explaining their reasons for establishing area management most authorities refer to the notion of responsiveness and include among their aims achieving sensitivity to local needs, achieving co-ordination at the local level and developing community involvement, even if not all of these are emphasised in practice. They appeal to the philosophy, yet rarely has the nature of the underlying problems been explicitly analysed and the way area management is intended to meet these problems elucidated. Thus the conflicts and incompatabilities which are contained within the philosophy have not been resolved prior to the implementation of the ideas, and are often reflected in the form of the schemes themselves.

In the same way that the ineffectiveness of government policies towards urban deprivation has been attributed to a failure to clarify and disaggregate the concept of urban deprivation itself (Edwards and Batley, 1978), the limited impact of area management approaches to policy-making could be interpreted, in part at least, as a result of the failure to clarify the notion of responsiveness and articulate the various problems to which area management was seen to be the solution. The concept of responsiveness has been used to encapsulate a number of different problems and has lent a degree of coherence to the aims of area management which does not in fact exist. If the three distinct aspects of the philosophy, namely, differentiation in policies and services to meet the diversity of needs, a co-ordinated response to local problems, and reflecting community-defined problems and preferences, were pursued separately then the impact of area management on policy-making might be enhanced, for the challenge to established interests within the authority would not be so great. More important, if the problems underlying these three aims were disaggregated and analysed more fully, more appropriate and effective measures to meet them might be identified. It may well be the case that different forms of area management are required to tackle different types of problem, that area management is not necessarily the most appropriate form of response to some problems, or even that certain problems require more fundamental changes in the relationship between the local authority and the public than can be brought about through internal management initiatives.

NOTES: CHAPTER 9

1 This chapter is based on the monitoring of eight area management schemes by a research team at the Institute of Local Government Studies, with the support of the Department of the Environment. It draws particularly on the experiences of the schemes in Stockport, Middlesbrough, Liverpool, Newcastle, Haringey and Dudley. A full description of the nature and development of each of these schemes is provided in Harrop, Mason, Vielba and Webster, 1978. I would like to acknowledge the invaluable contribution made by other members of the research team, especially Ken Spencer, Carol Vielba, Tim Mason, Ken Harrop and Neil Collins, who provided much of the information and helpful comments on the draft. I would also like to thank those officers and councillors in the authorities concerned who commented on the chapter and through discussions elucidated so much about how the schemes actually operate. The views expressed are, however, my own and do not necessarily reflect those of the local authorities or the Department of the Environment.

2 A detailed description of the formal objectives and structures of the schemes is provided in Horn *et al.*, 1977, and a fuller discussion of the way these have been

implemented and developed can be found in Harrop *et al.*, 1978.

3 Details of these budgets and an analysis of their use are provided in Spencer, Vielba, Webster *et al.*, forthcoming.

4 The community councils are non-party-political elected councils of local residents, which are intended to promote a representative community view. The authority applies certain criteria by which it determines whether a community council will be recognised, and 'recognised' community councils are entitled to a 'special relationship' with the authority. This includes the right to be represented at area committee meetings, to be consulted on local matters, to receive regular information on the authority's activities, and to some financial assistance. They are not unlike neighbourhood councils (Department of the Environment, 1977b).

5 The lack of concern with the development of policy-making was in two cases due to the fact that the schemes were primarily concerned with other objectives. In Haringey the main focus was community development and public involvement, and the councillor-officer priority area teams in Newcastle were designed to relieve the symptoms of urban stress by involving the community in the spending of special local budgets. The Haringey scheme has latterly been concerned with the development of a community plan for the area, and this has involved more attention being given to policy-making processes and policy analysis. Although in Dudley one of the main aims was to develop an area perspective in the corporate management system, this aspect was not really developed until the later stages of the project. See Harrop *et al.*, 1978, and Spencer *et al.*, forthcoming, for a full account of these changes.

6 For a discussion of this problem see Chapter 4 of this volume.

10

Comprehensive Community Programmes

KEN SPENCER

BACKGROUND

The concept of Comprehensive Community Programmes (CCP) was launched by Labour's Home Secretary, Roy Jenkins, on 18 July 1974.[1] He announced that CCP would deal with tackling manifestations of multiple deprivation in urban areas, they would relate to areas of about 10,000 people and would examine the nature of deprivation in the area and make proposals for its alleviation or solution. A five-year plan would be drawn up as part of this process which would be submitted to central government for approval and financial backing. The CCP would involve a range of urban governance agencies, with district council local authorities playing the leading role. The concept was that the work undertaken, including an action programme, would have a co-ordinated focus upon urban deprivation on an inter-agency basis including central government.

This brief statement was supported eleven days later by further details in the government's response to the parliamentary debate on urban deprivation.[2] This emphasised the role of CCP as a policy planning system to improve the effective use of existing resources as well as to provide additional resources. In the debate a desire for speedy implementation of CCP was stressed by the Home Office. In the event, however, CCP was to progress much more slowly than anticipated at that time.[3]

The 1974 announcements about CCP left issues to be resolved and this resolution took place over a period (1974–7) in which evidence from previous anti-poverty programme work was coming to light. It also took place in a climate of increasing economic stringency and a central governmental organisational climate which was to change ministerial responsibilities for the urban programme. Against this background and in the context of the wider work being undertaken by the Urban Deprivation Unit (UDU)[4] the development of CCP was subject to the varying pressures of the organisational climate within the Home Office including political pressures. The CCP provided a mechanism whereby the Home Office was able to continue its role in relation to the ongoing governmental debate about the future of programmes to relieve urban poverty. CCP development was undertaken by the UDU in conjunction with discussions with five potentially interested local authorities, Bradford, Gateshead, Wandsworth and Wirral, with Birmingham being added in 1976.

Four main changes affected the nature of the CCP. These were first, that the concept of relating a CCP to pockets of deprivation, that is, areas of 10,000 population, was dropped in favour of an authority-wide approach. Secondly, as the national economic climate became more stringent it became clear that CCP would have little, then no, central resources automatically allocated to its action programme.[5] However, CCP staff would be paid for by central government. The third change affecting the nature of CCP and its development was that there was growing rivalry between the Home Office and the Department of the Environment over future initiatives in the field of urban deprivation, and also over ministerial responsibilities. The UDU saw itself as the main co-ordinating body in considering the future of urban deprivation initiatives (Wasserman, 1975), but the Department of the Environment had developed increasing interest in this area, especially after the establishment of its Urban Affairs Division in the early 1970s.[6] The fourth change, related closely to the previous issue, was the establishment of a Cabinet subcommittee on inner city policy in 1976 chaired by Peter Shore, Labour's Secretary of State at the Department of the Environment. This threw urban poverty programme initiatives back into the melting pot. The result was the by-now-expected statement that the Home Office role in this area would be transferred to the Department of the Environment, to the Inner Cities Directorate. This transfer took place in June 1977.

However, shortly before this transfer the Home Office's UDU had agreed with Gateshead to go ahead with an experimental CCP in that authority.[7] Thus the CCP initiative was underway for only two to three months before the Home Office disengaged itself from the project and the Department of the Environment took over. The Gateshead CCP was thus launched by the Home Office, whereas one year later the Bradford CCP was launched by the Department of the Environment.

THE OUTLINE CCP MODEL

What was emerging towards the end of 1976, therefore, was a CCP experiment assisted by resources to cover CCP manpower costs but relying upon shifts in the main budgets of the partners involved in the CCP policy planning process. The emphasis of CCP was therefore upon concentrating on a policy planning system which could relate to the ongoing decision-making processes of those agencies involved in CCP. This instrument would provide a means by which the various agencies of urban government could try to develop more effective proposals for dealing with deprivation. It recognised that a fragmented approach was not adequate, while it also recognised that local authorities could not deal alone with the manifestations of multiple urban deprivation.

The UDU produced a short paper in November 1976 which outlined the CCP approach.

> Meeting the basic needs of the deprived calls for the use of a wide range of 'main' policies and programmes of both central and local government, such as those concerned with employment, housing, income maintenance, education and social services. This is the basis of the CCP approach. It is intended as an instrument for directing the major programmes and policies of government to those most in need. (Home Office Urban Deprivation Unit, 1976, p. 1)

The note leaves the definition of urban deprivation at a broad level being 'those people whose quality of life or standard of living is markedly below the average in our society' (ibid., pp. 1–2). In line with earlier urban programme means of dealing with definitions of urban deprivation this task was left as one which local authorities, with greater local knowledge, could more adequately determine. The CCP was to provide a policy planning framework to develop responsive policies to deal with the specific problems characterising urban deprivation within the local authority. The paper draws attention to the particular needs of racial minorities. The main part of the paper outlines the three-part CCP policy planning process. The CCP process was regarded as an annual cycle in the following terms.

Part 1: a description and analysis of the nature of deprivation throughout the authority, based on information provided by participating agencies. This would set the context for subsequent analysis and action. It would incorporate a scan of existing policies and activities to deal with deprivation and include a review of the appropriateness and effectiveness of those approaches to dealing with deprivation.

Part 2: based on the results of part 1 a number of specific deprivation issues would be selected for in-depth analysis. The issues for policy analysis would vary each year and the aim would be to develop practical proposals for ways of meeting the needs of the deprived, through resource shifts, policy change and procedural changes.

Part 3: a programme of action for the next financial year to tackle some of the issues identified in parts 1 and 2. Some urban programme grant could be provided, but the emphasis was upon redirecting the existing budgets of the agencies involved in CCP to those in most need. There would also be a review and monitoring element.

This three-part CCP process was seen as a policy planning system which would not operate in isolation, it would build on existing information and decision-making patterns on an inter-agency basis, assisted by a partnership link with central government. The CCP would link into existing policy planning systems at appropriate points in order to influence existing systems to take on board a deprivation perspective in their decision-making. In this sense the CCP was a corporate planning process with an inter-agency dimension and a specific focus upon the problems of deprivation.

The District Council was to be the prime agent responsible for the CCP, but CCP itself was to be an inter-agency approach and the control of the direction of CCP work was to be an inter-agency venture. The County Council and Area Health Authority were to be main participants along with the Home Office and Department of the Environment (Regional Office). Other agencies would attend as necessary (co-ordinated by the Home Office). Thus the stage was set for the first English CCP to become operational. However, an inner cities directorate had already been established, and the new policy was set out in a government White Paper of June 1977 (HMSO, 1977). Many of the ideas associated with inner city policy were related to those about CCP but with two main differences. Demarcation of the inner city zones and the allocation of urban programme funds to such zones provided an areal focus within the local authority (deliberately avoided through CCP) and a significant level of resourcing. Partnership authorities were declared in 1977 and they were to receive the lion's share of enhanced urban programme resources; thereafter programme authorities were designated where financial assistance was at a lower, but nevertheless reasonably substantial level (around £1–2 million).

Thus CCP would now operate in the context of a more politically significant inner city policy with broadly similar objectives though different means of attempting to achieve those objectives, CCP with its emphasis on policy planning processes and inner city policy with its emphasis on new project identification. The White Paper placed CCP on a similar footing to programme authorities.[8] Thus the concept that CCP would in 1976 have very little central government financial assistance for the action programme element of part 3 was changed to an expectancy level equivalent to that of programme authorities.[9]

The gestation period for CCP was protracted[10] but by April 1977 Gateshead had begun to operationalise the concept. The case of CCP in Gateshead is examined first, followed by the operation of CCP in Bradford.

GATESHEAD CCP, 1977–80

UDU staff had been liaising with Gateshead prior to 1977 through joint work on educational disadvantage. There was strong support for the CCP project from the Director of Social Services and Chief Executive. The experiment was seen as important in 'putting Gateshead on the map'. Initially senior local politicians were sceptical. Was Gateshead chosen because it had more deprivation than other places? Would it highlight problems about which they could do little? Would it put the past record of long Labour Party control under scrutiny? However they agreed to the project on the grounds that Gateshead was a 'typical urban environment' which had a representative range of the problems of deprivation.

A CCP team funded by the Home Office was appointed consisting of a team leader, two policy analysts and a clerk/typist. The team leader was a town planner and corporate planner by background. One policy analyst was a researcher, the other had management consultancy experience. Those appointed, by a joint panel of the agencies involved in CCP,[11] were new to Gateshead. They took up their posts between April and July 1977 with the team leader first in post. The project was envisaged as lasting for three years, by which time it was hoped that CCP would have incorporated a sufficient deprivation perspective into the ongoing processes of decision-making within the agencies concerned. Thus the CCP team and a separate CCP policy planning system were seen as temporary mechanisms. The team quickly produced the Gateshead CCP project report which outlined both what CCP hoped to accomplish and the means of achieving it (Gateshead CCP, 1977). The project report followed closely the CCP model produced by the Home Office (Home Office, Urban Deprivation Unit, 1976).

The Project Report

The project report identified the experiment as being different from previous initiatives because its basic aim was *'to direct the major policies and programmes of central and local government and other agencies to those most in need'* (Gateshead CCP, 1977, p. 3). The programme aimed specifically to assist those suffering multiple deprivation and identified four aspects of this initiative:

(i) an explicit focus on the problems of deprivation in Gateshead;
(ii) a new form of partnership between central and local government;
(iii) a comprehensive approach to bring together various public agencies;
(iv) the process was concerned with action and policy change.

The CCP process was envisaged diagrammatically as in Figure 10.1. It was seen as an integrated rolling programme based upon an annual planning cycle. Part 1 would be presented in an annual CCP review report. The series of review reports would help to support the ongoing development of CCP processes, primarily by developing an information base on the nature of deprivation. Part 2, the analysis of key issues, was seen as reflecting political priorities. This analysis would involve a search for new ways of looking at a problem or service; a concern to move beyond symptoms to underlying causes; an attempt to generate new forms of response and the submission of practical recommendations. Part 2 would lead to a series of issue reports. While the process of investigation was to be shared with those involved in service provision the effective operation of CCP required inputs not only of the CCP team but from officers of the agencies involved. This participation in investigation was seen as paramount in gaining subsequent commitment to action.

Part 3 was to be concerned with action programme formulation by

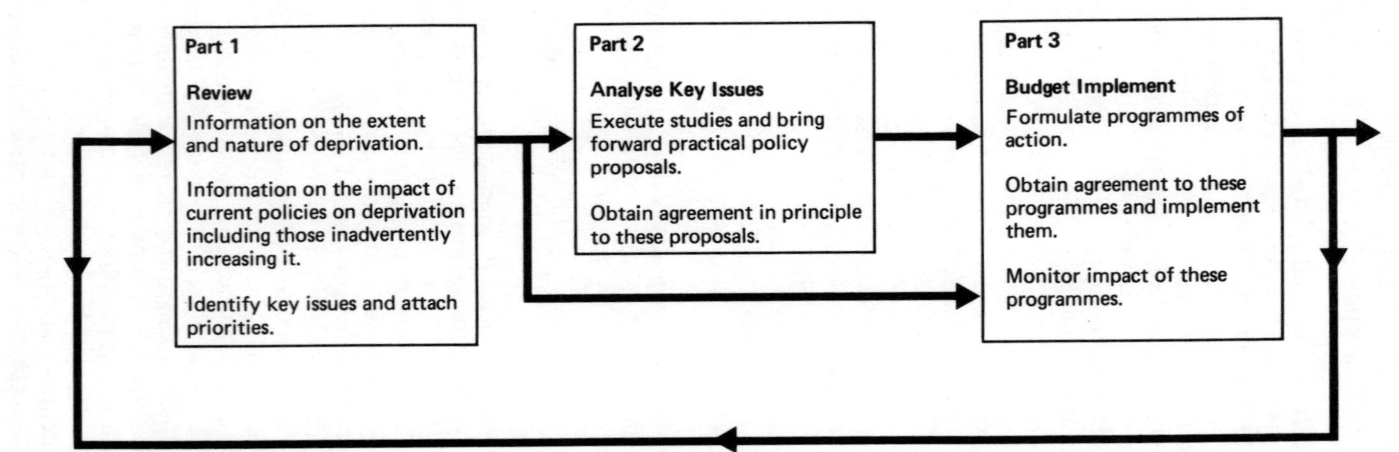

Source: Gateshead CCP, 1977.

Figure 10.1 *The CCP annual policy planning process.*

the agencies involved. It was envisaged that time-spans for programme implementation would vary. Three types of change were identified as relevant to the action programme.

(i) *Finance:* redirecting major policies and programmes of local and central government and other agencies involved; some assistance from Urban Programme funds for action programmes;
(ii) *Non-financial:* administrative, procedural, manpower and preventive strategy changes;
(iii) *Community*: the encouragement and fostering of self-help.

The project report foresaw some of the difficulties inherent in redirecting expenditure in an increasingly stringent financial climate. The monitoring of CCP progress in assessing policy impacts would be incorporated into the annual review reports. It would also include a systematic monitoring of the organisational framework of CCP. 'The "Review Report" therefore becomes the lynchpin of the CCP process' (Gateshead CCP, 1977, p. 9). The project report also considered the range of planning budgetary cycles to which the CCP would be linked and the need to inject a CCP influence at different times depending upon the particular nature and procedure of each planning cycle.

The Operation of CCP

Four groups were established as the formal structural elements of CCP.

(1) *The CCP team*, as an inter-agency unit, was regarded as independent, though links with Gateshead were strong. The team was primarily responsible to the CCP Steering Group and Members' Group.
(2) *CCP Working Group*, a team of mainly third- and fourth-tier officers of the key agencies involved in the CCP which provided the formal link with agencies on the general working arrangements of CCP. Others were invited to meetings as occasion demanded.
(3) *CCP Steering Group*, the group responsible for overall co-ordination of CCP at officer level. It was chaired by the Northern Region Director of the Department of the Environment, and was attended by the Chief Executives of Gateshead District and Tyne and Wear County, an Assistant Secretary from the Inner Cities Directorate and a representative of the Area Health Authority, together with their support staff.
(4) *CCP Members' Group*, the political link between the two tiers of local government and central government. It was chaired by a minister of the Department of the Environment and was attended by the local political leaders and key chairmen, together with their senior officers.

The groups changed elements of their roles over time. In particular the Working Group was unable to commit agency staff to much work on CCP issues. As a result it developed into a discussion forum for drafts of issue papers produced by CCP. Thus CCP had to develop informal networks to facilitate inter-agency working. Almost inevitably the CCP team was under pressure to do much of the work itself, whereas originally it had been envisaged that other departmental or agency staff would assist. This pressure led to a slowing-down of progress from the level envisaged at the outset and to a greater degree of concentration on selected aspects of CCP processes.

Three distinct phases of operation of the CCP can be identified. First, the preparation of the review report as part 1 of the CCP policy planning process. Secondly, the low profile given to CCP during the period of first-year Inner City Partnership programme preparation (Gateshead was announced as having joint partnership status with Newcastle in November 1977, several months after the first partnerships were announced). Thirdly, the emphasis of CCP on policy analysis. Thus what started out as an attempt by CCP to introduce a policy planning process was deflected by the advent of inner city policy and was subsequently developed on a more *ad hoc* basis of reports to influence specific policy areas. After the first phase the CCP experiment did not concern itself with the development of the CCP policy planning process as initially outlined. One could, therefore, argue that the Gateshead CCP has not in fact really attempted to develop a policy planning process, but that it has developed a policy analysis capacity. The latter is not an effective substitute for the former. These policy analysis skills were being operated in an authority with a weak, though slowly developing, corporate system. A consideration of the three phases of CCP work follows.

In the *first phase* of work attention focused upon providing information on the nature and extent of deprivation in Gateshead. In compiling the review report (Gateshead CCP, 1977) it was found that the information base of some of the organisations involved in CCP was weak. There were also problems about compatibility of information. Thus more time was spent in preparing the information base than had been anticipated. This early phase influenced agency attitudes towards CCP. It was seen by most of the agencies as a research and information role. The 1978 review report described the nature of deprivation in Gateshead and put forward a number of general principles about responsiveness to deprivation. However, agencies found it difficult to take any action on the basis of the report. Their reaction being that the information was generally useful, but that it was difficult to see what action was intended to flow from it. The report did not consider the impact of current policies on deprivation, and this general review, as outlined in the project report, was not carried out.

This early emphasis led to a labelling of CCP as being concerned with research and information. Even towards the end of the project many officers and politicians still saw CCP as being essentially a research tool and not about policy change, resource redistribution or priority setting. Thus the original concept, that CCP was about the development of a policy planning system with a focus on deprivation, soon began to lapse. This was strongly reinforced by the confusion created with the advent of inner city policy at an early stage in the life of CCP.

The original idea of developing the review report on an annual basis did not materialise. The first review report was the last. A selection of key issues for analysis was highlighted. Despite the CCP team's 'independent' stance, many of the issues identified at this stage and later stemmed primarily from interests within Gateshead Council. The review report lacked a clear link with action needed. Follow-up was essential to maintain commitment to and interest in CCP but at this point attention was diverted to Inner City Partnership work.

The *second phase* of CCP work involved the preparation of the Gateshead element of the first-year Newcastle–Gateshead Inner City Partnership Programme. Manpower working on CCP processes and issues was dramatically reduced. This decision to switch CCP staff to Inner City Programme preparation, though seen as complementary, dealt a blow to CCP progress from which it could not adequately recover. The three-year time-span of CCP was thrown out of joint. This phase of work emphasised that Inner City Partnership work had priority and most agencies' commitment to CCP, including that of the Department of the Environment, was reduced.

This phase was one of little CCP development other than an attempt to keep alive a minimum of policy analysis and work on the extent of deprivation. CCP effort continued for a year to concentrate on inner city project definition. On the one hand such an emphasis could be seen to fit into the CCP process as an opportunity to develop part 3, the action plan. Unfortunately, from a CCP process point of view, this action plan was based not upon bending main programmes, but upon a search for suitable projects on which extra (or windfall) resources could be spent. Thus the inner city programme was about spending extra resources although agencies had to find 25 per cent of the costs of the programme. However, background information from the review report, the contracts already established and some of the early policy analysis work were to contribute to influencing the type of programme eventually agreed for the Gateshead end of the partnership. Indeed CCP was able to inject projects stemming from CCP initiatives. Without the existence of CCP Gateshead may have found greater difficulty in coping with initial Inner City Partnership work.

The effects of this phase were to reduce agency commitment to CCP, to direct attention away from main service budgets and to create an atmosphere in which spending on deprivation in times of economic stringency was seen to be met by additional central government resources. Thus departments bid for extra resources to cope with their problems. In turn this detracted from attempts to assess needs in relation to priorities, resource allocation and new policies, the very crux of the CCP initiative. Departments felt under threat; the core of their activity base was increasingly being undermined by the harsher economic climate. Inner City Partnership provided a lifeline to extra resources; CCP did not. CCP questioned existing departmental approaches and priorities. CCP was about the processes of decision-making; it had the potential to influence ongoing main-line service activity. Inner city policy was generally seen as providing a resource pool. In Gateshead with its strong departmentalism there was some reluctance to become committed to a CCP policy planning system which was likely to raise basic issues of departmental decision making. On the other hand Inner City Partnership did not at that time raise any of these fundamental issues.

Though CCP identified concentrations of deprivation in the inner city zone, its analysis also showed much deprivation throughout the district. This drew attention to the need to reconsider departmental priorities and resource allocations but, except in a few cases, existing decision-making mechanisms did not take this on board.

The *third phase* of CCP work represented a strong commitment to policy analysis. By April 1979 the commitment of other agencies to participate actively in CCP had reduced considerably. Thus the emphasis of CCP policy analysis was on issues particularly relevant to Gateshead Council, the only agency remaining committed to the concept of CCP. However, this commitment was to a series of policy analyses, not to the development of a policy planning system. It was envisaged that rational policy analyses would lead to political commitment to action. At this stage staff appointed initially to the Inner City Partnership were transferred to develop the work of CCP. At this time there were also a number of staff changes in the CCP team.

In the absence of any corporate approach which could be effectively used to progress CCP policy planning attention turned to what was proving most useful to the local political leadership. Thus a series of policy analysis studies were prepared, for example, public sector housing allocation; educational disadvantage; the transition from school to work; social deprivation amongst children and young people; and business and employment in older housing areas. In the public housing allocation report recommendations for action were highly specific, in the other reports the identification of general principles dominated.

Co-operation between CCP team and agency staffs was variable but assistance was forthcoming on information provision about current needs and activities. Because of the nature of these investigatory pieces of work the CCP team was sometimes treated with caution; in a very few cases with hostility. Yet this was tempered by the commitment of the political leadership to this internal investigatory style. The Gateshead political and administrative leadership had a strong influence over the CCP team in the choice of issues to be investigated. Once prepared and processed through the Officer Working Group and the Steering and Members' Groups, the policy analysis reports were sent to relevant local authority and agency committees for their observations and action. Reports also went to the Gateshead chief officers' management team. However, progress on implementing proposals had by late 1980 shown little effect, though a number of proposals remained under active consideration.

Action by agencies other than Gateshead in response to CCP has been negligible, though in some cases report consideration has highlighted issues deemed to deserve further attention. Gateshead departments have taken up some specific issues, for example, the planning department's inner area policy plan, an interdepartmental group to consider the provision of children's play facilities. In other departments aspects of the policy analysis reports have been and still are under consideration in terms of individual departmental contributions or reassessments of approach, for example, education, housing, social services, leisure and recreation. Support for follow-up very much depends upon senior officers and members developing an interest in and seeking support on particular issues. Gateshead had no effective corporate mechanism for handling these reports and individual departments and committees have tended to adopt their own stances.

Policy analyses have been developed in response to a number of situations. First, reviews of an existing policy or procedure, for example, housing allocation, a proposed review of difficult-to-let high-density housing. Secondly, reviews of departmental service provision, for example, educational disadvantage. Thirdly, reviews of a problem area overlapping departmental and/or agency boundaries, for example, the transition from school to work, business and employment in an older housing area. CCP has been reluctant, except in the housing allocation case, to make specific recommendations for action, but has tended to rely upon the emergence of general principles. The danger is that general principles can be readily agreed and then forgotten. Perhaps service committees themselves should have been more involved in the selection of issues to be investigated.

Thus the operation of the CCP was not along the lines originally envisaged. Work on elements of part 1 and upon the detailed policy analysis of part 2 have been emphasised, but there has been no attempt to produce a CCP part 3. It could be argued that an *ad hoc*, rather than systematic, part 3 action programme for redirecting main services would arise from policy analysis studies. By late 1980, however, there was little evidence to support this view.

CCP Effectiveness in Directing Major Policies and Programmes to Those in Most Need

After the introduction of Inner City Partnership central government and the agencies, including Gateshead in 1978–9, lowered their commitment to CCP. Partnership and its available resources provided the new focus of the time. Thus CCP took on a low profile in the agencies, and though they continued to be involved it was with less enthusiasm and did not lead to their redirecting policies and programmes. The county council saw its main emphasis on the Partnership areas of Gateshead and Newcastle, and upon the areas designated as Programme authorities. Against this background it was difficult to argue that Gateshead should get two bites at the cherry, one as a Partnership authority, the other as a CCP authority. Nevertheless information provided through CCP, especially where relevant to county matters, was regarded as useful in informing and influencing the ongoing decisions of the county council. It was seen as helpful in providing background against which the Partnership operated. Gateshead was only one zone within the jurisdiction of the county which had to be considered against this wider background. Within the Gateshead Area Health Authority the priority was seen to be with the Inner City Partnership, which was viewed primarily as a joint funding mechanism in reverse. CCP was regarded as useful to the health authority because of its research and information role.

Central government, both at regional and central levels, saw the partnership status of Gateshead as its priority and its attention began to focus upon the CCP as a policy planning process for redirecting main spending programmes at local level. Central government was less concerned with individual policy analyses on which CCP began to concentrate. Other regional departments of government were involved in CCP through information provision and involvement with specific policy analysis issues. These officials saw CCP as a research- and information-based activity and several were not at all clear about its relationship to the Newcastle–Gateshead partnership. By the middle of the project emphasis on redirecting main programmes was generally viewed as a Gateshead Council affair. The advent of the Newcastle–Gateshead partnership provided a substitute inter-agency framework from which agencies could expect resources. CCP as an inter-agency policy planning system had largely fallen by the wayside.

Resource constraint was increasingly being felt within Gateshead and departments and committees were concerned with where cuts should fall. CCP created a pressure to improve and develop new services. At a time of cutback this produced a problem for many officers and politicians. Hence arguments about the need for a redirecting of main programme resources fell largely on barren ground. The urgent problem of the day was to survive the cuts as best one could. The maintenance of a basic level of resources to ensure adequate standards and service became the priority. Partnership resources could be used to top up departmental resources and to develop new initiatives. Thus the climate of organisational resource constraint was argued to militate against any redirecting of main programmes to those in greatest need.

It was argued by Gateshead's senior politicals and officers that CCP, having had a one-year disruption to cope with the first-year inner city programme, had too short a time-span to begin to assess the impact it would have on resource redistribution and on the working of the authority. A one-year project extension was sought by Gateshead but rejected by the Department of the Environment. Policy analysis appears to have had little success in this redistributive direction: the priorities are protecting one's service. There have, however, been some marginal resource shifts in relation to nursery education provision and play provision, while CCP has assisted in the preparation of the housing investment programme. CCP suggestions for additional resources are less likely to find favour than those which deal with procedural and administrative matters whose impact upon the deprived may nevertheless be potentially considerable, for example, the proposal to reshape the housing allocation system.

In Gateshead impending service cuts and their implementation appeared to threaten the small degree of corporate working that did exist. Against this background a strong commitment to redirecting resources is difficult. Decision-making was diffuse and decisions in one location were often independent of decisions elsewhere. The original CCP remit suggested the development of a CCP policy planning mechanism which would link to existing policy systems. The very subject matter of CCP is corporate. Yet where existing corporate planning exists only in embryo form and where CCP is seen by some departments and committees as creating tension, there could be perceived dangers in linking a more politically neutral corporate planning approach to a more politically sensitive CCP system for redirecting resources. Combined with economic restraint, commitment to CCP ideals can rapidly wane. However, it is possible to argue that CCP has drawn attention to issues about service provision and deprivation which has led to a higher level of political and administrative debate on these issues within the local authority, especially in education and housing.

The short-term effectiveness of CCP in redirecting priorities and resources to those in greatest need has been low. On the other hand there is growing awareness that elements of CCP work do form part of the background of information against which decision-making in the authority is undertaken. Similarly the existence of CCP has raised issues about the very nature of the processes of decision-making in Gateshead. The CCP experiment has therefore tended to raise issues about processes of decision-making rather than about greater organisational impact upon the problems faced by the deprived within Gateshead. For the future much depends upon whether these decision processes will be made more sensitive and responsive to the particular needs of the deprived.

The CCP experiment finished at the end of March 1980. Staff were transferred to a new central policy unit within Gateshead. Part of the work of this unit has been to progress some of the issues emerging through the CCP experience.

BRADFORD CCP, 1978–80

In May 1978 the Bradford CCP was launched. Earlier Bradford, a Conservative-controlled authority, had received a letter from the Department of the Environment offering a choice between either CCP or Inner City Programme Authority status. Bradford opted for CCP. In financial terms the choice was broadly similar for both options with £2 million allocated for first-year operation and resources promised for future years to fund new and ongoing projects. Bradford through CCP received the same resources as if it had opted for Programme Authority status. Bradford's CCP was established on the basis of a four-year life (to the end of March 1982), subject to review after two years (March 1980). In the event CCP was terminated at the earlier date because of local political pressures, though it had been winding down for several months before that.

Some of the reasons for the selection by Bradford of the CCP option were that the CCP was authority-wide, not inner-city-specific. Secondly, the resources offered were attractive and included assistance with staffing costs (unlike programme status). Thirdly, Bradford was familiar with the CCP concept, having been involved in earlier discussions with the Home Office. Fourthly, it was felt that CCP provided Bradford with better access to central government.

The CCP team, as in Gateshead, was created as an independent unit reporting to the inter-agency CCP administrative and political framework. But inevitably, because of its composition and physical location, it was closely allied to Bradford District Council itself. Bradford's Director of Social Services was appointed Comptroller of CCP on relinquishing his post. A team was quickly assembled. It had been decided as a matter of principle that the team would be recruited from among existing officers of the authority. Staff were appointed by Bradford, not by an inter-agency panel. The team was made up of a town planner, a social worker, a librarian, a finance officer and a corporate planner, together with secretarial/administrative support. The team was in post by May 1978.

The Bradford CCP prospectus was quickly prepared, setting out the approach to CCP (Bradford CCP, 1978). It provided a more philosophical approach than that of Gateshead.

The CCP Prospectus

This document was published in July 1978. The aim of CCP was:

> *to examine ways in which existing policies and programmes act upon those who are deprived in order to make practical recommendations which help to lessen inequalities in economic, social and physical conditions in the community* . . . CCP must be realistic and it must work through, and with, existing planning cycles and decision making processes of the agencies concerned and must involve the community in the process . . . The CCP must be practical. It is about changing situations on the ground. (Bradford CCP, 1978, p. 3)

The prospectus outlined the three-part CCP process in the following terms:

Part 1: Examination of the nature of multiple deprivation in Bradford

The CCP team would work with the agencies involved to encourage their understanding of deprivation in order to help them become more responsive to the needs of the deprived. This work would be developed in conjunction with the first part of the ongoing Metplan process, that of district trends analysis, already well established in Bradford [Metplan is Bradford's corporate planning system].

Part 2: Review of selected policies

(i) Critically examine the assumptions behind existing policies and programmes, including resource allocation.
(ii) Ask whether, if they are the correct policies and programmes, they are being implemented properly.
(iii) Ask all levels of government to consider the implications of policies and programmes beyond the achievement of narrow departmental or professional operational objectives.
(iv) Seek policies to discriminate in favour of particular client groups or resolve areas of concern for the wider disadvantaged community.

Part 3: Formulation of programme of action

In addition to determining the projects financed through urban programme resources the aim of CCP would be to encourage agencies to:

(i) improve the provision and quality of services;
(ii) make more accessible social and economic support;
(iii) encourage greater community participation.

The prospectus drew attention to the need to gear CCP to Metplan.[12] It was also recognised that the first-year CCP action programme (1979/80) would not benefit from the full three-part CCP process because of time shortage. The prospectus outlined the planning cycles of the agencies involved[13] and showed how the CCP would influence the 1979/80 programme of action. Thereafter subsequent action programmes would be built from the full three-part CCP process.

Organisational Structure

The CCP Members' Group was chaired by a Minister of State from the Department of the Environment and consisted of political representatives of the agencies involved. The Officer Steering Group was chaired by the Regional Director of the Department of the Environment and consisted of senior officer representation from the agencies involved. The CCP team reported to the Steering Group and Members' Group, the latter being responsible for CCP. There was no equivalent of the Gateshead Working Group. In parallel, CCP reported to Bradford's elected-member Corporate Planning Panel,[14] while the Comptroller reported regularly to Bradford's Chief Executive and Directors' Management Team. Strong links were developed with Bradford's Corporate Planning Co-ordinator in order to integrate CCP with the Metplan process. The purpose of Metplan is:

> through the declared philosophy, planning and managing the activities of the local authority (and as far as possible other agencies) so as best to meet the needs of the people, to the extent and in the ways decided by the elected politicians (with the benefit of good information and analysis), and to meet these needs efficiently and effectively. (Bradford City Council, 1978, p. 4)

In discussions about the organisation of CCP in Bradford one alternative had been to place CCP under the aegis of the corporate planning co-ordinator. In the event this alternative was not pursued. Bradford's Metplan system was highly regarded by leading politicians and political questions amongst Bradford's Conservatives were concerned with how to make Metplan more effective, not with whether corporate planning was a useful approach or not. In Bradford therefore controlling elected members had a highly developed concern for and interest in the nature of policy planning processes.

The first Five-Year Plan was produced for 1980–5; before that Three-Year Plans on a rolling programme basis were prepared. CCP input was for this Five-Year Plan, that is, the cycle starting in early 1979.

The Operation of CCP

Over the life of the CCP, effectively eighteen months out of an originally anticipated life of four years, it is possible to identify distinct phases of work. These were: preparing the first-year programme submission (1979/80) including the organisation of a Community Fund; secondly, issue analysis work; thirdly, integration with Metplan; fourthly, preparing the second-year programme submission (1980/1) and the rundown of CCP.

The first-year CCP spending programme. In this phase the CCP team were responsible for developing, with the co-operation of others, the first-year action programme (including both the main programme and the Community Fund). Much of the initiative and responsibility for highlighting projects was handled by the CCP team which meant that it could not, at this early stage, adequately develop CCP processes.

Some politicians and officers felt that spending programmes were too rushed and without adequate preparation. This concern was inevitable given central government's treatment of CCP in the same submission-phasing manner as Inner City Programme authorities. Yet it made the CCP highly visible as having resources and for those interested more in the idea of rapid action on the ground it proved attractive. The concept was that spending would be a form of pump-priming, with the aim of breaking into resource distributional changes in main programmes. In the first programme, as with partnership and programme authorities, projects were often those drawn off shelves, or projects pushed up the priority order list owing to CCP resource availability. Because of the central government-imposed constraint of having to spend within the particular financial year this meant that projects, especially capital projects, had to be at a relatively advanced stage of development. Otherwise the time-lag would mean that valuable resources would have been lost.

A further dilemma was created by central government's view that projects should not be main programme projects already in the pipeline, but should be additional, new ventures, which would affect future patterns of main programme spending. Central government felt initially that many of these projects should be innovative. The dilemma created was the feeling among local agencies that many suitable projects, on which a fair degree of preparatory work had been undertaken, were already waiting in the wings. A number of these projects found their way into the 1979/80 action programme. The broad areas in which first-year CCP resources for this action programme were spent were: social services, £150,000; educational services (including recreation), £795,000; development services (including housing), £627,000; Area Health Authority, £97,000; West Yorkshire County Council, £108,000, and Community Fund (voluntary group bids), £300,000, giving a total allocation of £2,077,000.

Through this early emphasis on the preparation of projects CCP became associated with project-funding rather than with developing a policy planning process. The team was aware of this situation and attempted to rectify the position subsequently. Nevertheless the £2 million for projects in 1979–80 had proved valuable to the CCP in developing contacts and insights into the attitudes and operations of agencies in relation to deprivation. CCP had proved a means of enabling it to participate with appropriate divisional staff in their ongoing thinking about service delivery and policy. It had provided a useful break-in point. The CCP team also established a monitoring system within Bradford, agreed by the Management Team and operated jointly by CCP and divisions concerned with project supervision and implementation. This was to enable slippage to be identified early and any necessary corrective action taken to keep the spending programme on target, for example, injection of projects on a reserve list.

Arising from this first CCP resource allocation exercise several important issues emerged. One was the concern of senior officers about the length of time taken to process project agreement through central government machinery. Projects had to be carried out in the year 1979–80 and as much notice as possible was needed. This was compounded by the amount of extra work some service officers responsible for planning of CCP projects had to undertake. Also the flow of project design work through the architect's division proved problematic because of the time constraint and bunching effect on capital projects.

From the local political viewpoint the programme was felt to be too 'social' in outlook, and too separate from the Metplan process (over which local political control was stronger). A particularly significant political issue was the availability of CCP specific resources in relation to the general level of resource availability for the authority as a whole. Some chairmen, as part of the Metplan process, were having to cut costs and reduce expenditure on services. They found it difficult to appreciate why they had to do this, only to be asked by CCP to come up with new spending projects. It was felt that greater control of CCP expenditures and linking projects with the priorities set by panels were important. Such change was developed through CCP linkages with Metplan for the second year. Local politicians had a similar concern about other 'funny monies', for example, section 11 grants under the 1966 Local Government Act, normal urban aid funds, operation cleanup money.

The Community Fund was one element of the first-year programme. A sum of £300,000 was set aside against which bids from voluntary organisations throughout the district could be made. Bids of about £1·5 million were made after widespread local publicity. The projects for forwarding to the minister for approval were selected by a panel consisting of local politicians, the vice-chairman of the local Council for Voluntary Service, and a representative of the Regional Office of the Department of the Environment.

The existence of the Community Fund helped the CCP and Bradford in their dealings with voluntary groups. It dispelled some of the doubt created early in the life of CCP when a senior Conservative politician stated that he did not see a role for community group participation in the CCP process. On the other hand, the government's White Paper on the Inner City stressed that such groups had a role to play (HMSO, 1977).[15] The Labour minister chairing the CCP Members' Group stressed the importance of community involvement.

Voluntary groups in Bradford generally welcomed the CCP. Subsequently they were to assist, through the local Council for Voluntary Service, with one of the CCP issue analysis topics on policy and procedural constraints preventing the community and agencies from dealing with deprivation. Community groups also played an active part in bidding for CCP resources in the second programme.

Issue analysis. The CCP team in conjunction with officers from Bradford and other agencies carried out a number of studies. Some related to ideas identified in the prospectus, others were highlighted because of local political and voluntary group concern. The issue papers were prepared ready for a Steering Group meeting in June 1979, but this meeting was cancelled because of government announcements about public expenditure cuts in local government. Thus senior officer attention in Bradford was diverted away from CCP papers and the future role of CCP to the more immediate concern of further expenditure constraint. Besides the issue papers a paper was prepared dealing with part 1 and entitled 'The examination of the nature of multiple deprivation in Bradford'. It was not a statistical profile (Metplan already covered this in District Trends, a major planning document in Bradford). The report was based upon the subjective and qualitative evidence of officers in the various agencies and upon material from the Chief Officers' Reports (again springing from the Metplan process). The report focused upon the allocation of resources as the critical factor and through selective case studies considered how resource allocation was decided and how these decisions related to problems of deprivation. One issue paper addressed constraints in policies, including rules and procedures, which prevented both the community and the agencies involved in CCP from tackling deprivation. A review of information and advice services was also undertaken. Voluntary groups had been particularly interested in this issue and the local political leadership had rejected a proposal to submit for approval to the minister (then a Labour minister) a scheme for CCP funding of a legal advice centre. The final report was concerned with service delivery and the impact of agency activities upon life in a peripheral council housing estate in Keighley. This work involved the participation of local residents and local field staff. The estate had received a significant injection of first-year CCP project funding, many of the projects being strongly influenced by local residents. It was felt that an inter-agency approach to dealing with the problems of the estate together with local resident participation would be a beneficial exercise which could provide lessons for other areas.

In the event the papers were eventually received but not proceeded with in terms of CCP action because CCP was being wound up. The effect upon the CCP team was demoralising. The documentation was passed to the central policy unit as the successor body to which a number of CCP staff were transferred early in 1980.

Integration with Metplan. There was pressure from local politicians, senior officers and the CCP team itself to develop a CCP–Metplan linkage. Politically it was felt that CCP resource guidelines should be integrated with Metplan thus providing an extra resource element for panels to exploit. At the same time elected members wanted to end the nonsense of different central government proposals and programmes being dealt with separately and in isolation from Metplan. It was also felt that CCP could make a major contribution to achieving the two main objectives of the authority by concentrating on industrial development and the physical environment. Bradford's Conservatives saw CCP as a means both of plugging their own service resource gaps and focusing more directly on their two main objectives. Attention dwelt on the CCP as a source of extra resources, not as a competing policy planning system. Despite the inter-agency nature of CCP Bradford's politicians wanted to control and direct the process more closely. This emphasis was boosted by a change of Conservative Party leader in May 1979, and was pursued with more vigour after that date. At the same time the new emphases for Metplan revision (stemming from the change of leadership) were to give greater stress to the role of performance review and policy analysis. Both of these were elements being developed by CCP itself.

The annual Metplan cycle starting in 1979 (for the 1980–5 Five-Year Plan) was the first full cycle upon which CCP could begin to have impact. In addition to political pressures pushing in this direction the CCP team had seen the wisdom and necessity of such integration as a step towards fuller directorate and divisional participation in the work of CCP. Some of the detailed timing of the Metplan process was altered to allow CCP processes to feed in at the appropriate stages. The significant links developed through Metplan were first an input through District Trends and second, influencing chief officers' service reports. These are considered in turn.

CCP had an input into the preparation of the District Trends document for 1979.[16] District Trends is one of the documents which helps councillors to plan the policies and services of Bradford over the next five years. District Trends highlighted nine key points which needed to be considered in formulating policy proposals for 1980–5. Among these key points were several concerned with aspects of deprivation in Bradford, for example, different educational attainment levels in different parts of the district, the concentration of certain economic and social problems in the inner city and some council estates, future non-white household size and its implications for housing provision.

On publication of the report the local, and indeed national, press highlighted the high infant morbidity and mortality rates, especially among Asian families. As a result the Area Health Authority began to develop its work in coping with those problems. Similarly the report put pressure on the education service to review its provision for meeting the education needs of the coloured immigrant community. The housing department, assisted by CCP urban programme funds, began to consider the particular housing needs of these families. Thus a series of policy reviews and proposed policy, programme and resource allocation changes were to result in the 1980–5 Five-Year Plan.

District Trends, together with the CCP report on the nature of deprivation in Bradford, began to affect thinking on a number of programme and policy developments, and teams of officers in the various divisions of the city council took up a number of points arising from these analyses. A number of schemes, either with CCP resource assistance or by financing from within normal budgets, have been developed.

The role of Chief Officers' Reports are important in Bradford because they feed directly into panel discussions by the elected members on the future development of services. CCP was able through Metplan to ask chief officers to provide information on the way resources were allocated and priorities decided. This attempt to lead towards new policy directions through influencing the nature and scope of Chief Officers' Reports was an element of CCP integration with Metplan. CCP issues were incorporated as part of the guidelines on the nature of Chief Officers' Reports.[17]

Chief officers were asked to comment upon specific CCP issues. One group of chief officers were asked to focus on their service provision to children of school age suffering educational and/or social disadvantage. Each division was asked to select an appropriate function and analyse its role in terms of its information base, criteria of service allocation and degree of co-operation with other divisions and agencies. The responses complemented other work in the authority on provision for the under-5s. As a result a number of programmes were implemented through CCP funding and through divisions' main programmes, including work by the educational advisory service, the monitoring of inner city school performance, library and other recreational facilities for the deprived, and social services work with disadvantaged youngsters.

Another group of chief officers commented upon a particular aspect of their service and its relation to deprived areas or individuals. Divisions involved in industrial promotion and development were asked to describe the way their work was organised and co-ordinated, to review their activities and to suggest changes for the future. These responses raised a number of policy and procedural issues with the result that the management of this hitherto disparate activity was centralised within the chief executive's aegis and responsibility placed in the hands of a newly created elected members' panel.

Thus CCP helped to focus organisational attention on aspects of deprivation in Bradford to a greater degree than previously. This was achieved through a combination of Metplan processes, CCP project-funding, decisions of service departments and committees and outside pressures.

The link of CCP with Metplan was difficult, not least because of local political feeling towards CCP during 1979 which saw it as too isolated and not politically central to the objectives of the council. One problem recognised by senior members was that Metplan was not itself a process linked to a political philosophy whereas CCP was seen as an explicitly political process. With increasing economic austerity Bradford under the Conservatives stressed the need to develop the economic prosperity of the area and to improve the physical environment, an emphasis heightened by the new Conservative government which came to power in 1979. Dealing with deprivation *per se* was not an item on the local political agenda.

Relationships with other CCP agencies require comment. Significant progress was made with the county council, particularly with the strategic planning division, the transport policies and programme section and those responsible for the county's ten-year finance plan. Relationships with the Area Health Authority (AHA) were more difficult to develop. There were different organisational cultures. The AHA saw itself as marginal and saw the CCP as an AHA joint funding exercise with the local authority in reverse. Thus the Joint Consultative Committee was seen by the AHA as a means by which Bradford gained access to health resources, while the CCP was a means by which the AHA gained access to Bradford's resources.

The CCP team generally found links with both central and regional levels of the Department of the Environment useful. The Department maintained a strong interest in the Bradford CCP, particularly in the development of the CCP policy planning system and its integration with Metplan. CCP was important in providing a useful means of dialogue between central government and Bradford, a dialogue which was often used for non-CCP purposes. The existence of CCP had enabled Bradford to benefit from some of the small resource shifts within central government programmes.

Preparing the second-year programme and the rundown of CCP. After the summer of 1979 political commitment to the idea of maintaining a separate CCP unit rapidly waned. The election of a Conservative central government in May 1979, coinciding with a change in local political leadership, led Bradford to regard CCP as a source of extra cash which Bradford itself should utilise through its service panels, particularly to plug gaps in services and to develop new ideas. CCP was regarded politically as a peripheral irritant; it had raised a number of issues which had been politically controversial. At the same time the concept of urban deprivation was not one readily espoused by the local political leadership. Some elected members saw CCP as leading to a criticism of the policies and work of the authority, while there was also a feeling that members had not been adequately consulted about the decision to opt for CCP status. Some members felt they lacked a sufficient awareness of the content and purpose of CCP.

As a result CCP was wound up, though it did spend time helping to co-ordinate the panels' bids for CCP resources for the second funding year 1980/1; it also handled community group applications for CCP resources. The title of CCP has been officially dropped and the experiment was terminated at the end of March 1980. In May, after ward boundary changes in the district with all elected members having to seek re-election, the Labour Party was returned with a clear majority. The fate of CCP had already been sealed by then, though the Labour majority has espoused within its philosophy and programmes several of the themes raised through CCP (Winchurch, 1980, pp. 27–32). Bradford's CCP team was posted to the central corporate planning unit which was being significantly enlarged in late 1979 and early 1980 by the drawing together of existing research, corporate planning, industrial development, CCP and some public relations staff. The new unit was seen as part of a wider intended reorganisation of the Bradford management structure. The Comptroller retired upon the termination of CCP.

Bradford continues to receive Programme Authority status resources, but was less directly committed to bending its own main programmes. Currently Bradford does not define an inner city area but uses urban programme resources to improve its services in line with local political aims. It is now treated in other respects by the Department of the Environment as a normal Programme Authority, though in Bradford the programme is referred to as a Community Programme.

Thus Bradford CCP, though short-lived, did create some awareness of the problems of deprivation and probed alternative forms of service provision. There are now a number of programmes, including, but not confined to, CCP project funding, which are presently attempting to alleviate deprivation in Bradford. Many of these programmes would not necessarily have been instituted without the presence of CCP, which also strengthened liaison with certain voluntary organisations.

CONCLUSIONS

What are the issues which emerge from the two experiences of attempting to develop a CCP policy planning process? A preliminary and very obvious point is that the context was different. One authority was Labour-controlled, the other Conservative. One had developed a systematic and workable policy planning process, the other had not.

Gateshead CCP operated in conjunction with partnership status which overshadowed it and reduced its inter-agency significance. Bradford had the more difficult local political environment. Bradford had CCP project resources, Gateshead did not.

It was difficult to introduce CCP as a policy planning process where no strength of corporate working or corporate management processes already existed. Similarly this affected the ability of CCP to link into existing processes and interdepartmental or departmental working group structures. In Gateshead CCP provided the authority with the basis of a corporate approach. The existence of other corporate processes affected the level of assistance given to the CCP teams, while it also influenced the pace at which CCP processes were developed. In the Gateshead case CCP moved away from developmental policy planning towards opportunistic policy analysis. In Bradford CCP more readily adapted to its role as a policy planning process assisted by Metplan.

CCP did not provide a route to effective inter-agency working and co-ordination. In both cases most of the political and day-to-day working pressures came from the district councils. It was easier for Bradford CCP team (all seconded staff) to adapt quickly to local circumstances, whereas in Gateshead (all outside appointments) this process took longer. This was compounded in Gateshead by the resignations of the team leader and one of the policy analysts during the experimental period. In both cases CCP staff were transferred to a central policy and research unit on the chief executive's staff once CCP had terminated.

The Home Office remit had not explicitly recognised the implications for CCP work of a period of increasing economic severity. Changed economic circumstances led to problems in both schemes. CCP demonstrated its usefulness in defining problems and issues; both schemes indicated a high level of analytical ability. However, both faced problems over introducing new policies and getting programmes implemented through service departments. The pattern of public expenditure cuts imposed by central government were often regarded as making the task of stemming the extent of deprivation even greater, for example, heavy cuts in local authority housing programmes. Locally public expenditure restraint was seen as central government's main political priority while that of redirecting resources to those most in need was seen as a marginal priority. It was also recognised, particularly after the Conservative government came to power in 1979, that concern with deprivation increasingly emphasised the productive base of local economies. The basic aims of CCP of developing a policy planning process and directing main policies, programmes and resources to those in greatest need were not fully understood and appreciated by agency staffs involved in CCP. The early work of both CCPs tended to create longlasting impressions of what CCP was about. In Gateshead it was seen as a research and information tool, in Bradford as a dispenser of urban programme project resources. In neither authority was it an easy task to develop an organisational focus upon deprivation.

Much depended upon adequate political understanding and commitment to the aims of CCP activity. Without strong political commitment CCP policy planning processes could not succeed in their aims. Indeed CCP was largely an explicitly political policy planning process, whereas many other policy processes were regarded as politically neutral, for example, Metplan, Area Health Authority plans, Transport Policies and Programme. The direct linking of CCP processes with ongoing decision processes was difficult because of its political implications.

The authority-wide perspective of the CCP raised a number of issues (see also Mason *et al.*, 1977).

(1) Deprivation though concentrated in the inner area was not exclusively located there. There were different spatial manifestations of various elements of deprivation.
(2) Most existing decision-making systems operated authority-wide. The area perspective as a basis of decision-making was less significant (with the exception of certain planning decisions). It was therefore more appropriate for a policy planning system dealing with deprivation to link into existing patterns of decision-making and influence these.
(3) Agencies often had problems in adjusting to decision-making in respect of only a part of their jurisdiction. Many agencies worry about 'creating a precedent'. Reaction against creating precedents serves to reinforce uniformity rather than the differentiation which may be required for a more sensitive response to the problems of deprivation.
(4) A CCP approach could readily be adapted to include less urbanised areas.
(5) Programmes to ameliorate deprivation may well include the need for action outside a defined inner area. Too often the geographical scale of analysis for problem definition was the same scale for programme implementation.
(6) Decisions about redirecting resources need to consider which programmes should be reduced as well as which should be enhanced. This is especially the case in times of economic restraint. Such decisions can lead to interdepartmental and professional rivalries.

In Gateshead the main achievements of CCP were concerned with internal organisational matters rather than with short-term impact upon the community. In Bradford the internal organisational concern was balanced by a small range of variously funded programmes to alleviate deprivation. CCP depended upon an organisational ability to work corporately. Where such a co-ordinated approach was lacking it was difficult for CCP itself to create that form of working. Without this pre-existing corporate approach CCP moved towards being a more *ad hoc*, opportunistic, enterprise. Such a movement is also likely where political and administrative commitment is low.

There was resistance to linking CCP to existing policy-making processes, especially where CCP might give rise to competition with departmental priorities, or where it might produce material putting outside pressure on departments to encourage change. CCP had the potential to highlight existing service deficiencies and weaknesses which could be politically embarrassing to departments and service committees.

CCP had no executive powers other than a link with decisions about urban programme resources (available in Bradford but not Gateshead). Thus the problem which CCP did not solve, of itself, was gaining sufficient leverage to tilt the balance of resource allocation decisions towards those individuals in greatest need. As resource constraints increase a narrower, more specific, focus for deprivation combating policies may be required. These approaches could be departmental or agency-specific. CCP has shown that effective inter-agency co-ordination is difficult to achieve, at central and regional levels of government as well as at local authority level.[18]

NOTES: CHAPTER 10

This chapter is based largely upon work supported first by the Home Office Urban Deprivation Unit and subsequently by the Department of the Environment, Inner Cities Directorate, over the period 1977 to 1980. The author thanks the officers and elected members of all the agencies involved in the two CCP experiments for their help and assistance. In particular help has been willingly forthcoming from the Inner Cities Directorate and from the two CCP teams in Gateshead and Bradford. The views expressed, however, are those of the author and do not necessarily reflect the views of all, or any specific, agencies or individuals involved in the CCP experiments.

1 *Hansard*, HC, vol. 877 (18 July 1974), col. 65.
2 *Hansard*, HC, vol. 878 (29 July 1974), cols 237–53.
3 For a more detailed account of the origin of the comprehensive community programme through to the first English operational scheme at Gateshead in 1977 see Spencer, 1980b, pp. 17–28. See also Stewart, Spencer and Webster, 1976, for ideas on urban deprivation plan initiatives, some of which were incorporated within the CCP approach. This report suggested 'that central government should pay grants for urban deprivation plans prepared by local authorities in association with the other agencies of government' (p. ii), that these plans 'would not contain a single, simple solution to the problems of urban deprivation . . . Rather they provide a possible approach within which policies can develop over time' (p. ii).
4 This work included responsibility for the ongoing urban programme, including urban aid grants and the community development projects, section 11 grants of the 1966 Local Government Act (assistance with staffing costs in areas of high coloured immigration) and liaison with government departments and local authorities.
5 One Minister of State at the Home Office has explained 'that Labour Ministers at the Home Office accepted too readily Treasury protestations that there was no money available'. See Lyon, 1979, p. 24.
6 See for example the urban guideline studies; Department of the Environment, 1973a, 1973b and 1973c (2 vols); and the inner area studies: Department of the Environment, 1977a, 1977b and 1977c.
7 This lapse of time from 1974–7 has been described as suffering 'from a lack of urgency, imagination and commitment, at both ministerial and civil service levels', see Wicks, 1980, p. 278. This article also provides a view on the development of the CPP concept.
8 HMSO, 1977, para. 64: 'Authorities who undertake inner area programmes or CCPs will, as far as is possible, be given preference in the allocation of grants after partnership authorities.'

9 For a brief outline of inner city policy evolution see Wicks, 1977; Spencer, 1979, pp. 59–62; D. L. Smith, 1978, pp. 193–202; Cox, 1979, pp. 2–17.

10 For For the development of the reasons for this situation, see Spencer, 1980b, and Wicks, 1980; see also Lawless, 1979, pp. 88–95, for an outline of the background of CCPs.

11 Home Office Urban Deprivation Unit; Gateshead District Council; Tyne and Wear County Council; Gateshead Area Health Authority.

12 For an introduction to Bradford's Metplan process see Hawkins and Tarr, 1980, pp. 43–51.

13 These were central government, represented by Department of the Environment (Inner Cities Directorate and the Yorkshire and Humberside Regional Office), Bradford City Council, West Yorkshire County Council and the Area Health Authority.

14 Bradford's panels are basically the equivalent of subcommittees. See Hawkins and Tarr, 1980.

15 In addition Bradford's CCP prospectus has also referred to community participation.

16 Bradford City Council, 1979a. The document provides a first stage to the Metplan process. It is updated annually and portrays the problems and changes facing the community. It provides one source from which needs are identified.

17 Chief officers' reports are in three parts. Part A reviews those services for which a chief officer is responsible, considering client group trends, service gaps, resources, unit costs, manpower, physical equipment. It also presents an assessment of current policies in meeting the needs identified. Part B is about the general philosophy of service provision, professional objectives and the direction in which the chief officer would wish to see the service developed. It also considers constraints on service development. Part C, which is prepared later than parts A and B, contains detailed, costed recommendations of the developments likely over the period of the five-year plan. For CCP influence in parts A and B see Bradford City Council, 1979b.

18 For other material on CCPs see K. M. Spencer, *The Comprehensive Community Programme Experiment in Gateshead, 1977–1980*, Institute of Local Government Studies, University of Birmingham 1981 and K. M. Spencer, 'Comprehensive Community Programmes – the practical experience', *Local Government Studies*, vol. 7, no. 3, 1981, pp. 31–49.

11

Planning Health Care Services

BRYAN STOTEN

The reorganisation of the National Health Service had been canvassed for many years before 1974. Guillebaud in 1956 had drawn attention to the difficulties created by a tripartite structure (Royal Commission on the National Health Service, 1956). The Porritt Report (Medical Services Review Committee, 1962) advocated a unified service under area health boards, a proposal endorsed by the British Medical Association in 1962. Proposals for local government reform, however, finally placed NHS reorganisation on the political agenda. Indeed the subsequent shape of that reform was largely to determine the overall administrative structure of the NHS.

The history of the negotiations over the reorganisation has been examined elsewhere (F. Stacey, 1973); of more importance for the development of health care planning, however, was the nature of the management arrangements within the reorganised service. In 1970 a working party was established

> to make recommendations on management systems for the services for which regional and area health authorities will be responsible and on the internal organisation of those authorities. (Department of Health and Social Security, 1972, p. 7)

The result of this study published as *Management Arrangements for the Reorganised National Health Service* and known popularly as the Grey Book, was a structure both hierarchical and centralised, designed to secure the twin principles of clinical involvement in the management of health care and centralised control exercised ultimately by the Secretary of State. These principles reflect two key political constraints in the management of the NHS: first, the tradition of clinical autonomy, which extends beyond the practice of medicine. Klein (1973, p. 7) has noted:

> The history of the British health service is the history of political power, Ministers, Civil Servants, Parliament accommodating itself to professional power. It is not so much that doctors dictate public policy as that they define the parameters of the politically possible.

Klein pointed to the role of the clinicians as policy-makers – not in Eckstein's (1960, p. 8) sense as a member of an influential pressure group, but as executant of policy: 'it is the doctor who determines how . . . the resources will be used: which patients will be treated when and how.' To avoid suspicion that such autonomy was threatened by a bureaucratic structure great emphasis was laid upon 'maximum decentralisation and delegation of decision making' (Department of Health and Social Security, 1972, p. 8, para. 15).

The second feature of the service since its inception has been its centralised nature, particularly within the largest sector: the hospital service. Centralised policy-making in the service has tended to be negative rather than positive. Although macro-resource allocation decisions have been centralised the nature of professional practice has remained largely unaffected. The University of Hull's pre-reorganisation study of area joint liaison committee activity makes the point economically. The first volume, *Preparations for Change*, in which locally generated plans began to develop, was followed by a second volume, *Waiting for Guidance* (Humberside Reorganisation Project, 1973, 1974).

Powell (1966) has stressed the centralised nature of the service:

> in effect the Board and Committee represent an administrative chain for the transmission of central policy and decision, all the more formidable for being in appearance bodies with an existence of their own and not merely a bureaucracy.

While Crossman (1972) pointed to the difficulty of achieving change through such policy transmission: 'the centre is weak and the Regional Hospital Boards are strong . . . [with the result that there is] . . . a consultant dominated service.' These two aspects of the service are crucial for understanding the management and planning arrangements for reorganisation. As one senior civil servant in the Department of Health pointed out, at the centre of DHSS thinking was the task of 'squaring the circle' of maximum delegation to the point of service delivery and maximum accountability to those politically responsible. Thus the principles of peripheral consensus and central accountability were introduced in an attempt to reconcile the claims of political control and clinical autonomy.

An annual planning cycle was to be the mechanism through which this reconciliation was to be achieved.

> . . . this systematic planning process will be in the form of an interactive dialogue between DHSS, RHAs and AHAs and their District Managements in which the main management control exercised by one level over another is the allocation of resources and the setting of guidelines to the level below, followed by review and approval of their plans. Once these have been agreed, operating authority can be delegated and accountability will be affected through monitoring performance in relation to agreed plans.

(Department of Health and Social Security, 1972, para. 1.31)

Thus between the publication of the Grey Book and the Royal Assent it became increasingly apparent that the planning system was to occupy a central role and to be more concerned with supporting the management structure than improving health care policy-making. Planning procedures provided the main system of relationships between the tiers of authorities, local authority services, health care planning teams, joint consultative committees (with local authorities), community health councils and an elaborate structure of professional advisory committees. As Sir Keith Joseph stated, the planning system was to be the 'principal means of achieving accountability between the statutory authorities' (Department of Health and Social Security, 1973a). The contrast, then, between the role of planning in the NHS and in local government is significant:

> the Health Service has developed its planning system as a mechanism to make its management arrangements work. Local Government management proposals are designed to facilitate planning itself. The former approach leads to uniformity, the latter to variety. (Thomas and Stoten, 1974)

PLANNING WEAKNESSES – THE NEED FOR CHANGE

A major objective of NHS reorganisation was to improve the planning and allocation of health care resources through organisational change, but the task of introducing the proposed structural changes drew attention away from 'the more systematic and comprehensive analysis of needs and priorities that will lie behind the planning and operations of each area' (Department of Health and Social Security, 1973b). Indeed in the service as a whole the reorganisation was seen primarily as an administrative tidying-up. Brown (1979, p. 143) has commented:

> Professional, technical and nursing staff seemed fairly satisfied that their own work would continue regardless of the administrative changes and that April 1974 would be relatively unimportant for them.

Even so the shape of the planning system reflected a desire to remove some of the more widely criticised weaknesses in health care planning. These criticisms took a number of forms.

(1) Cochrane (1972, p. 12) has argued that the NHS failed to consider the effects of the service which it provided.

> I once asked a worker at a crematorium who had a curiously contented look on his face, what he found so satisfying about his work. He replied that what fascinated him was the way in which so much went in and so little came out. I thought of advising him to get

a job with the NHS, it might have increased his job satisfaction, but decided against it. He probably got his kicks from a visual demonstration of the gap between input and output. A statistical demonstration might not have worked so well.

This problem of output management, of influencing the *effects* produced by health care service provision rather than merely the *level* of service provision, produced most of the other weaknesses that the new planning system was to remedy. Almost all routinely available NHS information had been collected for budgeting or managerial control purposes. Epidemiological information on the effect of services on health care was scarce and little used in planning.

(2) Because NHS planning had concentrated upon the provision of services rather than the achievement of health objectives health care planning had been limited to the development of particular specialities or disciplines rather than planning the delivery of a comprehensive service to patients. The tendency to plan for services rather than to plan for patients' needs was exacerbated by a tripartite structure which afforded little opportunity for the provision of an integrated service. In the absence of any output criteria health care activities became ends in themselves. Thus the increase in the number of health visitors at a time when most observers expressed doubts about the value of the role altogether epitomised the problem (see Committee on Nursing, 1972). The development and improvement of the *service* took precedence over changing health care needs. In the absence of long-term, patient-oriented, objectives the goal of health care planning had become the maintenance and development of existing services. Such an environment for policy-making inevitably favours professional imperialism. Growth in existing services swamped innovation. Furthermore because of the distribution of influence within the health service high-status clinical activities tended to attract a disproportionate share of NHS resources. The service thus became increasingly drawn toward the provision of high-technology medical care culminating in the series of scandals about long-stay patients in the late 1960s. Concern about redressing the balance of care in favour of the latter group of patients informed much of the thinking behind the development of planning in the post-1974 service.

(3) Coupled with the tendency to plan for the performance of an activity rather than the health care needs of the patient was a failure to review existing activities. While the health care planning task was primarily to expand the services provided to the patient no criteria could be developed to appraise existing services. In the absence of output criteria about the health of the community the different contributions of different activities to health care could not be assessed. Further, 'nor [was] there any proper analysis of alternatives along cost benefit or cost effectiveness lines' (Department of Health and Social Security, 1974).

(4) Because NHS planning lacked criteria by which to appraise existing services it concentrated essentially upon new expenditure.

Planning in the NHS meant primarily development planning with little emphasis on redeployment. However, with a planned growth rate of less than 3 per cent (HMSO, 1974, table 2.11), major policy changes could not be implemented through development planning alone. As Klein has pointed out:

> the hospital sector so dominates the health and personal social services that it would need a switch of resources, rather than a different rate of expansion, to make a more immediate and dramatic difference to the distribution of the total even over a 10 year period. (Klein *et al.*, 1974, p. 31)

In consequence NHS planning activity had been concentrated at the margins of the service and had failed to develop any comprehensive priorities or strategic plans based on an analysis of health care needs for the community as a whole. Health care policy-making was, therefore, highly susceptible to planning by decibel count (see Oldham HMC/Manchester Regional Hospital Board, 1973) – whoever shouted loudest got most. The process was one likely to exacerbate existing imbalances. Again Klein has pointed to the consequences of such incrementalism:

> the White Paper is clearly on strong grounds in using the growing numbers of the elderly as the rationale for increasing expenditure. The trouble is that it is by no means clear that the elderly are, in fact, the main beneficiaries of such extra expenditure as is incurred . . . Between 1963–64 and 1971–2 the Central Statistical Office Study shows health and welfare spending on the elderly rose by 23·7% in constant terms. But total non capital spending in this period rose by 45·8%. (Klein *et al.*, 1974, p. 37)

(5) In summary, the NHS had been planned and managed for twenty-five years with little reference to explicit health objectives, mainly because of the importance attached to achieving consensus amongst the health care professions, a task more easily secured by agreement on means rather than ends.

There is a major conceptual problem of relating patient-oriented health care objectives to specific programmes. Godber has pointed out:

> It might be thought that we should be able to demonstrate the effect of a comprehensive service upon 'the state of the public services'. In most respects the health record has improved throughout the period . . . But there is no way of proving that these things have happened because of the National Health Service. (Department of Health and Social Security, 1973c, p. 1)

If broad health care objectives (set in terms of reducing the experience of morbidity or mortality for specific groups) are difficult to operationalise, then they are likely to prove an inappropriate basis for central government's resource allocation decisions. The need to provide common standards of care throughout the service had been accepted by government for many years. If such common standards could not be set in output terms, then they had to be set in the form of standards or norms for services provided.

In such a way were the ultimate objectives of the NHS of improving the health of the community replaced by arbitrary goals expressed as bed-norms and staffing ratios (see especially Bosanquet, 1980). The exercise reflected more the exigency of constitutional accountability through a hierarchically managed service than it did any understanding of the health care outcomes of different levels of provision. Thus excessive supervision by each tier of the one below was substituted for the proposed Grey Book model of inter-tier relationships characterised by proper delegation and accountability based upon output targets set in terms of improved patient care.

(6) Planning in the NHS had the characteristics of being both centralised (Eckstein, 1959) and arbitrary in nature. Central government had since the inception of the NHS adhered to the principle of a national service in which inter-authority variations should be minimised and centrally determined policies should be pre-eminent. The result had been, however, to increase the irrational element in health care planning:

> the best example is hospital finance. The greater the need has been for a really rational distribution of funds among the hospitals the more have financial procedures been centralised; the more these procedures have been centralised, the more they have been dominated by routine and arbitrary formulas, by snap decisions in place of rational calculations . . . the process seems impelled, for logical reasons, to enlarge the area of factors which are subject to the control of a single authority as much as possible; in the second, it is impelled, for psychological as well as logical reasons, to reduce the scope of rational decision making as much as possible, and the more the range of calculation is enlarged the more it is necessary to reduce it. (ibid., p. 280)

Such centralising tendencies have further weakened the ability of chronic and preventive spheres of health care to attract resources. Statistics are compelling especially in so far as they conceal the subjectivity present in the policy-making process (Codlington, 1970, pp. 579–80). Centralised planning requires quantitative data to aid comparability when allocating resources between authorities. The 'softness' of data on many non-acute and community services, however, while capable of appreciation at the local level, is difficult to comprehend or employ in centralised planning. However, reliance on statistical data reporting bed occupancy rates and length of occupancy exaggerates the more measurable curative activities of the acute sector and sheds little light on the more intangible nature of prevention and long-term care. Such criticisms continue to be made of the service even after the 1974 reorganisation. The Merrison Report expressed its own misgivings about the nature of NHS strategic planning saying:

> even after listening to careful explanation by representatives of the DHSS about the way in which the needs of particular priority groups are taken into account in the allocation of resources to health authorities we remain mystified. We are bold enough to think that this is because there is some cloudiness in the Department's thinking about these matters, which are as important as anything in the Department's care. (Royal Commission on the NHS, 1979, p. 56)

One further central feature of pre-reorganisation planning proved the most intractable feature of the old system:

> Planning is too heavily biased towards capital development which is allowed to pre-empt revenue and manpower. Effective programming for more than one or at most two years ahead is limited to capital by present methods of resource allocation, there is often no adequate assessment of the other implications of capital development until too late. (Department of Health and Social Security, 1974, p. 27)

The long-term consequence of this manner of planning was effectively to denude the NHS of a field planning capability. The regional tier has always had the main planning role in the service. Eckstein wrote:

> The Boards are, first and foremost, planning agencies in that they make plans for the development of medical specialities in each region, control the distribution of specialists, and determine the grouping of individual hospitals under their jurisdiction. The Boards supervise the budgetary arrangements of lower hospital authorities and themselves administer all but the most minor capital expenditures, in other words, expenditures for plant and equipment – an indispensable adjunct to their planning functions. (ibid., pp. 180–1)

The bounded rationality engendered by this process of centralised planning at regional level resulted in an obsession with bricks and mortar. In the climate of the post-reorganisation service it is difficult to understand the lack of epidemiological or medical sociological contributions to this planning activity. NHS planning has rested primarily upon the shoulders of surveyors, architects, engineers and general administrators. Perhaps as important has been the social and professional distance that exists between the regional planners and field authorities. Many regional officers have not worked in the NHS other than at regional level. Before reorganisation the capital planning task did not involve the generation of alternative futures, an examination of alternative strategies, or evaluation of programmes in cost benefit terms. The planning role was essentially commissioning, hence the apparently arbitrary changes in national norms (Central Health Services Council, 1969; Ministry of Health, 1962).

In consequence planning in the pre-reorganised NHS was separated from main-line administration and management. Thus although authorities at the periphery of the service were able to be most sensitive to the environmental demands on the service, they were encouraged to pursue an essentially maintenance function. The regional authority charged with adapting the service to its environmental circumstances has in the past been the one least sensitive to the needs and developments of that environment.

The operational levels of the NHS, while concerned with maintenance issues, have been divorced from the wider issues of planning and policy-making. The consequent vacuum has been filled by clinicians with no responsibility to take a balanced overview of health care needs but rather with narrower commitment to the particular patients in their care.

PLANNING IN THE REORGANISED SERVICE

In introducing a national health care planning system DHSS has embraced the purest form of the rational model. In the *Guide to Planning in the NHS* (DHSS, 1975) the Department emphasises the stages through which a health plan must pass. Together with a system of programme areas based upon client groups this approach is designed to resolve many of the past problems of NHS planning.

Initially, however, the system was more piecemeal in character. In 1973 DHSS conducted a series of field trials to test the viability of a national planning system. Paradoxically the system, emerging out of the failure of the DHSS exercise with PPBS between 1970–2, was primarily a programming system requiring resource allocation statements and development proposals for the next three years. The basic building blocks of the system were health care planning teams (made up of practitioners, nurses, doctors, administrators, paramedicals and relevant local authority officers) whose task was to identify 'improvement opportunities' and make proposals for a range of client groups, including the elderly, the mentally ill and handicapped, and children. These proposals together with, in effect, a three-year budget were to be aggregated to form a district (or area) plan for transmission to the next tier up in the service. In addition a ten-year 'forward look' was to be included indicating longer-term development objectives. The system said little about the role of regional health authorities or DHSS, the assumption being that guidelines based upon aggregated statements of need, derived from health authority submissions, would be handed down to field authorities in response to their previous year's submissions. There was no place for ongoing policy analysis in the proposed system and the link between programme submissions and longer-term statements of intent was tenuous. In essence although no one appeared to know where they were going the system did ensure they would know how they were going to get there!

The change of government in 1974, however, produced a radical revision of these proposals. Crossman's complaint that 'the centre is weak and the Regional Hospital Boards are strong' encouraged ministers to place greater emphasis on the strategic role of DHSS in determining national priorities. The essentially 'bottom-up' programming system was replaced by a 'top-down' strategic planning system fully embracing the rational model's cycle, and the first national strategic health plan was published in 1976 as *Priorities for Health and Personal Social Services* (PHPSS) (Department of Health and Social Security, 1976).

The post-1976 system emphasised the importance of strategic planning at area level (strategic plans being required every three years) in addition to the ongoing programming activity culminating in the annual submission of a three-year operational plan. In addition, with the publication of PHPSS, the whole NHS planning system was given a firm push towards 'joint planning' with coterminous and complementary local authority services. Circular HC76(18), and more forcefully HC77(17), replaced at area level health care planning teams with joint care planning teams, which had a membership drawn from senior health and local authority officers with special planning responsibilities rather than fieldwork staff and health care practitioners. Planning had become professionalised at AHA level. The new planning system now differentiated between the strategic planning task of areas and the operational programming role of health care districts.

The disjunction between operational and strategic planning caused some confusion. The initial strategic submissions in 1976–7 indicated how little the NHS had come to terms with the intentions of the system. Strategic submissions ranged from those with vague philosophical statements of intent to those which were essentially lists of existing and proposed capital developments. The DHSS was disappointed and indicated its expectation that plans should improve with further submissions. Furthermore district operational plans with their own shorter time horizon tended not to reflect the longer term strategic thinking of planners at area level. In particular the elaborate procedures (with the professional advisory bodies; community health councils and local authorities) produced an incremental and horse-trading environment within which district operational plans were prepared.

The single-district areas (one-third of all AHAs) where district and area planning tasks were merged found much less difficulty in preparing coherent and internally consistent proposals. So striking was their success that both the Royal Commission and the incoming administration recognised the advantages of an integrated approach to strategic and operational planning. *Patients First* states: 'what is needed in England is a pattern of operational authorities throughout the Service, similar in the main to the present single-district areas' (Department of Health and Social Security, 1979, para. 15). None the less at a time of financial constraint the NHS planning system has succeeded to an enviable degree in (*a*) focusing health planning upon services as well as capital provision; (*b*) developing an appreciation that planning can be effective in reallocating existing services as well as managing capital and service development; (*c*) convincing the service that longer time horizons are necessary, particularly when major demographic, clinical and epidemiological changes are being experienced; and (*d*) widening the institutional horizons of health service planners to embrace not only primary care and community medical care but also the non-NHS functions of social services, housing and education in shaping their proposals.

Many tensions, however, exist within the present system. Different health authorities experience them to varying degrees. The tensions arise in part from the various organisational and epidemiological situation of authorities. But some are inherent in the nature of the service itself. For the NHS, however, the problem of rational planning lies not merely in the conceptual difficulties of implementation but in the variety of actors involved in health care policy-making, each group of whom adheres to fundamentally different planning models. In dialogue between the groups incomprehension is mutual.

The Rational Model

The rational model is overwhelmingly the most widely articulated approach to planning in the service. The Blue Book (Department of Health and Social Security, 1976) identified five steps in strategic and operational planning.

(*a*) Taking stock. Examining where the organisation is now and forecasting where it is likely to find itself at the end of the planning period if nothing is done to change course. This will require discussion of current services, resources and their use, and existing constraints on operation.
(*b*) Objective setting. Reviewing what the organisation will seek to achieve in the time span being considered – i.e., its aims or objectives. This will require consideration of needs, demands and resources. It should take into account the values of all concerned as well as the general social, economic and political climate.
(*c*) Defining strategy. Defining how to move the organisation from where it is now to its agreed objectives. This requires considering alternative routes to the goals, the costs and other implications quantitative and qualitative of each, and the organisation's ability to match each routing. A selection between the options is then made leading to the definition of an overall strategy or programme.
(*d*) Developing a detailed plan. Deciding how this general strategy or programme is to be implemented. This means working out financial, staffing and other implications and preparing a formal plan for the period involved.
(*e*) Monitoring implementation. Assessing during and after implementation whether the plan is still relevant to the objectives

and whether performance is in line with the plan. This requires some means of monitoring process and evaluating results.

This model is clearly close to the rational model emphasising, as it does:

(1) problem identification;
(2) objective setting;
(3) the identification of alternative means of reaching such objectives;
(4) policy analysis of such alternatives;
(5) implementation;
(6) monitoring implementation in order to review initial strategy.

Such a model is explicitly adopted by civil servants in the DHSS together with service planning officers at regional health authority and (in multi-district areas) area health authority level.

Partisan Mutual Adjustment
This model interprets policy-making as part of a political bargaining process in which the forces of competing interest groups evolve a mutually acceptable solution. The complex process of consultation machinery within the national health service together with the principle of multidisciplinary management teams operating on a consensus basis provides an ideal environment for policy-making of this kind. Indeed the model is institutionalised in the role of the health service administrator whose key role has been described as that of 'facilitator', 'fixer', 'fire-fighter'. It is apparent that the more senior officers at regional and area health authority level celebrate such skills and find difficulty in adjusting this approach to the rational model employed by service planners with whom they must negotiate in determining future planning strategy. Such conflicts arise especially in the relationship between regional service planners and area management teams/area teams of officers and between regional teams of officers and their service-planner support systems.

Incrementalism
The incrementalist approach to planning, essentially concerned with change at the margin, is concerned with problem solution rather than goal achievement. We have already suggested above that the NHS policy-making process had been characterised by development planning, that is, planning the allocation of new monies (and therefore marginal resources) rather than holistic planning of all health care resources. The incrementalist approach is most noticeable in published area and district management teams' operational plans which are both short-term (three to four years) and therefore of necessity incrementalist in nature. In contrast the strategic plans of region and area (in multi-district areas) tend to adopt a rational model approach to planning.

Mixed Scanning

The mixed scanning approach advocated by Etzioni (1968) attempts to resolve the apparent conflict between the rational model and the incrementalist and partisan mutual adjustment models:

> What is needed for active decision making is a strategy that is less exacting than the rationalistic one but not as constricting in its perspective as the incremental approach, not as Utopian as rationalism but not as conservative as incrementalism, not so unrealistic as model that it cannot be followed but not one that legitimates myopic, self-oriented, non-innovative decision-making. The strategy of mixed scanning . . . assumes that the criticisms of the rationalistic model are valid . . . rationalistic models do not provide an effective descriptive, normative or analytical model for the conduct of macro-actors. Incrementalism, we suggest, is descriptive of the sub-set of decisions but not of the more effective decisions. (pp. 282–3)

Etzioni argues that mixed scanning strategies discriminate between fundamental decisions and tactical decisions. Fundamental decisions are goal-related, lacking detail, concentrating on the overview. Short-term tactical decisions are made 'incrementally' but within the context set by the fundamental decisions.

> But incrementalism overcomes the unrealistic aspects of comprehensive rationalism (by limiting it to contextuating divisions), and contextuating rationalism helps to right the conservative bias of incrementalism. (ibid., ch. 12)

The practical difficulties that arise when incongruent planning models come into conflict have led to just such an approach to operational planning in the NHS planning system. The mixed scanning model is especially explanatory when we consider the role of the monitoring function in NHS planning. In such an approach a delicate balance is struck between 'maximum delegation downwards and accountability upwards'. Indeed at the core of health service planning has been an attempt to balance ongoing scrutiny of lower-tier activities against short-term crisis intervention.

Such problems as occur in health service planning in the next few years are likely to emerge from the conflicting approaches of adherents to these different models. It is not uncommon to find all four approaches within any organisational context; but what makes planning in the NHS especially fraught is the institutionalised place each model occupies at different points and among different groups in the service. Such conflicting approaches to planning are common in local authorities. They are exacerbated in the NHS because of the centralised and administratively hierarchical nature of the service and the enormous power of the clinician in the exercise of professional autonomy. The differences are highlighted when the two systems interact.

THE FUTURE OF PLANNING IN THE NHS

Ambiguities about accountability and democratic legitimacy in national health service management and planning are likely to continue. Even with the present Conservative government's commitment to reduce central government functions it is doubtful if the principle of decentralisation, which is at the core of the NHS planning system, will prove durable. To achieve the full effect of maximum delegation downwards combined with accountability upwards a firmer conceptual grasp on the issues of output measurement must be developed than exists in the NHS at present. At its most forceful such delegation would require inter-tier agreement on objectives, leaving the resource management necessary to achieve such objectives to the operational tier. In practice, however, such delegation requires the capacity to assess whether health objectives have actually been met. While such measures are lacking the principle of accountability cannot be satisfied. The alternative, however, is for objectives to be set in input terms, as levels of service to be met. But to the extent to which plans are approved in terms of standards of service to be provided, so delegated authority to lower management tiers is eroded. The fundamental problem of health care planning is that insufficient attention has been given to the development of serious policy analysis of health care issues. Research and analysis have either been contracted out or remained the preserve of DHSS officers insensitive to the 'soft' issues which are more capable of appreciation at the periphery of the organisation. In place of such analyses the planning system offers inchoate informational support for intuitive judgements made in a political bargaining environment. As Wildavsky (1969, p. 842) has said about the application of PPBS in the United States,

> hence the agency is at once over-supplied with masses of numbers and under-supplied with propositions about the impact of any action he might undertake. He cannot tell, because no one knows, what the marginal change he is considering will mean for the rest of his operation.

In such uncertainty the task of maintaining the existing patterns of health service is likely to take precedence over the kind of analysis necessary to adapt the service to the needs of those who receive it.

12

Choice in the Design of Policy-Making Systems

JOHN STEWART

I CHOICE FOR POLICY-MAKING PROCESSES

The design of policy-making processes is an exercise in organisational choice. If one regards the rational model as the basis of policy-making then choice is barely involved. But the rational model belongs to the domain of justification. Sufficient was said in Chapter 2 to show that in the domain of policy derivation (and it also holds in the domain of policy adoption) there are no single models to be followed. The various chapters in this book have shown variety in policy-making processes. In design, the constraints of context and the possibility of choice have both to be allowed for and to be used.

Context influences choice. The complexity of the environment and its degree of stability will or can affect the type of policy to be adopted and the nature of the policy-making processes. A stable environment may encourage stable policies and requires policy-making processes little concerned to extend the bounds of possibility. In Chapter 7 it has been shown that the contexts of regional planning have to be understood in order to understand the processes that are adopted.

Context does not determine policy-making processes. There is no deterministic relationship between context and policy or policy-making systems. The design (or, if that is the choice, the non-design) of a policy-making system is an exercise in organisational choice. Context constrains the choices. It cannot determine the choice actually made.

Choice is not easily made. It has many aspects. In many cases choice is not normally made in absolute, but as to the point on a continuum between conflicting values. In policy-making processes, balance is sought between ideas and the values and interests expressed in those ideas. There is no final point on the continuum of organisational choice. There are arguments for decentralisation expressed in such terms as the need for responsiveness and the encouragement of responsibility. There are, however, arguments for centralisation – expressed in such terms as the need for co-ordination or the need for common standards.

There are arguments for the specialist – well put by those who call attention to the special skills needed to deal with the mentally ill. There are arguments for the generalist – well put by those who stress the limitations of the specialist in dealing with issues beyond the bounds of the specialist. Over time in organisations balance is sought between conflicting points on the continuum of change. Each change alters the direction as in the institution balance is sought over time between conflicting pressures. Such choices confront all those concerned with the design of policy processes.

This book has shown the variety in the choices to be made in the design of policy-making processes. The variety can be presented as dimensions on which choice has to be made. This chapter sets out some of those dimensions. In each dimension choice is posed between two conflicting sets of ideas. The choice, at any one moment of time, is likely to be resolved not in favour of one set of ideas but at a point on the continuum between the ideas, which will represent the point of balance between the strength of the conflicting ideas and the values they represent. Choice is made in a context, within the constraints imposed by the context, but it also reflects the relative strengths of the ideas and the values and interest that they represent.

In what follows a number of the dimensions of choice are described. Choice is presented as between two sets of ideas, each of which is shown as having force and legitimacy within processes of policy-making. No attempt is made to predict the point of choice, because the choice will vary over time and context. The dimensions provide a framework for the analysis of the choices made on the form of policy-making processes.

II FUNCTIONAL/ANTI-FUNCTIONAL

The functional principle which organises tasks in accordance with major functions such as education and social services is deeply embedded in the institutions of government. It is given expression in certain policy planning processes, as Chapter 11 illustrates. It structures the internal framework of organisations, the divide between organisations and the procedures linking them. The functional principle has strength in securing organisational effectiveness in action. Policy-making based on the functional principle fits more easily into organisational requirements.

The functional principle is challenged by corporate, community or cross-functional approaches. Issues that cross the functional led to the development of corporate planning described in Chapter 3. Awareness of the cross-functional issues of urban deprivation led to the experiment in CCPs described in Chapter 10. Policy-making processes, it can be argued, should not be based on the same principle as the system for running operational services but should express a wider perspective.

Comprehensive/Selective

The comprehensive ideal has a powerful appeal. Because it can be shown that issues are interrelated in the complex environment of government then policy processes should give expression to that same complexity. The case for comprehensive planning is powerful. Divisions in the planning process as discussed in Chapter 8 on land use planning are not easily handled. The idea of an all-purpose authority (and a genuinely all-purpose authority would go far beyond present local government functions) attracts.

The case for the comprehensive approach is easily made. It is frustrated by its impossibility. The change within corporate planning for the comprehensive ideal to an emphasis on selectivity is described in Chapter 3.

Uniformity/Diversity

Any level of government has a tendency to uniformity. At national level there is concern for the maintenance of common national standards. National government exists to unite not to differentiate. At local level, professional standards and political pressures unite to ensure formal uniformity. Uniformity simplifies policy processes.

Formal uniformity may lead to actual inequity. Uniformity of provision may lead to differential uptake. Chapter 4 discusses the distributional effects of local authority services. Libraries for all means resources used by some but not all. Needs vary and so should response. The need for diversity and difference have forced recognition in regional planning described in Chapter 7, as in concern for urban deprivation described in Chapter 10. The deprived areas require difference in response. The movement to area management described in Chapter 9 reflects an awareness of the need for diversity and difference.

Intervenes/Permits

Policy-making processes can meet problems by direct government interventions. Government legislates. It lays down standards. It provides common services.

Yet there is a set of ideas that centre on the retreat from government. Intervention should be curbed. Standards should not be enforced automatically. Government should permit individuals and private organisations to deal with problems. Chapter 8 on regional planning shows the dilemma, but also the potential, of a policy planning system that is concerned with more than the planning of intervention.

Participatory/Directive

Participation involves a cluster of ideas. Industrial democracy, worker participation, consumer participation and public participation all provide ideas. Participation cannot necessarily be restrained by the rules management often seeks to set. If participation is powerful then it will break out of present forms.

Participatory ideas are challenged by other ideas. The job of government is to govern. Action is required, not consultation. Plans must not be deflected by every passing view. These propositions reflect ideas of purposive directive government.

Certainty/Flexibility

Deep in one approach to policy-making is the desire to impose certainty in an uncertain world. A set of processes can be designed for stability and to achieve certainty. Chapter 11 on health care planning could be said to describe just such an approach.

A planning process may, however, be concerned to increase flexibility. It may centre on the need to maintain adaptability in institutions as the environment changes. Chapter 6 on monitoring reflects aspirations to such processes.

Incremental/Radical

There is a case for gradual change. Adjustments will be found. Ways through will be found. Any system can be made to work. The costs of disturbance are great. There is more faith in the safety of marginal change (and the capacity for gradual learning), than in the capacity of the designers of significant change. Policy planning if required operates at the margin.

Yet there is a case too for radical change that challenges the capacity of incrementalism. The weight and scale of problems cannot be met by gradual adjustment. Policy planning processes have to confront sharply the rigidity of existing activities.

Political/Neutral

Policy planning in government is about politics. It involves elections and political parties. It implies political pressures and their handling. Politics is not to be denied but welcomed. Politics legitimates policy planning. Policy processes can be designed to maximise political input.

To politics and elections are opposed professional purpose and appointed boards. Some tasks of government are argued to be beyond politics. Certain tasks are seen as value-free, calling for management and professional skills. Policy processes can be designed to minimise political input.

Centralised/Devolved

Many ideas support centralised policy planning. Powerful pressures support the centre. Economies of scale, uniformity of standards, national unity express ideas and values supportive of such policy processes. There are powerful forces for centralisation and powerful justifications, although Chapter 4 shows that within formal unity there are important differences in distribution.

There are countervailing pressures. These are expressed in different ideas and values: diversity; the pluralistic society; devolution; community politics; 'small is beautiful'. All these are pressures for devolved policy-making. Chapter 9 on area management shows such ideas but also the forces constraining them.

Quantitative/Qualitative

Planning methods and procedures have been influenced by technological approaches during the last decade using hard quantitative data.

There has been a considerable use made of computers, complex and large-scale mathematical models.

Each trend creates its opposite. New trends move from the 'high science' approach to policy-making and towards a 'softer' method, placing greater stress on qualitative data. Chapter 6 on monitoring reflects this movement.

III CONCLUSIONS

There are choices to be faced in the form of policy processes. Choice is made in a context and to a degree context determines choice, but it is to a degree only. Choice is influenced by the framework of values and ideas in which the choice is made. There is determination and there is choice.

The many dimensions that can be given to the policy system give a perspective that is not given by a simple model – be it the rational model or disjointed incrementalism. It enables the design or redesign of different types of policy processes to match differing needs, needs that must be assessed in the domain of policy derivation and policy bargaining as well as the domain of policy justification.

Processes of policy planning can be developed on different models. To see difficulties in the rational comprehensive model does not necessarily mean opposition to systematic processes of policy planning. It means merely that the choices made will represent different positions on the dimensions of choice. The emphasis of this book has moved towards policy processes:

- that accept the reality of the political process rather than an illusion of political neutrality;
- that accept the impossibility of the comprehensive ideal and the necessity of selectivity;
- that match the complexities of the planning context by a diversity of organisational perspectives rather than the single perspective functionalism;
- that can use the 'soft' data of opinion and thought as well as the 'hard' data of quantitative analysis.

In the richness of the variety of policy context choice has to be made. A variety of response is required if choice is to be adequate. It is the richness of choice brought by the varying responses that is nearer reality than the simple choices between the comprehensive rational and disjointed incrementation. Policy processes cannot be restricted by such a simple choice.

References

Ackoff, R. L. (1967), 'Management misinformation systems', *Management Science*, vol. 14 (December).

Ackoff, R. L., and Emery, F. E. (1972), *On Purposeful Systems* (London: Tavistock).

Alden, J., and Morgan, R. (1974), *Regional Planning: A Comprehensive View* (London: Leonard Hill).

Aldrich, H. (1974), 'The Environment as a network of organisations: theoretical and methodological implications', paper to the International Sociological Association, Toronto, Canada.

Allen, R. (1979), 'Area analysis of resources in Glamorgan CC', in E. M. Davies (ed.), *Research and Intelligence*, papers delivered at the Inlogov annual conference, 1978 (Birmingham: Institute of Local Government Studies, University of Birmingham).

Allison, G. T. (1971), *Essence of Decision: Explaining the Cuban Missile Crisis* (Boston, Mass.: Little, Brown).

Alt, J. E. (1971), 'Some social and political correlates of County Borough expenditures', *British Journal of Political Science*, vol. 1, pp. 49–62.

Anderson, J. E. (1975), *Public Policy-Making* (London: Nelson).

Anthony, R. N. (1965), *Planning and Control Systems: A Framework for Analysis* (Boston, Mass.: Harvard University Press).

Antunes, G., and Mladenka, K. (1976), 'The politics of local services and service distribution', in L. H. Masotti and R. Lineberry (eds), *The New Urban Politics* (Cambridge, Mass.: Ballinger), pp. 147–69.

Aristotle (1941), *Politics* (London: Oxford University Press).

Arnstein, S. (1969), 'A ladder of citizen participation in the USA', *Journal of the American Institute of Planners* (July), pp. 216–24.

Bachrach, P., and Baratz, M. (1970), *Power and Poverty* (London: Oxford University Press).

Banfield, E. C. (1973), 'Ends and means in planning', in Faludi (1973a).

Barnes, J. A. (1954), 'Class and committees in a Norwegian island parish', *Human Relations*, vol. 7, pp. 39–58.

Barras, R., and Geary, K. (1979), 'A review of the Cleveland county plan cycle 1977/78', *Local Government Studies*, vol. 5, no. 1, pp. 39–54.

Batley, R. (1972), 'An exploration of non-participation in planning', *Policy and Politics*, vol. 1, no. 1, pp. 95–114.

Batley, R. (1980), 'The political significance of administrative allocation', *Papers in Urban and Regional Studies*, No. 4, pp. 17–44.

Beer, S. (1973), 'Fanfare for effective freedom', Richard Goodman Memorial Lecture, unpublished paper.

Bell, C., and Newby, H. (1976), 'Community, communion and community action: the social sources of the new urban politics', in D. T. Herbert and R. J. Johnson, *Spatial Perspectives on Problems and Policies* (New York: Wiley).

Benington, J. (1976), *Local Government Becomes Big Business* (London: Community Development Project Information and Intelligence Unit).

Benington, J., and Skelton, P. (1972), 'Public participation in decision-making by governments', paper given at the annual meeting of the Institute of Municipal Treasurers and Accountants.

Benson, J. K. (1975), 'The interorganisational network as a political economy', *Administrative Science Quarterly*, vol. 20, pp. 229–49.

Berkshire County Council (1979), *The Policy Planning Process 1979–80* (Reading: Berkshire C.C.).

Berry, D. F., Metcalfe, J. L., and McQuillan, W. (1974), 'Neddy – an organisational metamorphosis', *Journal of Management Studies*, vol. 11, pp. 1–20.

Birmingham Inner Area Study (1975), *Small Heath, Birmingham: A Social Survey* (London: Department of the Environment).

Blau, P. M. (1964), *Exchange and Power in Social Life* (New York: Wiley).

Boaden, N. T. (1971), *Urban Policy Making* (Cambridge: Cambridge University Press).

Boaden, N. T., and Alford, R. R. (1969), 'Sources of diversity in English local government decisions', *Public Administration*, vol. 47, pp. 203–23.

Bolan, R. S. (1973), 'Community decision behaviour: the culture of planning', in Faludi (1973a).

Bosanquet, N. (1980), 'Inequalities in health', in Bosanquet and Townsend (1980).

Bosanquet, N., and Townsend, P. (eds) (1980), *Labour and Inequality* (London: Heinemann).

Bott, E. (1957), *Family and Social Network* (London: Tavistock).

Bovaird, A. G. (1979), 'Output measurement for local authority services: a review', in E. M. Davies (ed.), *Research and Intelligence*, papers delivered at the Inlogov annual conference, 1978 (Birmingham: Institute of Local Government Studies, University of Birmingham).

Bradford CCP (1978), *Prospectus* (Bradford: Bradford City Council).

Bradford City Council (1978), *Metplan: Corporate Management in Bradford* (Bradford: Bradford City Council).

Bradford City Council (1979a), *District Trends: 1979* (Bradford: Bradford City Council).

Bradford City Council (1979b), *Corporate Plan 1980–85: Chief Officers' Reports, Parts A and B* (Bradford: Bradford City Council).

Bradshaw, J. (1972), 'The concept of social need', *New Society*, vol. 19, no. 496 (30 March); repr. in G. McLachlan (ed.), *Problems and Progress in Medical Care* (London: Oxford University Press, 1972).

Brazier, S., and Harris, R. (1975), 'Inter-authority planning: appreciation and resolution of conflict in the new local authority system', *Town Planning Review*, vol. 46.

Brown, K. G. S. (1979), *Re-organising the National Health Service* (Oxford: Blackwell).

Bulpitt, J. (1967), *Party Politics in English Local Government* (London: Longman).

Bunge, W., *et al.* (1972), 'A report to the parents of Detroit on school decentralisation', in P. W. English and R. C. Mayfield (eds), *Man, Space and Environment* (London: Oxford University Press).

Burnett, A. D. (1980), 'The distribution of local political outputs and outcomes in British and North American cities: a review and research agenda', paper delivered to the Anglo-American seminar on research in political geography, Institute of British Geographers Annual Conference, Lancaster University, January.

Butcher, E., and Dawkins, J. (1978), 'The corporate approach in local government – an education viewpoint', *Local Government Studies*, vol. 4, no. 1, pp. 49–62.

Byrne, D., Williamson, W., and Fletcher, B. (1975), *The Poverty of Education* (London: Martin Robertson).

Cambridgeshire County Council (1979), *Medium Term Planning, 1980–1983* (Cambridge: Cambridgeshire C.C.).

Carter, K. R., Friend, J. K., and Norris, M. E. (1978), *Regional Planning and Policy Change: The Formulation of Policy Guidelines in Regional Strategies* (London: Department of the Environment).

Carter, K. R., Friend, J. K., Pollard, J. de B., and Yewlett, C. J. L. (1975), *Organisational Influences in the Regional Strategy Process* (Coventry: Institute of Operational Research/Department of Urban and Regional Planning, Lanchester Polytechnic).

Central Health Services Council (1969), *The Functions of the District General Hospital*, Report of the Committee (London: HMSO).

Chadwick, G. (1971), *A Systems View of Planning* (Oxford: Pergamon).

Chervany, N. L., and Dickson, G. W. (1974), 'An experimental evaluation of information overload in a production environment', *Management Science*, vol. 20, no. 10, pp. 1335–44.

Churchman, C. W., Ackoff, R. L., and Arnoff, E. L. (1964), *Introduction to Operations Research* (New York: Wiley).

CIPFA (1972), *Output Measurement*, discussion papers, (London: Chartered Institute of Public Finance and Accountancy).

City of Sheffield (1978), *Inner Area Programme 1979–82*, appendix B (Sheffield: Sheffield City Council).

Clegg, S. (1975), *Power, Rule and Domination* (London: Routledge & Kegan Paul).

Cochrane, A. L. (1972), *Effectiveness and Efficiency*, Rock-Carling Lectures, Nuffield Provincial Hospital Trust (mimos).

Cockburn, C. (1977), *The Local State* (London: Pluto Press).

Codlington, A. (1970), 'Soft numbers and hard facts', *New Society*, vol. 14, pp. 577–580.

Coleman, R. J., and Riley, J. (1973), *MIS: Management Dimensions* (San Francisco: Holden Day).

Committee on the Management of Local Government (1967), *Final Report* (Maud Report).

Committee on Nursing (1972), *Final Report*, Cmnd 5115 (London: HMSO).

Coote, A. (1979), 'Behind the town-hall pin-up row', *New Statesman*, vol. 98, p. 891.

Corporate Planning Journal (1977), 'The Birmingham saga', vol. 4, no. 2, pp. 1–22.

Corporate Planning Journal (1978), 'Profile: Clwyd', vol. 5, no. 1, pp. 37–46.

Corporate Planning Journal (1979), 'Profile: central region', vol. 6, no. 2, pp. 17–34.

Coventry City Council (1978), *City Policy Guide 1979–1988* (Coventry: Coventry City Council).

Cox, A. W. (1979), 'Administrative inertia and inner city policy', *Public Administration Bulletin*, no. 29 (April), pp. 2–17.

Crossman, R. H. S. (1972), *A Politician's View of Health Service Planning*, (Glasgow: University of Glasgow).

Culyer, A. J. (1976), *Need and the National Health Service* (London: Martin Robertson).

Culyer, A. J., Lavers, R. J., and Williams, R. (1972), 'Health indicators', ch. 6 in A. Shonfield and S. Shaw (eds), *Social Indicators and Social Policy* (London: SSRC).

Damer, S., and Hague, C. (1971), 'Public participation in planning: a review', *Town Planning Review*, vol. 42, no. 3, pp. 217–32.

Davidoff, P. R., and Reiner, T. A. (1973), 'A choice theory of planning', in Faludi (1973a).

Davies, B. (1968), *Social Needs and Resources in Local Services* (London: Michael Joseph).

Davies, B. (1978), *Universality, Selectivity and Effectiveness in Social Policy* (London: Heinemann).

Davies, J. G. (1972), *The Evangelistic Bureaucrat* (London: Tavistock).

Davis, A., McIntosh, N., and Williams, J. (1977), *The Management of Deprivation*, Final Report of the Southwark Community Development Project, Polytechnic of the South Bank (London: Polytechnic of the South Bank).

Dearlove, J. (1973), *The Politics of Policy in Local Government* (Cambridge: Cambridge University Press).

Dearlove, J. (1979), *The Reorganisation of British Local Government* (Cambridge: Cambridge University Press).

Dennis, N. (1968a), *People and Plans* (London: Faber).

Dennis, N. (1968b), 'The popularity of the neighbourhood community idea', in R. Pahl (ed.), *Readings in Urban Sociology* (Oxford: Pergamon).

Department of the Environment (1972), *The New Local Authorities Management and Structure* (Bains Report) (London: HMSO).

Department of the Environment (1973a), *The Sunderland Study: Tackling Urban Problems: A Working Guide* (London: HMSO).

Department of the Environment (1973b), *The Oldham Study: Environmental Planning and Management* (London: HMSO).

Department of the Environment (1973c), *The Rotherham Study: A General Approach to Improving the Physical Environment* (London: HMSO).

Department of the Environment (1974), consultation paper sent to urban authorities in England with a population over 200,000.

Department of the Environment (1975), *Regional Strategy for the North West: Government Response to the Strategic Plan* (London: Department of the Environment).

Department of the Environment (1977a), *Change or Decay*, Final Report of Liverpool Inner Area Study (London: HMSO).

Department of the Environment (1977b), *Unequal City*, Final Report of Birmingham Inner Area Study (London: HMSO).

Department of the Environment (1977c), *Policies for Dispersal and Balance*, Final Report of Lambeth Inner Area Study (London: HMSO).

Department of the Environment (1977d), *Inner Areas Studies – Summaries of the Consultants' Reports* (London: HMSO).

Department of the Environment (1977e), *Recreation and Deprivation in Inner Urban Areas* (London: HMSO).

Department of the Environment (1977f), *A Voice for Your Neighbourhood: The Neighbourhood Council* (London: HMSO).

Department of the Environment (1978), *Strategic Plan for the South East Review – Government Statement* (London: HMSO).

Department of Health and Social Security (1972), *Management Arrangements for the Reorganised National Health Service* (London: HMSO).
Department of Health and Social Security (1973a), *Health Reorganisation Circular*, No. 3 (London: HMSO).
Department of Health and Social Security (1973b), *A Planning Guide for Shadow Health Authorities* (London: HMSO).
Department of Health and Social Security (1973c), *The State of Public Health* (London: HMSO).
Department of Health and Social Security (1974), *Planning in an Integrated Health Service* (London: HMSO).
Department of Health and Social Security (1975), *Guide to Planning in the NHS* (London: HMSO).
Department of Health and Social Security (1976), *The National Health Service Planning System* (London: HMSO).
Department of Health and Social Security (1979), *Patients First: Consultative Paper on the Structure of Management of the National Health Service in England and Wales* (London: HMSO).
Dill, W. R. (1958), 'Environment as an influence on managerial action', *Administrative Science Quarterly*, vol. 2, pp. 409–43.
Douglas, J. (1964), *The Home and the School* (London: MacGibbon & Kee).
Dror, Y. (1968), *Public Policymaking Re-Examined* (New York: Chandler).
Dror, Y. (1971), *Ventures in the Policy Sciences* (London: Elsevier).
Dror, Y. (1973), 'The planning process: a facet design', in Faludi (1973a), pp. 332–53.
Duerden, B. (1979), 'Local planning in Liverpool', in C. Fudge (ed.), *Approaches to Local Planning*, Working Paper No. 3, School for Advanced Urban Studies (Bristol: School for Advanced Urban Studies, University of Bristol).
Dunleavy, P. (1977), 'Protest and quiescense in urban politics: a critique of some pluralist and structuralist myths', *International Journal of Urban and Regional Research*, vol. 1, no. 2, pp. 193–218.
Dunsire, A. (1978), *Implementation in a Bureaucracy* (London: Martin Robertson).
Earwicker, J. (1976), 'Corporate planning: the ideas and their search for methods', M. Soc. Sc. dissertation, Institute of Local Government Studies, University of Birmingham.
East Anglia Regional Strategy Team (1974), *Strategic Choice for East Anglia* (SCEA) (London: HMSO).
Easton, D. (1965), *A Systems Analysis of Political Life* (New York: Wiley).
Eckstein, H. (1959), *The English National Health Service* (Cambridge, Mass.: Harvard University Press).
Eckstein, H. (1960), *Pressure Group Politics* (London: Allen & Unwin).
Eddison, T. (1973), *Local Government: Management and Corporate Planning* (London: Leonard Hill).
Edwards, J., and Batley, R. (1978), *The Politics of Positive Discrimination: An Evaluation of the Urban Programme 1967–1977* (London: Tavistock).
Etzioni, A. (1967), 'Mixed-scanning: a "third" approach to decision-making', *Public Administration Review*, vol. 17, no. 6, pp. 385–92.
Etzioni, A. (1968), *The Active Society* (London: Collier Macmillan).
Evan, W. M. (1972), 'The organisation set: toward a theory of inter-organisational relations', in M. B. Brinkerhoff and P. R. Kunz, *Complex Organisations and Their Environments* (Dubuque, Iowa: Brown), pp. 326–40.
Faludi, A. (1970), 'The planning environment, and the meaning of planning',

Regional Studies, vol. 4, pp. 1–9.

Faludi, A. (ed.) (1972), 'The "systems view" and planning theory', in B. Dimitriou *et al.*, *The Systems View of Planning*, Oxford Working Papers in Planning Education and Research, No. 9 (Oxford: Department of Town Planning, Oxford Polytechnic).

Faludi, A. (ed.) (1973a), *A Reader in Planning Theory* (Oxford: Pergamon).

Faludi, A. (1973b), *Planning Theory* (Oxford: Pergamon).

Feyeraband, P. (1975), *Against Method* (London: New Left Books).

Firth, C. (1979), article in *Municipal Journal* (23 March 1979), p. 300.

Foley, D. L. (1963), *Controlling London's Growth* (Berkeley, Calif.: University of California Press).

Friedmann, J. (1965), *The Social Context of National Planning Decisions: A Comparative Approach* (Bloomington: Comparative Administration Group, American Society of Public Administration).

Friend, J. K. (1980), 'Planning in a multi-organisational context', *Town Planning Review*, vol. 51, no. 3, pp. 261–9.

Friend, J. K., and Jessop, W. N. (1969), *Local Government and Strategic Choice* (London: Tavistock).

Friend, J. K., Power, J. M., and Yewlett, C. J. L. (1974), *Public Planning: The Intercorporate Dimension* (London: Tavistock).

Friend, J. K., and Spink, P. (1978), 'Networks in public administration', *Linkage*, no. 3, pp. 18–22.

Galbraith, J. K. (1967), *The New Industrial State* (Boston, Mass.: Houghton Mifflin).

Galloway, T. D., and Mahayni, R. G. (1977), 'Planning theory in retrospect: the process of paradigm change', *Journal of the American Institute of Planners*, vol. 43, pp. 62–71.

Gash, R. (1979), 'Policy planning', *County Councils Gazette* (August 1979), pp. 146–7.

Gateshead CCP (1977), *Gateshead Project Report* (Gateshead: Gateshead Borough Council).

Gateshead CCP (1978), *Review Report* (Gateshead: Gateshead Borough Council).

Gillingwater, D. (1975), *Regional Planning and Social Change* (Farnborough: Saxon House).

Gillis, J. D. S., Brazier, S., Chamberlain, K. J., Harris, R. J. P., and Scott, D. J. (1974), *Monitoring and the Planning Process* (Birmingham: Institute of Local Government Studies, University of Birmingham).

Gray, F. (1976), 'Selection and allocation in council housing', *Transactions of the Institute of British Geographers*, vol. 1, no. 1.

Greenwood, R., and Stewart, J. D. (1974), *Corporate Planning in Local Government* (London: Charles Knight).

Greenwood, R., Hinings, C. R., and Ranson, S. (1975), 'Contingency theory and the organisation of local authorities: part 1 – differentiation and integration', *Public Administration*, vol. 53, pp. 1–23.

Greenwood, R., Hinings, C. R., Ranson, S., and Walsh, K. (1976), *In Pursuit of Corporate Rationality: Organizational Developments in the Post-Reorganization Period* (Birmingham: Institute of Local Government Studies, University of Birmingham).

Greenwood, R., Hinings, C. R., and Ranson, S. (1977), 'The politics of the budgetary process in English local government', *Political Studies*, vol. 25, pp. 25–47.

Gutch, R. (1972), *Goals and the Planning Process*, Oxford Working Papers in Planning Education and Research, No. 11 (Oxford: Department of Town

Planning, Oxford Polytechnic).
Gyford, J. (1976), *Local Politics in Britain* (London: Croom Helm).
Habermas, J. (1971), *Towards a Rational Society* (London: Heinemann).
Hall, A. S. (1974), *The Point of Entry* (London: Allen & Unwin).
Hall, P. (1970), *The Theory and Practice of Regional Planning* (London: Pemberton).
Hall, P., Gracey, H., Drewett, R., and Thomas, R. (1973), *The Containment of Urban England, Vol. 1: Urban and Metropolitan Growth Processes* (London: Allen & Unwin).
Hall, R. H., Clark, J. P., Giordano, P. C., Johnson, P. C., and Van Roekel, M. (1977), 'Patterns of interorganisational relationships', *Administrative Science Quarterly*, vol. 22, pp. 457–74.
Hambleton, R. (1975), 'Preferences for policies', *Municipal Journal* (25 July), pp. 979–83.
Hambleton, R. (1978), *Policy Planning in Local Government* (London: Hutchinson).
Hanf, K. (1978), 'Introduction', in Hanf and Scharpf (1978).
Hanf, K., and Scharpf, F. W. (1978), *Inter-organisational Policy-Making: The Limits to Coordination and Central Control* (Beverly Hills, Cal.: Sage).
Harris, R. J. P., and Scott, D. J. (1974), 'Perspectives on multi-organisational design', *Local Government Studies*, no. 8 (first series), pp. 31–46.
Harrop, K., Mason, T., Vielba, C. A., and Webster, B. A. (1978), *The Implementation and Development of Area Management* (Birmingham: Institute of Local Government Studies, University of Birmingham).
Hart, D. A. (1976), 'Planning as an iterative process', *Local Government Studies*, vol. 2, no. 3., pp. 27–42.
Hart, D. A., Skelcher, C. K., and Wedgwood-Oppenheim, F. (1978), 'Goals and objectives in regional planning', *Public Administration Bulletin*, no. 26 (April 1978), pp. 32–45.
Harvey, D. (1973), *Social Justice and the City* (London: Edward Arnold).
Hatch, S., and Sherrott, R. (1973), 'Positive discrimination and the distribution of deprivations', *Policy and Politics*, vol. 1, pp. 223–40.
Hatry, H. P. (1976), 'Measuring the quality of public services' in W. D. Hawley and D. Rovers (eds), *Improving Urban Management* (Beverly Hills, Cal.: Sage), pp. 3–27.
Hawkins, K., and Tarr, R. J. (1980), 'Corporate planning in local government – a case study', *Long Range Planning*, vol. 13, no. 2 (April), pp. 43–51.
Haynes, R. J. (1978), 'The rejection of corporate planning in Birmingham – a theoretical perspective', *Local Government Studies*, vol. 4, no. 2, pp. 25–38.
Healey, P. (1979), 'Networking as a normative principle – with particular reference to land use planning', *Local Government Studies*, vol. 5, pp. 55–66.
Hepworth, N. P. (1978), *The Finance of Local Government*, 4th edn (London:, Allen & Unwin).
Hereford and Worcester County Council (1978), *Rural Community Development Project – Final Report* (Worcester: Hereford and Worcester C.C.).
Hill, M. (1976), *The State, Administration and the Individual* (London: Fontana).
Hill, M. (1978), 'Implementation in the central local relationship', in SSRC *Central–Local Relationships: A Panel Report to the Research Initiatives Board* (London: SSRC).
Hinings, C. F., Greenwood, R., Ranson, S., and Walsh, K. (1979), 'The organizational consequences of financial restraint in local government', in M. Wright (ed.), *Public Spending Decisions: Growth and Restraint in the 1970s*

(London: Allen & Unwin).

Hinings, C. R., Greenwood, R., Ranson, S., and Walsh, K. (1980), *Management Systems in Local Government* (Birmingham: Institute of Local Government Studies, University of Birmingham).

HMSO (1971), *Local Government in England: Government Proposals for Reorganization*, Cmnd 4584 (London).

HMSO (1974), *Public Expenditure to 1977/78*, Cmnd 5519 (London).

HMSO (1977), *Policy for the Inner Cities*, Cmnd 6845 (London).

Holtermann, S. (1976), 'Areas of urban deprivation in Great Britain: an analysis of 1971 census data', *Social Trends*, vol. 6, pp. 33–47.

Homans, G. C. (1958), 'Social behaviour as exchange', *American Journal of Sociology*, vol. 63, pp. 597–606.

Home Office, Urban Deprivation Unit (1976), *Comprehensive Community Programmes, CCP (76) 1: 2nd Revise* (London: Home Office).

Honey, M. (1978), 'Corporate planning: myth or method?', paper to the London Group of Corporate Planners (typescript).

Honey, M. (1979), 'Corporate planning and the chief executive', *Local Government Studies*, vol. 5, no. 5, pp. 21–34.

Hood, C. C. (1976), *The Limits of Administration* (New York: Wiley).

Horn, C. J., Mason, T., Spencer, K. M., Vielba, C. A., and Webster, B. A. (1977), *Area Management: Objectives and Structures* (Birmingham: Institute of Local Government Studies, University of Birmingham).

Humberside Reorganisation Project (1973), *Preparations for Change* (Hull: University of Hull).

Humberside Reorganisation Project (1974), *Waiting for Guidance* (Hull: University of Hull).

Jencks, C. (1973), *Inequality: A Reassessment of the Effect of Family and Schooling in America* (New York: Basic Books).

Jenkins, W. (1978), *Policy Analysis* (London: Martin Robertson).

Joint Monitoring Steering Group (1975/6), *A Developing Strategy for the West Midlands: First/Second Annual Report, Birmingham, 1975/1976* (Birmingham: Joint Monitoring Steering Group).

Joint Monitoring Steering Group (1979), *A Developing Strategy for the West Midlands: Updating and Rolling Forward of the Regional Strategy to 1991 – Report of the JMSG* (Birmingham: Joint Monitoring Steering Group).

Jones, B. D. (1977), 'Distributional considerations in models of urban government service provision', *Urban Affairs Quarterly*, vol. 12, pp. 291–312.

Jones, B. D., and Kaufman, C. (1974), 'The distribution of urban public services: a preliminary model', *Administration and Society*, vol. 6, pp. 337–60.

Jones, B. D., Greenberg, J. R., Kaufman, C., and Drew, J. (1978), 'Bureaucratic response to citizen initiated contacts', *American Political Science Review*, vol. 71, pp. 148–65.

Jones, B. D., Greenberg, J. R., Kaufman, C., and Drew, J. (1979), 'Service delivery rules and the distribution of local services: three district bureaucracies', *Journal of Politics*, vol. 40, no. 2, pp. 332–68.

Jones, G. W., and Norton, A. (1978), *Political Leadership in Local Authorities* (Birmingham: Institute of Local Government, Studies, University of Birmingham).

Kershaw, P. (1978), 'Area teams', *Corporate Planning Journal*, vol. 5, no. 1, p. 50.

Kershaw, P. (1977), 'Developments in Sunderland', in Roy Darke and Ray Walker, *Local Government and the Public* (London: Leonard Hill).

King, A. (1975), 'On studying the impact of public policies: the role of the political scientist', in M. Holden and D. L. Dressang (eds), *What Government Does* (London: Sage).

Kirwan, R. W., and Martin, D. B. (1972), *The Economics of Urban Residential Renewal and Improvement*, Centre for Environmental Studies, Working Paper 77 (London: Centre for Environmental Studies).

Klein, R. (1973), *Complaints Against Doctors* (London: Routledge & Kegan Paul).

Klein, R., *et al.* (1974), *Social Policy and Public Expenditure*, Centre for Studies in Social Policy (London: Centre for Studies in Social Policy).

Knox, P. L. (1978), 'The intra-urban ecology of primary medical care: patterns of accessibility and their policy implications', *Environment and Planning*, series A, vol. 10, pp. 415–35.

Lambert, C., Penny, J., and Webster, B. (1980), 'The impact of services on the inner city: the case of housing improvement', unpublished Inlogov report to the Department of the Environment.

Lambert, J. R. (1970), *Police and Race Relations* (London: Oxford University Press).

Lambert, J., Paris, C., and Blackaby, R. (1978), *Housing Policy and the State: Allocation, Access and Control* (London: Macmillan).

Lambeth Inner Area Study (1974), *People, Housing and District* (London: Department of the Environment).

Lawless, P. (1979), *Urban Deprivation and Government Initiative* (London: Faber).

Lawrence, P. R., and Lorsch, J. W. (1967), *Organisation and Environment: Managing Differentiation and Integration* (Boston, Mass.: Harvard University Press).

Leach, S. N. (1978), 'County/district relations in shire and metropolitan counties', M. Soc. Sc. dissertation, Institute of Local Government Studies, University of Birmingham.

Leach, S. N., and Moore, N. (1978), 'County/district relations in a shire county', unpublished paper, Institute of Local Government Studies, University of Birmingham (typescript).

Leach, S. N., and Moore, N. (1979), 'County/district relations in shire and metropolitan counties in the field of town and country planning: a comparison', *Policy and Politics*, vol. 7, no. 2, pp. 165–79.

Lee, J. M., Wood, B., Solomon, B. W., and Walters, P. (1974), *The Scope of Local Initiative* (London: Martin Robertson).

Levine, S., and White, P. E. (1961), 'Exchange as a conceptual framework for the study of interorganisational relationships', *Administrative Science Quarterly*, vol. 5, pp. 583–601.

Levy, F. S., Meltsner, A. J., and Wildavsky, A. (1974), *Urban Outcomes: Schools, Streets and Libraries* (Berkeley, Calif.: University of California Press).

Lewis, J. (1975), 'Variations in service provision: politics at the lay-professional interface', in K. Young (ed.), *Essays on the Study of Urban Politics* (London: Macmillan).

Lewis, J., and Flynn, R. (1979), 'The implementation of urban and regional policies', *Policy and Politics*, vol. 7, no. 2, pp. 123–44.

Lindblom, C. (1959), 'The science of muddling through', *Public Administration Review*, vol. 9 (Spring), pp. 70–88.

Lindblom, C. (1979), 'Still muddling: not yet through', *Public Administration Review*, vol. 29, no. 6, pp. 517–26.

Lineberry, R. L. (1977), *Equality and Urban Policy* (Beverly Hills, Cal.:

Sage).

Lineberry, R. L., and Welch, R. E. (1974), 'Who gets what: measuring the distribution of urban public services', *Social Science Quarterly*, vol. 54, pp. 700–12.

Lipsky, M. (1976), 'Toward a theory of street-level bureaucracy', in W. D. Hawley and M. Lipsky (eds), *Theoretical Perspectives in Urban Politics* (Englewood Cliffs, NJ: Prentice-Hall).

Lister, R. (1974), *Take-Up of Means Tested Benefits*, Poverty Pamphlet 18 (London: Child Poverty Action Group).

Liverpool Inner Area Study (1974), *Proposals for Area Management*, Inner Area Study L1/3 (London: Department of the Environment).

Liverpool Inner Area Study (1976), *District 'D' Tables, 1973–74*, Inner Area Study L1/9 (London: Department of the Environment).

Local Government Act 1972 (London: HMSO).

Local Government Planning and Land Act 1980 (London: HMSO).

Lyon, A. (1979), 'A Labour view', in M. Loney and M. Allen (eds), *The Crisis of the Inner City* (London: Macmillan).

Macdougall, G. (1972), 'The systems approach to planning: a critique', in B. Dimitriou *et al.*, *The Systems View of Planning*, Oxford Working Papers in Planning Education and Research, No. 9 (Oxford: Department of Town Planning, Oxford Polytechnic).

Marcuse, H. (1964), *One Dimensional Man* (London: Sphere Books).

Marshall, J. D. (ed.) (1977), *The History of Lancashire County Council 1889–1974* (London: Martin Robertson).

Mason, R. O., and Mitroff, I. I. (1973), 'A programme for research on management information systems', *Management Science*, vol. 19, no. 5 (January), pp. 475–87.

Mason, T., Spencer, K. M., Vielba, C. A., and Webster, B. A. (1977), *Tackling Urban Deprivation: The Contribution of Area-Based Management* (Birmingham: Institute of Local Government Studies, University of Birmingham).

Mawson, J., and Skelcher, C. K. (1980), 'Updating the West Midlands regional strategy', *Town Planning Review*, vol. 51, no. 2, pp. 152–70.

McConaghy, D. (1978), 'Setting up six towns: an urban strategy gap', *Town Planning Review*, vol. 49, no. 2, pp. 184–94.

McLoughlin, J. B. (1969), *Urban and Regional Planning* (London: Faber).

Medical Services Review Committee (1962), *A Review of the Medical Services in Great Britain*, Porritt Report (London: HMSO).

Merrington, S. (1974), *A Review of Corporate Planning Developments in English Local Authorities*, Inlogov Discussion Paper No. 4 (Birmingham: Institute of Local Government Studies, University of Birmingham).

Metcalfe, J. L. (1976), 'Organisational strategies and inter-organisational relations', *Human Relations*, vol. 29, pp. 237–343.

Metcalfe, J. L. (1978), 'Policy-making in turbulent environments', in Hanf and Scharpf (1978).

Meyer, Marshall W. (1975), 'Organisational domains', *American Sociological Review*, vol. 40, pp. 599–615.

Meyerson, M., and Banfield, E. (1955), *Politics, Planning and the Public Interest* (Glencoe, Ill.: The Free Press).

Middlesbrough Borough Council (1979), *Policy Plan 1979–80* (Middlesbrough: Middlesbrough Borough Council).

Midwinter, A. F. (1978), 'The implementation of the Paterson Report in Scottish local government, 1975–77', *Local Government Studies*, vol. 4, no. 1, pp. 23–38.

Mills, C. W. (1958), *The Power Elite* (London: Oxford University Press).

Ministry of Health (1962), *Hospital Plan for England*, Cmnd 1604 (London: HMSO).

Mintzberg, H. (1973), *The Nature of Managerial Work* (New York: Harper & Row).

Mitchell, J. G. (1969), *Social Networks and Urban Situations* (Manchester: Manchester University Press).

Mottley, C. M. (1978), 'Strategic planning', in F. J. Lyden and E. G. Miller, *Public Budgeting: Programme Planning and Evaluation*, 3rd edn (Chicago: Rand McNally).

Muchnick, D. (1971), *The Politics of Urban Redevelopment* (London: Bell).

Mumford, E., and Banks, O. (1967), *The Computer and the Clerk* (London: Routledge & Kegan Paul).

Negandhi, A. R. (1975), *Interorganisation Theory* (Kent, Ohio: Kent State University Press).

Newton, K. (1976), *Second City Politics* (London: Oxford University Press).

Newton, K., and Sharpe, L. J. (1977), 'Local outputs research: some reflections and proposals', *Policy and Politics*, vol. 5, pp. 61–82.

Nicholson, R. V., and Topham, N. (1971), 'The determinants of investment in housing in local authorities: an econometric approach', *Journal of the Royal Statistical Society*, series A, vol. 134, pp. 273–320.

Nivola, P. S. (1978), 'Distributing a municipal service: a case study of housing inspection', *Journal of Politics*, vol. 40, pp. 59–81.

North West Joint Planning Team (1973), *Strategic Plan for the North West* (SPNW) (London: HMSO).

Northern Region Strategy Team (1977), *Strategic Plan for the Northern Region* (SPNR), 5 vols, (London: HMSO).

Offe, K. (1975), 'The theory of the capitalist state and the problem of policy formation', in L. Lindberry, R. Alford *et al.*, *Stress and Contradiction in Modern Capitalism* (Lexington, Mass.: Lexington Books).

Oldham HMC/Manchester Regional Hospital Board (1973), *Field Trial Evaluation Report* (Manchester: Manchester Regional Hospital Board).

Oliver, F. R., and Stanyer, J. (1969), 'Some aspects of the financial behaviour of county boroughs', *Public Administration*, vol. 47, pp. 169–84.

Ostrom, E. (1974), 'Exclusion, choice and divisibility: factors affecting the measurement of urban agency output and impact', *Social Science Quarterly*, vol. 54, no. 4, pp. 691–700.

Ostrom, V. (1975), 'Political orders and public service structures', paper to the conference on inter-organisational decision-making and public policy at the International Institute of Management in Berlin, quoted in Rich (1977).

Pahl, R. E. (1971), 'Poverty and the urban system', in M. Chisholm and G. Manners (eds), *Spatial Policy Problems of the British Economy* (Cambridge: Cambridge University Press), pp. 126–54.

Painter, C. (1972), 'The repercussions of administrative innovation: the West Midlands Economic Planning Council', *Public Administration*, vol. 50, pp. 467–84.

Paris, C., and Blackaby, Bob (1979), *Not Much Improvement: Urban Renewal Policy in Birmingham* (London: Heinemann).

Paterson Committee (1972), *The New Scottish Local Authorities: Management and Structure* (London: HMSO).

Payne, R., and Pugh, D. S. (1976), 'Organisational structure and climate', ch. 26 in M. D. Dunnette (ed.), *Handbook of Industrial and Organisational Psychology* (Chicago: Rand McNally), pp. 1125–74.

Perloff, Harvey S. (1968), 'Key features of regional planning', *Journal of the*

American Institute of Planners, vol. 34, pp. 153–9.

Peston, M. (1972), *Public Goods and the Public Sector* (London: Macmillan).

Pfeffer, J., and Salancik, G. R. (1978), *The External Control of Organisations: A Resource Dependence Perspective* (London: Harper & Row).

Pinch, S. (1980), 'Local authority provision for the elderly: an overview and case study of London', in D. T. Herbert and R. J. Johnston (eds), *Geography and the Urban Environment*, Vol. 3 (New York: Wiley), pp. 295–343.

Planning Advisory Group (1965), *The Future of Development Plans* (London: HMSO).

Pondy, Lewis R. (1969), 'Varieties of organisational conflict', *Administrative Science Quarterly*, vol. 14, pp. 499–505.

Popper, K. (1957), *The Poverty of Historicism* (London: Routledge & Kegan Paul).

Powell, A. J. (1978), 'Strategies for the English regions: ten years of evolution', *Town Planning Review*, vol. 49, pp. 5–13.

Powell, E. (1966), *Medicine and Politics* (London: Pitman Medical).

Pressman, J., and Wildavsky, A. (1973), *Implementation* (Berkeley, Calif.: University of California Press).

Prottas, J. M. (1978), 'The power of the street-level bureaucrat in public service bureaucracies', *Urban Affairs Quarterly*, vol. 13, no. 3, pp. 285–312.

Public Finance and Accountancy (1979), *Financial Planning* (July), pp. 25–38.

Puffitt, R. (1977), 'Comprehensive community programmes and environmental health functions', paper to the Home Office Urban Deprivation Unit, Institute of Local Government Studies, University of Birmingham.

Ramirez, Ronaldo (1974), 'Planning in a social vacuum', *Proceedings of the Town and Country Planning Summer School* (London: Royal Town Planning Institute), pp. 80–7.

Randall, G. W., Lomas, K. W., and Newton, T. (1973), 'Area distribution of resources in Coventry', *Local Government Finance*, vol. 77, pp. 396–400.

Ranson, S., Hinings, C. R., and Greenwood, R. (1980), 'The structuring of organizational structures', *Administrative Science Quarterly*, vol. 25 (March), pp. 1–18.

Read, W. (1962), 'Upward communication in industrial hierarchies', *Human Relations*, vol. 15, pp. 3–16.

Rees, S. (1978), *Social Work Face to Face* (London: Edward Arnold).

Rein, M. (1979), *Social Sciences and Public Policy* (Harmondsworth: Penguin).

Rich, R. C. (1977), 'Equality and institutional design in urban service delivery', *Urban Affairs Quarterly*, vol. 12, no. 3, pp. 383–410.

Rich, R. C. (1979), 'Neglected issues in the study of urban service distributions: a research agenda', *Urban Studies*, vol. 16, pp. 143–56.

Richards, P. G. (1975), *The Local Government Act 1972: Problems of Implementation* (London: Allen & Unwin).

Rondinelli, Dennis A. (1971), 'Adjunctive planning and urban development policy', *Urban Affairs Quarterly*, vol. 7, pp. 13–39.

Rondinelli, Dennis A. (1975), *Urban and Regional Development Planning: Policy and Administration* (Ithaca, NY: Cornell University Press).

Rothenberg, J. (1976), 'Inadvertent distributional impacts in the provision of public services to individuals', in R. E. Grierson (ed.), *Public and Urban Economics* (Lexington, Mass.: D. C. Heath).

Royal Commission on Local Government in England (1969), *Report*, 3 vols, (London: HMSO).

Royal Commission on the National Health Service (1956), *Final Report* (London: HMSO).

Royal Commission on the National Health Service (1979), *Final Report* (London: HMSO).

Rutter, M., Maugham, B., Mortimore, P., and Ouston, J. (1979), *Fifteen Thousand Hours* (London: Open Books).

Salisbury, R. H. (1968), 'The analysis of public policy: a search for theories and roles', in A. Ranney, *Political Science and Public Policy* (Chicago: Markham).

Saunders, D. L. (1977), 'The changing planning framework', in F. Joyce, *Metropolitan Development and Change: The West Midlands* (Farnborough: Saxon House).

Saunders, P. (1979), *Urban Politics: A Sociological Interpretation* (London: Hutchinson).

Schmandt, H. J. (1969), 'Municipal decentralization: an overview', *Public Administration Review*, pp. 571–88.

Schon, D. A. (1973), *Beyond the Stable State* (Harmondsworth: Penguin).

Schroeder, H. M., Driver, M. J., and Streufert, S. (1965), *Information Processing Systems in Individuals and Groups* (New York: Holt, Rinehart & Winston).

Self, P. (1972), *Administrative Theories and Politics* (London: Allen & Unwin).

Self, P. (1975), *Econocrats and the Policy Process* (London: Macmillan).

Selznick, Phillip (1949), *TVA and the Grass Roots* (Berkeley, Calif.: California University Press).

Shaw, J. Martin (1975), *Regional Planning in East Anglia*, Discussion Paper No. 7, Regional Studies Association (London: Regional Studies Association).

Shelter (1973), *Another Chance for Cities: Shelter Neighbourhood Action Project, 1969/72* (London: HMSO).

Simkins, A. (1975), 'Towards area management', *Municipal Journal* (21 March 1975), pp. 390–2.

Simmie, J. M. (1974), *Citizens in Conflict: The Sociology of Town Planning* (London: Hutchinson).

Simon, H. (1957), *Administrative Behaviour* (New York: Collier Macmillan).

Skelcher, C. K. (1979a), 'Corporate activity in the districts', *District Councils Review* (June), pp. 150–1.

Skelcher, C. K. (1979b), 'The corporate approach and the districts', *The Corporate Planning Journal*, vol. 6, no. 1, pp. 1–46.

Skelcher, C. K. (1980a), 'From programme budgeting to policy analysis: corporate approaches in local government', *Public Administration*, vol. 59 (Summer), pp. 155–72.

Skelcher, C. K. (1980b), 'The changing shape of regional planning', *Town Planning Review*, vol. 51, no. 3, pp. 324–9.

Skinner, B. F. (1953), *Science and Human Behaviour* (New York: Macmillan).

Smith, B. (1976), *Policy Making in British Government* (London: Martin Robertson).

Smith, B. M. D. (1972), *The Administration of Overspill*, Occasional Paper No. 22 (Birmingham: Centre for Urban and Regional Studies, University of Birmingham).

Smith, D. L. (1978), 'Policy making for urban deprivation', *Public Administration*, vol. 56, no. 2, pp. 193–202.

Smith, D. M. (1977), *Human Geography: A Welfare Approach* (London: Edward Arnold), ch. 6.

South East Joint Planning Team (1970), *Strategic Plan for the South East* (SPSE) (London: HMSO).

South East Joint Planning Team (1976), *Strategy for the South East: 1976*

Review (London: HMSO).

Spencer, K. M. (1979), 'Inner city policy', *Local Government Studies Annual Review*, vol. 5, no. 2, pp. 59–62.

Spencer, K. M. (1980a), 'Inner city policy and urban development corporations', *Local Government Studies Annual Review*, vol. 6, no. 2, pp. 47–50.

Spencer, K. M. (1980b), 'The genesis of Comprehensive Community Programmes', *Local Government Studies*, vol. 6, no. 5, pp. 17–28.

Spencer, K. M., Vielba, C., and Webster, B. A. (1982), *Deprivation, Urban Neighbourhoods and the Policy Process* (London: Allen & Unwin).

Spencer, K. M., Webster, B., Collins, C. A., and Lomer, M. (1980), *Area Management Monitoring Study: Final Report* (Birmingham: Institute of Local Government Studies, University of Birmingham).

Stacey, F. (1973), *The Reorganisation of the National Health Service*, Public Administration Committee Third Annual Conference.

Stacey, M. (1969), 'The myth of community studies', *British Journal of Sociology*, vol. 20, pp. 134–47.

Stamper, R. (1973), *Information in Business and Administrative Systems* (London: Batsford).

Stewart, J. D. (1971), *Management in Local Government* (London: Charles Knight).

Stewart, J. D. (1973), 'Developments in corporate planning in British local government', *Local Government Studies*, no. 5 (First series), pp. 13–29.

Stewart, J. D. (1974), *The Responsive Local Authority* (London: Charles Knight).

Stewart, J. D. (1975), 'The government of cities and the politics of opportunity', *Local Government Studies*, vol. 1, no. 1, pp. 3–20.

Stewart, J. D. (1977), *Management in an Era of Restraint* (London: The Municipal Group), pp. 14–16.

Stewart, J. D. (1980), 'The governance of the conurbation', in G. C. Cameron (ed.), *The Future of the British Conurbations* (London: Longman).

Stewart, J. D., and Eddison, T. A. (1971), 'Structure planning and corporate planning', *Journal of the Royal Town Planning Institute*, vol. 57, no. 8, pp. 367–69.

Stewart, J. D., Spencer, K. M., and Webster, B. A. (1976), *Local Government: Approaches to Urban Deprivation*, Occasional Paper No. 1, Home Office Urban Deprivation Unit (London: HMSO).

Stringer, J. (1967), 'Operational research for multi-organisations', *Operational Research Quarterly*, vol. 18, pp. 105–20.

Struthers, W. A. K., and Williamson, C. B. (1979), 'Local economic development integrated policy planning and implementation in Merseyside', *Town Planning Review*, vol. 50, no. 2, pp. 164–84.

Thamesdown Borough Council (1978), *Villages in Thamesdown*, Corporate Planning Unit (Swindon: Thamesdown Borough Council).

Thomas, N., and Stoten, B. (1974), 'The NHS and local government' in K. Jones (ed.), *Yearbook of Social Policy in Britain 1973* (London: Routledge & Kegan Paul).

Thompson, James D. (1967), *Organisations in Action* (New York: McGraw-Hill).

Titmuss, R. M. (1962), *Income Distribution and Social Change* (London: Allen & Unwin).

Townsend, P. (1979), *Poverty in the United Kingdom* (Harmondsworth: Penguin).

Tuite, M., Chisholm, R., and Radnor, M. (1972), *Interorganisational Decision*

Making (Chicago: Aldine).

Tunley, P., Travers, T., and Pratt, J. (1979), *Depriving the Deprived: A Study of Finance, Educational Provision and Deprivation in a London Borough* (London: Kogan Page).

Turk, H. (1970), 'Interorganisational networks in urban society: initial perspectives and comparative research', *American Sociological Review*, vol. 35, pp. 1–19.

Vickers, G. (1965), *The Art of Judgement: A Study of Policy-Making* (London: Methuen).

Walton, R. E. (1972), 'Interorganisational decision-making and identity conflict', in Tuite *et al.* (1972).

Warren, R. L. (1967), 'The interorganisational field as a focus for investigation', *Administrative Science Quarterly*, vol. 12, pp. 396–419.

Warren, R. L. (1972), 'The concerting of decisions as a variable in organisational interaction', in Tuite *et al.* (1972).

Warren, R. L., Burgander, A. F., Newton, J. W., and Rose, S. M. (1975), 'The interaction of community decision organisations: some conceptual considerations and empirical findings', in Negandhi (1975).

Wasserman, G. (1975), 'Urban deprivation', in J. Brand and M. Cox (eds), *The Urban Crisis: Social Problems and Planning*, Royal Town Planning Institute (London: Royal Town Planning Institute).

Webster, B. A. (1977), 'Distributional impacts of local government policy', unpublished conference paper, Institute of British Geographers, Urban Geography Study Group, Leicester.

Webster, B. A., and Stewart, J. D. (1974), 'Area analysis of resources', *Policy and Politics*, vol. 3, no. 1, pp. 5–16.

Webster, B. A., Lambert, C., and Penny, J. (1979), 'The impact of local authority services on the inner city', first interim report to the Department of the Environment, Inlogov, unpublished.

Wedgwood-Oppenheim, F., Hart, D., and Cobley, B. (1976), *An Exploratory Study in Strategic Monitoring: Establishing a Regional Performance Evaluation and Policy Review Unit for the North West*, Progress in Planning, vol. 5, pt 1 (Oxford: Pergamon).

West Midlands Economic Planning Council/West Midlands Planning Authorities' Conference (1979), *A Developing Strategy for the West Midlands: Updating and Rolling Forward of the Regional Strategy to 1991 – the Regional Economy: Problems and Prospects* (Birmingham: West Midlands Economic Planning Council).

West Midlands Planning Authorities' Conference (1974), *A Developing Strategy for the West Midlands: Report of WMPAC with statement by the Secretary of State* (Birmingham: West Midlands Economic Planning Council).

West Midlands Regional Study (1971), *A Developing Strategy for the West Midlands: Report of West Midlands Regional Study* (Birmingham: West Midlands Economic Planning Council).

Whistler, T. L. (1970), *Information Technology and Organisational Change* (Belmont, Cal.: Wadsworth).

White, P. E., Levine, S., and Vlasak, C. J. (1975), 'Exchange as a conceptual framework for understanding interorganisational relationships', in Negandhi (1975), pp. 182–95.

Wicks, M. (1977), 'Social policy for the inner cities', in M. Brown and S. Baldwin (eds), *The Yearbook of Social Policy in Britain* (London: Routledge and Kegan Paul).

Wicks, M. (1980), 'Urban deprivation', in Bosanquet and Townsend (1980).

Wildavsky, A. (1964), *The Politics of the Budgetary Process* (Boston, Mass.:

Little, Brown).

Wildavsky, A. (1969), 'Rescuing policy analysis from PPBS', *Public Administration Review*, vol. 19, no. 2, pp. 189–202.

Wildavsky, A., and Dempster, M. (1979), 'On change: or there is no magic size for an increment', *Political Studies*, vol. 27, no. 3, pp. 371–89.

Williams, A. J. (1977), 'The relationship between regional water authorities and local authorities', in P. J. Drudy, *Water Planning and the Regions*, Discussion Paper no. 9, Regional Studies Association (London: Regional Studies Association).

Williams, F. (ed.) (1977), *Why the Poor Pay More* (London: National Consumer Council).

Winchurch, D. (1980), 'Political values in corporate planning', *The Corporate Planning Journal*, vol. 7, no. 2, pp. 27–32.

Yates, D. (1974), *Neighbourhood Democracy* (Lexington, Mass.: Lexington Books).

Yates, D. (1976a), 'Political innovation and institution building: the experience of decentralization experiments', ch. 6 in W. D. Hawley (ed.), *Theoretical Perspectives on Urban Politics* (Englewood Cliffs, NJ: Prentice-Hall).

Yates, D. (1976b), 'Urban government as a policy making system', in L. H. Masotti and R. L. Lineberry (eds), *The New Urban Politics* (Cambridge, Mass.: Ballinger), pp. 235–64.

Young, K. (1977), 'Values in the policy process', *Policy and Politics*, vol. 5, pp. 1–22.

Young, K. (1978), 'Of rules and roles: approaches to the study of policy implementation', unpublished paper, School for Advanced Urban Studies, University of Bristol (typescript).

Young, R., and Jay, C. (1979), article in *Social Work Today*, vol. 10, no. 26 (27 February 1979), pp. 13–19.

Zeitz, G. (1975), 'Interorganisational relationships and social structure: a critique of some aspects of the literature', in Negandhi (1975), pp. 39–48.

Index